THE LATER CHRISTIAN FATHERS

A selection from the writings of the Fathers
from St. Cyril of Jerusalem to
St. Leo the Great

Edited and translated by
HENRY BETTENSON

OXFORD NEW YORK
OXFORD UNIVERSITY PRESS

Oxford University Press, Walton Street, Oxford OX2 6DP

London Glasgow New York Toronto
Delhi Bombay Calcutta Madras Karachi
Kuala Lumpur Singapore Hong Kong Tokyo
Nairobi Dar es Salaam Cape Town
Melbourne Auckland

and associated companies in
Beirut Berlin Ibadan Mexico City Nicosia

Oxford is a trade mark of Oxford University Press

Introduction, selection, translation and annotation,
© Oxford University Press, 1970

First published by Oxford University Press, London, 1970
First issued as an Oxford University Press paperback 1972
Reprinted with corrections 1974, 1977
Reprinted 1982, 1983

ISBN 0 19 283012 0

Printed in Great Britain by
The Guernsey Press Co. Ltd.
Guernsey, Channel Islands

Contents

Introduction

The century and a quarter after the Council of Nicaea was mainly concerned, theologically, with the working out of the Nicene conclusions in the formulation of the doctrine of the Trinity, and the enunciation of the doctrine of the divinity and humanity of Christ. What was achieved was not a solution of the problems, but a clarification of their statement in terms which were given, if not a precise definition, at least a manageable circumscription of connotation.

The aim of this introduction is to give a brief sketch of the life of each of the Fathers represented in the selections, and some account of his more important contributions to doctrinal development.

Cyril of Jerusalem

Only one occupant of the see of the metropolis of the Christian faith attained a place among the foremost teachers of the Church, and even he is not regarded as a teacher of the first rank: Cyril's main importance is as a witness to the liturgical practice of the fourth century. He was, it is thought, born about 315, in Jerusalem, and was elected bishop of the city in 348. Soon after his consecration he found himself at odds with his Arian metropolitan, Acacius of Caesarea, and he was expelled from his see for a year in 357, and for two years in 360. Even the death of Acacius in 366 did not bring him tranquillity; for in the following year the Emperor Valens deposed him, and Cyril did not return till after the Emperor's death in 378. He took part in the Council of Constantinople in 381, and died five years later. His *Catechetical Lectures* were delivered during the Lenten season, probably in 350, in the church of the Holy Sepulchre, to candidates who were to be baptized at Easter. Some of the manuscripts preserve a note recording that the text is a transcript of shorthand notes taken at the time of the delivery of the lectures. The *Mystagogic Catecheses* were addressed to neophytes during Easter Week, and are based on the ceremonies of the sacraments administered at Easter: Baptism, Laying on of Hands, and the Eucharist. There is doubt about the date of their delivery; and even about their attribution to Cyril, since one manuscript assigns them to his successor, John; and three others jointly to Cyril and John.

Apart from his importance in the history of liturgy and the development of sacramental teaching, Cyril has a minor part in the history of Christological and Trinitarian doctrine as a representative of the cautious 'conservative' wing of the defenders of Nicene orthodoxy. The Council of Nicaea had affirmed the *homoousion*—that the Son is 'of the same substance' as the Father. But the Nicene decision had been largely the work of a determined minority. Many were suspicious of the *homoousion* because it was novel and unscriptural: and its advocates were exposed to the charge of Sabellianism, of identifying the Father and the Son. Besides that, the term contained an ambiguity: it could be, and had been, employed in a generic sense, whereby things similar in *nature* could be described as 'of the same substance'; and many of the illustrations used by theologians to illustrate the relationship of Father and Son might suggest that the *homoousion* meant no more than this: light and radiance, seed and plant, source and river. And Nicaea was concerned with the divinity of the Son, rather than with the unity of God; and since Constantine desired the widest possible agreement, a certain ambiguity was perhaps not unwelcome.

There followed a period of controversy, when synod succeeded synod, and creed jostled creed in what often seems to the student a bewildering phantasmagoria; when the Christian is tempted to sympathize with the sardonic comment of the pagan historian Ammianus Marcellinus: 'Bishops bustled about to one council after another, each trying to impose on the rest his own interpretation of the faith. And the only noticeable result was the imposition of an intolerable burden on the means of public transport.' The reaction against Nicaea, under the leadership of Eusebius of Nicomedia, produced the formulas of Antioch (341), Philippopolis (342), and the 'Macrostich' of Antioch (344). All these were moderate in tone; critical of Arianism, but omitting the *homoousion*. From 350–61, when the Arian Constantius was sole emperor, there followed a determined attempt to crush the Nicene definition, and the Arians were triumphant at the Third Council of Sirmium (357—the creed which Hilary called 'The Sirmian Blasphemy'), Nice (359), and Constantinople (360—when the authorization of the 'Dated Creed'[1] led Jerome to declare that 'the world groaned in amazement at finding itself Arian'). The period from 361 to 381 saw the triumph of the *homoousion*, mainly through the winning

[1] Formulated at Sirmium in 359.

over of the 'conservatives' and 'moderates' by the patient diplomacy of Athanasius and Hilary.

Thus there were, after Nicaea, three main parties in theology antagonistic, in a greater or less degree, to the Nicene formula. There were the full-blooded Arians, led by Aetius and Eunomius, who were responsible for the 'Sirmian Blasphemy', who condemned both *homoousios* (of the same substance) and *homoiousios* (of like substance). The Son, in their view, was *unlike* the Father; and hence they were called the 'Anomoeans'. There were the conservatives, who disliked the *homoousion* but who preferred no alternative technicality. The 'Dedication Creed' of Antioch in 341 expresses their position; anti-Sabellian, but leaving a loophole for the less crude forms of Arianism by asserting that the Son is 'not a creature as one of the creatures': the three divine *hypostases* are, on this view, separate in rank, but united in will and activity. The moderates, faced with the denials of the Anomoeans, were attracted to the 'homoiousian' position, formulated in the 'Dedication Creed' of Antioch and the 'Dated Creed' of Sirmium. This party included some who accepted the *homoousion* in theory, but preferred not to employ the term in practice; among these were Melitius of Antioch and Cyril. Cyril speaks of the Son as 'like to the Father in all things', sharing in divinity and united in will. Some of the moderates were more subordinationist in their teaching, like Basil of Ancyra, under whose presidency the Synod of Ancyra in 358 produced the formula 'like the Father' with the significant omission of 'in all things'.

The dispute with the Arians after Nicaea was about the divinity of the Son. The divinity of the Holy Spirit was not yet fully defined, and the Church had not reached the formulation, in acceptable terms, of the Trinity. The first step towards general agreement was the reconciliation of conservative opinion to the *homoousion*. Athanasius and Hilary of Poitiers both endeavoured to convince the 'homoiousians' that their essential belief was best safeguarded by the 'homoousian' formula, which barred Arianism, and Hilary insisted that if the 'likeness' was complete, then the conservatives should not boggle at 'one substance' to express identity of nature, provided that the distinction of persons closed the door to Sabellianism.

In 361 the Arianizing Emperor Constantius died, and was succeeded by the apostate Julian. The cessation of political interest in theological discussion provided a climate favourable to the eirenic deliberations of a council at Alexandria in the following year, when an attempt was made to mitigate confusions caused by differing interpretations of the terms *hypostasis* and *ousia*. These had often been used interchangeably (Athanasius himself equated them), and to speak of a plurality of *hypostases* might be taken as declaring an Arian distinction in essential nature: this was especially true in the West, since the precise Latin translation of ὑπό-στασις is *sub-stantia*, the word used to translate οὐσία; while the consequent assertion of 'one hypostasis' would have a Sabellian ring in the ears of those accustomed to distinguish essential nature (*ousia*) from subsistent reality (*hypostasis*). By explaining these confusions, and sanctioning the use both of 'three *hypostases*' and of 'one *hypostasis*', provided the divergent meanings of hypostasis were understood, the Council of Alexandria helped to unite 'homoousians' and 'homoiousians,' and paved the way for the later acceptance of the standard formula 'one *ousia* and three *hypostases*'.

The divinity of the Spirit was implicitly pronounced at Nicaea; but the creed was content with the bald affirmation '(I believe) in the Holy Spirit', without any explicit declaration of his equality with Father and Son, or any attempt to define his relation to them. Athanasius, in correspondence with Serapion of Thmuis, taught that the three Persons of the Trinity are inseparable and identical in activity, and that all therefore share the same *ousia*. Cyril of Jerusalem had given much the same teaching some ten years before; the Spirit shares in the inseparable life and work of the Trinity, and is glorified with Father and Son. 'The Father gives to the Son, and the Son communicates to the Holy Spirit'; a formula which foreshadows the later orthodoxy of 'proceeding from the Father through the Son'.

Cyril's *Catechetical Lectures* were addressed to candidates for baptism; and they are of great importance in their witness to the ritual and the theology of baptism in the fourth century. Baptism, it is explained, has a negative and a positive effect: the forgiveness of sins, the washing away of the impurities of the pagan life; and the positive gift of the Holy Spirit which is to lead to enlightenment and sanctification (for which Cyril employs the typically Eastern term, 'deification').

In Cyril's Lectures to the newly baptized we find the first clear teaching of a 'conversion' of the bread and wine of the Eucharist into the Body and Blood of Christ. He stresses that the elements undergo no physical change: they are described as 'symbols' or 'types'. But the effect of the prayer of consecration is to 'convert' them, through the activity of the Holy Spirit, in response to the celebrant's invocation (*epiclesis*), into the Body and Blood, as the water was converted into wine at Cana; not, it may be thought, a happy illustration. Then, by the assimilation of the Eucharistic Body, the faithful become 'Christ-bearers'. Χριστοφόροι. Cyril also develops the language of sacrifice. It was already customary to speak of the sacrament as not only a memorial of Christ's sacrifice, but as also, in some sort, itself a 'bloodless and spiritual sacrifice'. Cyril goes further in describing it as a 'tremendous (φρικωδέστατος) sacrifice of propitiation, an intercessory offering for temporal and spiritual wants—for the benefit of the living and the departed'.

Hilary of Poitiers

Hilary was born in 315, of a noble pagan family, and received a good pagan education. Converted in 350, he was elected bishop, while still a layman, in 353. He did not take part in two Arianizing synods in Gaul, neither in that of Arles in 353, nor in the synod of Milan, which in 355 decreed the third deposition of Athanasius. In 355 Hilary led the resistance of the Gallic bishops to their Arian metropolitan, Saturninus of Arles, and in the next year the Emperor Constantius exiled him to Asia Minor, where he lived for three years, during which he wrote the *de trinitate*. In 360 he was recalled to Gaul, at the earnest request of the Eastern Arians, who complained of him as 'the mischief-maker of the East'. In 361 he compassed the excommunication of Saturninus, at the Council of Paris; and in 364 he presided over a synod of Italian bishops at Milan, which tried, without success, to get the Arian Auxentius of Milan deposed. He died in 367.

The 'Athanasius of the West' was of a positive, rather than a speculative, cast of mind. His teaching was based on that of the Greeks, which he was concerned to interpret to the West, while at the same time seeking to ensure that the East should have a better appreciation of Western points of view; and in his interpretation of his Eastern teachers he shows some independence.

We have seen his conciliatory attitude towards those who shied at the *homoousion* formula, in the great debate which followed Nicaea, and how his endeavours were paralleled by the generally successful endeavour of Athanasius to win over the 'homoiousians' at the Council of Alexandria. Hilary insisted that *homoousios* was the more adequate formula, while admitting that *homoiousios* could express the full Nicene belief: perfect likeness implies identity of nature in Father and Son.

When he comes to consider the theory of Christ's person, Hilary, like Western teachers in general, goes to Tertullian for his formulation. In the one Person of Christ the divine and the human nature are united; he is fully man, in soul as well as body (the Arians, in ascribing to the Logos the human experiences of Christ, had derogated both from the divinity and the humanity): yet fully divine, in that the Person of the man Jesus is identical with the Person of the Logos. The incarnation entailed a renunciation of outward glory, a submission to human conditions; but not an abdication of power or a change in essential nature: *evacuatio formae non est abolitio naturae*. But when he ventures on to more speculative ground, Hilary is less happy. He speaks (as Clement of Alexandria had done before him) of Christ's body as 'celestial', since it was conceived by the operation of the Holy Spirit, and of the Transfiguration as a natural manifestation. Thus he has more than the usual difficulty in accounting for the recorded human weakness and the sufferings of Jesus: such experiences must, for him, be regarded as made possible by an act of free condescension, an assertion of his humanity rather than a consequence of it. Similar explanations were offered by other teachers, to avoid the attribution of human suffering to the Godhead. But some of Hilary's statements seem to topple over into Docetism, making the suffering illusory. And in this aspect of his thought he seems to join with his contemporary, Apollinarius of Laodicea, though the correspondence is undoubtedly fortuitous. It cannot be claimed that Hilary has anything useful to contribute on this point: for to assert, as he does, that Christ 'had a body capable of suffering, and therefore Christ suffered, although his nature was not susceptible of suffering', is surely to darken counsel.

The Cappadocians

The period of controversy which succeeded Nicaea resulted in the general acceptance of the *homoousion* formula. We have seen that this was mainly due to the patient statesmanship of Athanasius and Hilary, in alleviating the misunderstandings arising from 'speaking with other tongues' in respect of technical vocabulary, a 'glossolalia' without the benefit of an agreed glossary. There was need for a formulation of the Trinitarian faith in terms of as much precision as the subject-matter would admit, and, as part of this project, the status of the Holy Spirit called for determination. In these two connected enterprises the contribution of the Cappadocian Fathers was decisive. In themselves they constituted a triad of complementary qualities: Basil, the practical organizer and administrator; his friend, Gregory of Nazianzus, the orator and, if not exactly a poet, a man of poetical turn of mind, with no liking for the episcopal responsibilities which circumstances (and Basil's importunity) imposed upon him; and Basil's brother, Gregory of Nyssa, another reluctant administrator; an indifferent stylist (though his preaching was highly esteemed in his day), but the most gifted of the three as a speculative theologian, and a philosopher in the Platonic tradition.

Basil of Caesarea

Basil's life started in 330 in happy auspices: his family was noble and wealthy: his father's mother was rated a saint, and his mother was a martyr's daughter. Of the ten children born to this well-connected pair, three sons became bishops, two of them achieving canonization, while their elder sister gained the title of St. Macrina the Younger, to distinguish her from her grandmother and namesake. Basil was educated for a rhetorician's career at his home town of Caesarea in Cappadocia, at Constantinople, and at Athens, where he met another student from Cappadocia, Gregory, the son of the bishop of Nazianzus, who was to become his friend for life. He returned to Caesarea in about 356 to follow in his father's footsteps as a rhetorician, but he soon abandoned his ambitions for a worldly career, received baptism, and, after a Grand Tour of the eremitical establishments of Egypt, Syria, and Mesopotamia, he was fired by these ascetic examples to give his patrimony to the poor and embrace a life of solitude near Neocaesarea. Companions joined him; the hermitage became a cenobium; and his experiences issued in the two Rules which made Basil the legislator of the social monasticism of the Eastern Church, whose principles, adopted in the main by Benedict at Monte Cassino, fixed the pattern for the cenobitic life in the Western Church also. In 364 he advanced to the priesthood, under the persuasion of Eusebius, metropolitan of Cappadocia, whom he succeeded in 370. He was energetic in the founding of monasteries, of hospitals for the sick, of asylums for the poor, and of hospices for the traveller. He was equally untiring in combating Arianism, in defiance of the Emperor Valens, who was so impressed by the intrepidity of his resistance as to abandon his intention to sentence Basil to exile. As an ecclesiastical statesman, he bent his efforts towards the establishment of better understanding between Western and Eastern churchmen, as he saw the geographical, historical, and linguistic forces which underlay the disintegration of an Empire already in decline, exercising the same disruptive force in the Church. Little success attended his efforts: and he was equally frustrated in an endeavour to heal the Meletian schism at Antioch, a local symptom of the wider lack of unity. But it may be that his endeavours paved the way for the Council of Constantinople, in 381, two years after Basil's death, which brought a substantial unity to the Eastern Church. And though the West seems not to have taken any part in the deliberations of the Council, it showed no hesitation in the general acceptance of its conclusions.

That the Holy Spirit is 'of the same substance' as the Father and the Son had been implied by Cyril of Jerusalem, and explicitly asserted by Athanasius: but neither had directly spoken of him as God. The main body of the 'homoiousian' party apparently accepted, at Alexandria in 362, a position something like that of Cyril, which associated the Spirit inseparably with the activity of the First and Second Persons in the Trinity. But it was probably from the extreme section of this party that there emerged the group who won the nickname of 'Fighters against the Spirit'—the *Pneumatomachi*—because they resisted the ascription of the fullness of Godhead to the Third Person. The followers of Athanasius showed extreme caution in countering this position. The *Pneumatomachi* appealed to Scripture, using in particular the argument from silence: they also argued that the Athanasian position credited the Father with two Sons, no other relationship being possible; and, if unrelated, then, if divine, he would be an independent divinity. Gregory of Nazianzus tells us that Basil in this controversy exercised the greatest reserve, in order to win over the moderates in the opposing party: no doubt he hoped that such tactful accommodation might have the same happy result as the diplomatic handling of the conservatives by Athanasius and Hilary in the matter of the *homoousion* of the

Son. At first Basil was content that the controverters should deny that the Spirit was part of the created order: and from that requirement he passed to the insistence on the inseparability of his activity in the Trinity, which was taught implicitly by the Trinitarian formula in baptism. Even when he comes to deal with the topic at length in his treatise *On the Holy Spirit*, he does not commit himself to the direct appellation of 'God', nor even to an explicit assertion of consubstantiality; though this, without doubt, is implied in his affirmation of equality of worship, and of inseparability of activity in personal relationship.

Basil's most important contribution to Trinitarian theology is his establishment of the technical terms of the standard formulation. He distinguishes *ousia* and *hypostasis*, which hitherto had been used as synonyms. *Ousia*, in his acceptation, denotes essence, *hypostasis* a mode of being in which that *ousia* is manifested. He compares the difference with that obtaining between the universal and the particular: he does not equate these two differences, though it must be admitted that the Cappadocians sometimes seem to be arguing for a generic rather than a substantial unity in the Godhead. The *hypostases* are distinguished by their special characteristics; according to Basil these are 'fatherhood', 'sonship', 'sanctifying power': not, perhaps, a fruitful suggestion, since the first two are relations, not characters, and they are internal to the Trinity; while the third has an external reference. These distinctions are, as it were, balanced, in Basil's teaching,[1] by the mutual interpenetration of the *hypostases* by which the *hypostasis* of the Son manifests the Father. It does not appear that Basil clearly states the converse: that the *hypostasis* of the Father displays the Son; nor does he apply this notion to the Spirit. But we may see here at least the germ of the later doctrine of the *perichoresis* (*circumincessio*, 'co-inherence') formulated by John of Damascus.

Gregory of Nazianzus

An almost exact contemporary of Basil, born in 330, and from a very similar background, Gregory pursued a similar course of study;

[1] If it is Basil's. The letter (38) which expounds the doctrine is now often ascribed to Gregory of Nyssa.

the two young men met in their student days, and they were closely linked throughout their lives. Though Gregory outlived his friend by some nine years, his active life was nearly over when in 381 he pronounced the funeral oration over Basil's body. He was ordained at the age of thirty-two after he had spent a year or two in withdrawal from the world in Basil's cenobium at Neocaesarea where he collaborated in the production of the *Philocalia*, a collection of extracts from Origen, and in the devising of the two versions of the *Rule*. He did not desire ordination, but accepted it so as to help his father, the bishop of Nazianzus, whose health was failing. Soon afterwards he took refuge once more with Basil, but in a short time he returned to help the ailing bishop. In 372 Basil persuaded him, again much against his will, to become bishop of Sasima (a move dictated rather by Basil's desire to assert his metropolitan rights than by any pastoral concern for the local population), and Gregory became nominally responsible for a place he described as a 'horrible and detestable village'. In fact he did not reside there, but continued at Nazianzus as coadjutor to his father; and on the latter's death in 374 he took over the diocese, but only till a suitable successor could be found; when that requirement was fulfilled, he once more went into retirement. Four years later the Nicene minority at Constantinople summoned him to help them reorganize, now that Valens was dead; and for two years Gregory was a leading figure in that church; and when, in 380, Theodosius restored to the Catholics all their churches and buildings, Gregory was installed in the Church of the Apostles, conducted thither by the Emperor in person. Although the Council of Constantinople, in the following year, recognized him as bishop of the Imperial City, Gregory resigned almost immediately because canonical objections were raised against his nomination. He returned to Nazianzus, administered the diocese for two years, before retiring, this time finally, to the family estate. He lived on in failing health for some five years, confining his activity to writing, and to the following of the monastic way of life.

In his teaching on the Trinity Gregory follows the main lines of Basil's doctrine: the three *hypostases* and the one *ousia*. But he is bolder than his 'guide of life and doctrinal leader' in respect to the divinity of the Spirit: and, for the first time, the question 'Is the Spirit God?' is answered with a blunt affirmative, and his consubstantiality is asserted as a corollary. The Old Testament, says Gregory, revealed

the Father, and pointed towards the Son: the New Testament revealed
the Son and spoke of the Spirit in terms whose meaning was only
understood when he had revealed himself in the lives of Christ's
followers. Basil had failed to find a satisfactory way to describe the
mode of origin of the Spirit in terms which would evade the Pneumato-
machian jibe about the 'two Sons'. Gregory is content to echo the
statement of the Fourth Gospel: the Spirit 'proceeds' from the Father.
The formulation which was to satisfy the thought of the Church had
to wait for Gregory of Nyssa. But the elder Gregory improves on
Basil's differentiation of the *hypostases* in the Trinity by substituting
for 'fatherhood', 'sonship', 'sanctifying power', the characteristics of
'ingeneratedness', 'generatedness' (the Greek terms are not so ungainly)
and 'procession'. Gregory of Nyssa followed him in this, and this
way of speaking was generally adopted: he is also more careful than
Basil to emphasize the danger of the analogy between the universal-
particular relation and that between *ousia* and *hypostasis*. He contrasts
the 'conceptual' unity that subsists between particular men in virtue
of their sharing in 'manhood' with the real unity which informs the
Trinity. This evidence surely disposes of the charge, made by Harnack
and others, that the Cappadocians were, in effect, 'homoiousians',
because they taught a unity of *hypostases* which proved, if closely
examined, merely generic; that the two Basils, of Ancyra and Caesarea,
were in effect teaching the same doctrine.

The Cappadocian doctrine of Christ—as divine and human—was
developed in opposition to what seemed to them the docetic teaching
of Apollinarius, a zealous supporter of Athanasius, who became bishop
of Laodicea in 360. His teaching represents, in extreme form, the
'Word–flesh' Christology of Alexandria in contrast with the 'Word-
man' Christology found in Antiochene thought. The tendency of the
former was to find no place for the human soul in Christ, the humanity
being represented only by the 'flesh'. It has often been pointed out
that Arius had substituted the Logos for the soul of Christ, and thus,
paradoxically, Arianism has been regarded as the source of the teaching
of Apollinarius, one of its most vigorous opponents. The truth seems
rather to be that the resemblance derives from the Alexandrian 'Word-
flesh' approach which Apollinarius shared with the Arians; and the
common account of his teaching, that for him the Logos took the
place of the 'rational soul' in Christ, functioning in him as his will and
intellect, is an over-simplification. Apollinarius detested the dualist

tendency in the Word–man doctrine of Antioch: such Antiochenes as Eustathius of Antioch and Diodore of Tarsus seemed to him to be renewing the errors of Paul of Samosata,[1] and preaching an adoptionist Christology, a Christ who was not incarnate God but a man 'attached to God'; to be distinguishing between the Son of Mary and the Son of God. A man 'attached to God' could be neither the object of worship nor the author of salvation. Against such teaching he insisted on the unity of Christ's nature, resulting from the fusion of Logos and flesh. The Logos, to Apollinarius, was not just the 'rational soul' of the incarnate, it was his 'soul' in the wider sense of ψυχή, the life-giving principle of his whole being. Thus, as any man is a unity of body and soul (in the wide sense), so Christ is 'physical unity' of Word and flesh. And Apollinarius used a phrase which Cyril of Alexandria was later to adopt, under the belief that its author was Athanasius: 'one incarnate nature of the divine Word'. This fusion of Word and flesh makes it natural for him to speak of the 'divine flesh' (we have found similar language in Hilary of Poitiers, without the same presuppositions).

Teaching of this kind was condemned at the Council of Alexandria (362), without mentioning names: but in 377 Apollinarius was condemned at a council in Rome; and this decision was repeated in 378 at Alexandria and in the next year at Antioch, and finally by the Oecumenical Council of Constantinople in 381. The opposition to Apollinarianism was led by the Cappadocian fathers, and the arguments can best be seen in the writings of the two Gregories. They contended that the Apollinarian Christ must lack the element that makes man truly human: he would not be 'God made man', but a monstrous hybrid: to speak of 'divine flesh' implied that Christ's manhood was a mere illusion; and in that case the ascription to Jesus of human experiences of suffering and ignorance must be erroneous or deceitful. But the clinching argument was held to be the phrase of Nazianzen, often repeated: 'What was not assumed was not healed'. Apollinarius had made much of the plea that a fully human Christ would have no saving power: the retort was that Christ could not represent us, nor could he unite us to himself, without becoming 'in all points' like his brethren.

This controversy forced theologians to consider their positive doctrine of the person of Christ. Gregory speaks of 'two natures coming together in unity': there are two elements presented to thought,

[1] A 3rd century 'Unitarian', for whom Christ was supremely inspired by the Word.

but only one person. It must be admitted that he comes near to Apollinarian teaching when he uses the language of 'mixture' and 'fusion' to describe this union, and such expressions did not ultimately find favour: and he is as embarrassed as his opponents when he comes to consider the ignorance and sufferings attributed to Jesus, and the 'Eli, Eli' from the cross.

In one important matter Gregory diverged sharply from his friend and his brother. Basil and Gregory of Nyssa (Gregory more emphatically) made much of the idea of the ransom in expounding the saving work of Christ. The notion that the Devil had acquired a right over mankind, through man's sin, and that his claim must somehow be honoured, haunted the minds of most of the fathers. Gregory of Nazianzus would have none of it. What rights could a robber enjoy? And why such a price? And the Father could not require such a ransom. The Devil is conquered, not paid: man is restored and sanctified, not bought. A metaphor has been taken too literally.

Gregory of Nyssa

The most gifted of the Cappadocians, as a thinker, was born in 335, five years after the birth of his brother Basil. He does not seem to have travelled for his education, like the other two: and he himself gives his brother the credit for his education. He embarked, like Basil, on the career of a rhetorician, and married: but he soon repaired to Basil's cenobium in Pontus, and in 371 he was appointed bishop of the small town of Nyssa, in Basil's province of Caesarea. As a bishop, appointed against his will, he disappointed his brother by his incompetence in organization, and his weakness in discipline; and in 376 a synod of Arian bishops and prelates deposed him on charges of misappropriation of church funds. We are told that the charges were trumped up, and we certainly would never suspect the saint of dishonesty; but the financial inefficiency which his own brother criticizes in him doubtless lent colour to the charge: we may imagine that the books were in some disorder. However, the motives for the deposition were theological (or theologico-political), and on the death of Valens Gregory was restored to his see, in 378. In the following year he attended the synod of Antioch, and was sent by that conference on a visitation of the diocese of Pontus: while on that mission he found himself elected, to his dismay, as archbishop of Sebaste: but he administered this diocese for only a few months. In 381 he was a prominent figure, with the other Gregory, at the Council of Constantinople. The latter part of his life is scantily documented: and the last recorded event is his presence at a synod at Constantinople in 394.

Gregory is the first systematic theologian since Origen, whom he greatly admired, and whose disciple he professed himself. Like his master, he thought pagan philosophy could be used, and should be used, in the service of the Christian faith—'the Egyptians should be spoiled'; and he uses the terms and concepts of Platonism and Neo-platonism. Yet on the whole his dependence on those philosophies is more literary than philosophical: his ultimate appeal is to the Scriptures, and to the tradition of the Fathers.

We have already seen that Gregory of Nyssa provided the statement of the Spirit's place in the Trinity which became accepted as the most adequate formulation: the Spirit proceeds from God, and receives from the Son: the Father is the cause, the Son is caused directly, the Spirit is caused through the Son's intermediation. Gregory uses the image of a torch lighting another torch, which in its turn gives its light to a third. We have also seen that it was probably Gregory who first expounded the doctrine of 'circumincession', in a letter which was attributed to Basil. Like his fellow Cappadocians, but with even more emphasis, Gregory found the unity of the Godhead revealed in the inseparability of activity. He dangerously outdoes them in comparing the unity-in-plurality of the Trinity to the unity of the universal in its particulars. Perhaps it was the Platonist in him that led him to confuse the abstract which excludes plurality with the concrete particulars which impose it, when he states that three men should be called one man, in virtue of their common nature. It may be that he expresses what he is driving at here when in another place he argues that number indicates mere quantity, the unitary essence denotes nature.

There is a marked difference between the two Gregories in their Christology. Though firmly opposed to Apollinarius, Gregory of Nazianzus favours the 'Word-flesh' approach typical of Alexandria; and we have noticed that his language often approximates to that of his opponents, and that he has difficulty in dealing with the marks of human weakness and limitation in the Gospel portrait of Christ. Gregory of Nyssa is more 'Antiochene'. He can speak of 'the God-receiving man', and ascribe Christ's sufferings to 'the man united to the divinity'. Though he uses such terms as 'mixture' to describe the union, he distinguishes the two natures in the historical sense: it is only after the resurrection that this 'transformation' is completed, and the human nature absorbed into the divine 'like a drop of vinegar swallowed up in the sea'. Yet even in the earthly life of Jesus the conjunction (Gregory uses a word, *synapheia*, which was later to be rejected after the Nestorian controversy) made one person (*prosopon*). But the *communicatio idiomatum*, in accordance with which the 'Alexandrians' find it easy to interchange the characteristics of the divine and human natures, in virtue of the unity of person, was not congenial to his way of thinking, as it was to Gregory of Nazianzus.

In Christian thought about the redemptive work of Christ there are two main lines of interpretation: one which regards Christ as, in some sense, our representative, who identifies himself with us, and enables us to identify ourselves with him: the other views him as, in some way, a substitute for us, his sacrifice effecting 'a ransom for many'. It may be held that there is truth in both these interpretations, since the saving work has many facets: and most of the Fathers speak of the redemption in both these ways, often with some loss of consistency. Athanasius, in his *de incarnatione*, tries to combine them; but his ruling thought is that of the kinship between Christ and mankind, which enables us to share his victory. The Cappadocians followed him in this: and Gregory Nazianzen repudiated a literal interpretation of the ransom metaphor. Basil on occasions employs the language of substitution, and the image of the ransom, with its implication of the Devil's right over mankind in consequence of the fall: but it is Gregory of Nyssa who has the dubious credit of introducing the image of the baited hook which exerted an unfortunate fascination on many Christian minds. While he has much to say of the restoration of man through identification with the Incarnate, and in the sharing of the victory of the second Adam which cancelled the defeat of the first, he treats also of the liberation of mankind from the power of evil in terms of the 'ransom'. The Devil had acquired rights over mankind which God's justice could not deny (this is in line with one strain in the thought of Athanasius): Satan was delighted to accept the man Jesus in payment of the debt; but he failed to discern the divinity concealed in the human flesh, and was caught, as a fish is caught by the hook concealed in the bait. If the justice of this transaction seems to savour too much of Portia's Venice, it is perhaps relevant to observe that Satan himself is one of the ultimate beneficiaries of Christ's saving work: for Gregory follows Origen in looking forward to the final restoration of all things, when even the 'inventor of evil' will be reconciled to his Creator in the harmonious conclusion of the history of all creation.

Gregory carries further the teaching of Cyril of Jerusalem about the 'change' or 'conversion' of the elements in the Eucharist. Cyril's word was vague in meaning; to describe this change Gregory employs a rare word which, strictly interpreted, denoted a transformation of the physical constituents of the bread and wine. Although Gregory was not followed in this attempt to define the change effected by the eucharistic consecration, various words were employed by other eastern writers to emphasize that a conversion of some kind did take place. The use of such terms as 'symbol', 'figure', 'type', is still found at this period in western writers: the East in general had adopted the language of 'realism'.

Theodore of Mopsuestia

The two most famous exponents of the Antiochene school of biblical exegesis, the school which eschewed the allegorical interpretations canvassed at Alexandria, were Diodore of Tarsus and his pupil Theodore. Diodore was a doughty defender of the Nicene faith against the Arians, and of the Christian faith in opposition to the Emperor Julian's effort to revive classical paganism. Banished from Antioch by Valens in 372, he returned after that emperor's death, to become bishop of Tarsus in 378: and he attended the Council of Constantinople in 381. He died some ten years later, respected as a pillar of orthodoxy who had been named by Theodosius, in his edict confirming the decisions of the Second Oecumenical Council, as one of the 'arbiters of the faith'. But his 'Antiochene' Christology (which has come down to us only in scattered fragments, and in quotations from his opponents) excited the hostility of Cyril of Alexandria, who traced to him and his pupil Theodore the source of the Nestorian heresy. Diodore was condemned as a heretic by a synod at Constantinople in 499.

Theodore also was born at Antioch, about 350, and there he studied rhetoric at the feet of the celebrated Libanius, and listened to the theological and exegetical discourses of Diodore. In the school of Libanius he began a friendship, which was to last through his life, with a certain John, whose eloquence was later to win him the name of Chrysostom —'John of the Golden Mouth'. John persuaded his friend to enter a monastery; but Theodore soon found the life there uncongenial, and he left it, with the intention of pursuing a legal career. Soon, however, he was persuaded by John to return to the community. He received ordination; and in 392 he was consecrated bishop of Mopsuestia, in Cilicia, and administered the diocese till his death in 428. In his life he won the highest praise for learning, especially in his exposition of Scripture, and for sound doctrine: but Cyril condemned him as the proximate source of the errors for which Nestorius was condemned, and although he was not mentioned by name at the condemnation of Nestorius at Ephesus in 431, he was repudiated as a heretic after his death, as Diodore had been, when, mainly at the instance of the Emperor Justinian, the Second Council of Constantinople passed judgement on a number of writings held to be 'Nestorian'. After this condemnation his works were destroyed, or allowed to perish, by his opponents, though some of his commentaries survived in a Latin translation under a false ascription to St. Ambrose: his doctrinal statements were only known in tendentious quotations and collections of extracts prepared by those who secured his condemnation. But many of his works survived in a Syriac translation. His *de incarnatione*, the work most quoted for his Christological teaching, was discovered, in a Syriac version, in 1905, but was lost during the 1914 war, before it had been published. However, the discovery of his *Catechetical Homilies* in 1932 enables us to form a more balanced estimate of Theodore's teaching than was possible when the only evidence was provided by the statements of Cyril and the excerpts from Theodore presented for condemnation at Constantinople.

Theodore's Christology developed in opposition to the Alexandrian 'Word–flesh' doctrine which he encountered in extreme form in Apollinarius. The 'Word–man' theory he thus evolved was more thorough-going than any doctrines hitherto put forward by the 'Antiochene' school. He insists on the completeness of the humanity of Christ, on the reality of his human experiences, of his moral, as well as his physical growth. The relation between the humanity and the divinity is variously described: 'the man assumed' has an echo of Gregory of Nazianzus, but his language is sometimes patient of an 'adoptionist' interpretation; while the image of the humanity as a

'garment', 'dwelling', or 'temple' might suggest a 'Word–flesh' scheme:
but the phrase that his opponents seized on (though it may be garbled,
or quoted misleadingly out of context) was the statement that the
Word and the man were united 'by favour', which might suggest the
relation obtaining between God and any human being who conveyed
God's message or was chosen in any way to further God's purpose.
And Theodore employed the term 'conjunction', which was later to
be found the most misleading element in Nestorianism, with its
suggestion of collocation rather than union. No doubt Theodore
insisted that the result of this connexion was one person (*prosopon*),
and his intention was to preserve the integrity of the two natures.
But his way of putting it was precarious. He was no heretic: or if he
was, he was less of a 'Nestorian' than Cyril of Alexandria was a
Monophysite. The question of Christological statement was still under
debate, and the terms in use had not been defined with even the modest
precision that such terms admit.

John Chrysostom

The third Oecumenical Doctor of the Eastern Church (the others were
Basil and Gregory of Nazianzus) was born in an eminent family of
Antioch about 350. With Theodore, he studied rhetoric under
Libanius and learnt his theology from Diodore. At an early age he
aspired to an ascetic life of withdrawal from the world, and for many
years led a life of extreme discipline at home, being unable to fulfil
his ambition because of the claims of his widowed mother; but in the
end he steeled himself against her protestations and retired to spend
four years in a hermitage. Then, because of a serious illness, he
returned to Antioch and was ordained, becoming priest in 386, when
he was given the charge of the principal church in that city. There he
remained for twelve years, during which time he gained the reputation
for pulpit eloquence which won him the title of 'John of the Golden
Mouth'. When he was elected bishop of Constantinople, in 397, he
tried to evade the responsibility, but the Emperor Arcadius forced his
acceptance and he was consecrated in 398. It was a position requiring
more diplomatic tact than eloquence, and John had these qualities in
inverse proportion: he made many enemies, among whom the most
bitter, or the most able to exercise her bitterness, was the Empress

Eudoxia, who dominated the weak-willed Arcadius. John had another enemy in Theophilus, the patriarch of Alexandria, who had resented being forced to consecrate Chrysostom as bishop: and this resentment was not mitigated when in 402 he was summoned to Constantinople to answer charges brought against him by Nitrian monks at a synod over which John presided. Theophilus obtained his revenge, with the eager support of Eudoxia, when he summoned a synod of thirty-six bishops (twenty-seven from Egypt and all of them enemies of John) which condemned the bishop of Constantinople on various insubstantial charges. John refused to recognize the competence of this 'Synod of the Oak' (named after the suburb of Chalcedon where it met), and Arcadius exiled him to Bithynia: but he recalled him next day, in response to the riotous clamour of the people; which the Empress seconded because she saw, in a tragic accident in the palace, a sign of divine displeasure at the injustice dealt to the bishop. But there was not room in Constantinople for both Eudoxia and Chrysostom. The months of peace ended when John began his sermon on the Decollation of St. John the Baptist with dramatic words in which his hearers could scarcely fail to see an allusion to the scandalous diversions which had attended the unveiling of the Empress's statue near the cathedral. 'Once more Herodias rages in fury; once more she dances; once more she seeks to get the head of John on a platter.' This conflation of Herod's Queen with her daughter seemed to point the allusion; Arcadius inhibited John from his episcopal functions; and when the bishop proved obdurate, the Easter baptism next year was stopped by a troop of soldiers, and the baptismal water was tinged with the blood of clergy and laity. Soon after this, John was exiled to Armenia, where he stayed for three years: but to the chagrin of his enemies his place of retreat became a goal of pilgrimage for his admirers from Antioch. These enemies therefore contrived his banishment to the remote eastern shores of Pontus: but John was already broken in health; he was forced to travel on foot through difficult country, in stormy weather, and he died before reaching the journey's end, in September 407.

John was not a speculative thinker, nor a systematic theologian: he was essentially a pastor, a preacher, a reformer. In his Trinitarian theology he expands the Nicene faith; though it appears that, while he employs the *homoousion* formula, he was happier to speak of 'equality in essence'. In Christology he is generally classed with the 'Antiochenes';

and it is true that he asserts the reality of the two natures in Christ, and the unity of the Person. 'He (the Logos) assumed what he was not. ... There is no confusion, but no separation. ... One Christ, by union, not by commixture. ... The Logos and the flesh are one by a union and conjunction (συναφεία) ... ineffable and inexplicable.' But in John's teaching the divine nature preponderates over the human nature in Christ to such a degree that his teaching often approximates to the 'Alexandrian'. He asserts the human soul and intellect in Christ, but it plays little part in his thought: he cannot admit any human development, any human ignorance in Christ. It is the Logos who chooses to 'do the will of the Father' and decides to 'lay down his life'. There is an Apollinarian strain in this, and it is significant that Chrysostom appears undisturbed by that heresy: he only mentions Apollinarius once.

John has been entitled (unofficially) *Doctor Eucharistiae*: and he develops the 'conversion' teaching of Gregory of Nyssa to the extent of a startling 'realism', or materialism, of language: the Christian 'bites into the body of Christ'; the body which was unbroken on the cross is 'broken in pieces in the sacrifice of the altar'. No doubt such expressions should be interpreted as oratory, rather than theology. But the language of 'conversion' had come by this time to be the accepted teaching of the Eastern Church: there was no divergence here between 'Alexandria' and 'Antioch': Chrysostom only gave it sharper emphasis. And he carries forward Cyril of Jerusalem's teaching of the 'tremendous sacrifice' offered once for all on the cross: in both these sacrifices Christ himself is both priest and victim.

Ambrose

Ambrose was born in 339 when his father, a member of a noble Roman family, held high office in Gaul. His father died in that office, and his mother took the three children back to Rome. Ambrose received the training in rhetoric and law which was customary in his class, and at the age of thirty was appointed to a responsible post as the Emperor's representative in the district of Liguria and Aemilia. The headquarters of this district was in Milan; and four years after his appointment Ambrose was compelled, in his official capacity, to try to mediate between the Catholics and the Arians when the election of a new bishop to succeed the Arianizing Auxentius led to dangerous violence. To his amazement, the contending parties united to elect the arbitrator, who was at the time only a catechumen: this sudden coalition of opponents seemed evidence of divine intervention and in spite of a *nolo episcopari* which seems to have been quite sincere, Ambrose was consecrated, eight days after his baptism. The rapidity of his elevation might very well have left him breathless: and indeed he spent much of his time, at the start of his episcopate, in studious retirement, where he applied himself to the study of the Fathers, Latin and Greek: he gave away his inherited wealth, and followed a strict rule of life. Ambrose was an essentially Roman character: practical rather than speculative; a great churchman and ecclesiastical statesman; an organizer, pastor, and teacher. As the champion of the Church's rights he fought without remission against the claims of paganism and heresy, and against the encroachments of the State, even when the head of the State was the orthodox Theodosius I, the Emperor who virtually 'established' the Christian Church in the Roman Empire. 'The Emperor,' said Ambrose, 'is inside the Church, not above it.' Thus in 384 he successfully opposed the Roman senate's project of restoring to the senate-house the pagan statue of Victory: and the proposal of Justina, the Empress-Dowager, that one of Milan's churches should be granted to the Arians. He played a prominent part in the synods of Aquileia (381) and Rome (382), which saw Arianism in retreat: and in 390 a massacre in Thessalonica, ordered by the Emperor, brought Ambrose to impose a public penance on Theodosius, which points forward to Canossa. He was the first prince of the Church (for all his personal humility) to speak with the princes of the world on equal terms; whose advice was sought by them as the advice of a fellow-statesman. He died in 397.

In his Trinitarian theology Ambrose carries on in the West the work of Hilary of Poitiers in championing the Nicene formulation which the Eastern Church had produced. He succeeded Hilary as the foremost Western defender of the orthodox position against the attacks of all forms of Arianism, and of the divinity of the Holy Spirit in face of the attempts of the *Pneumatomachi*. But he has no distinctive contribution of his own to make.

Nor is there anything original in his Christological teaching: in this, as elsewhere, he depends on the Greek Fathers. But as a teacher of the Western Church he supplies on this topic a wholesome corrective to the 'Alexandrian' teaching—verging on Docetism—we have noticed in Hilary. Ambrose is quite clear about the reality of Christ's human nature, and his human soul. There is one person in two natures, each distinct and complete, the human nature including a human soul. Yet the unity of the Person admits the *communicatio idiomatum*, so that we can speak of the crucifixion of the Lord of glory.

The interests of Ambrose were predominantly pastoral, rather than theological, and it is appropriate that we have two treatises—*de mysteriis* and *de sacramentis*—which are of importance for the history of baptismal and eucharistic practice and teaching. The authenticity of the second of these works was for long in doubt: but modern scholarship seems to allow us to regard it as the work of Ambrose. In regard to baptism Ambrose is a witness to the growing tendency to separate the two main elements in the rite: the baptismal washing, and the consignation with oil; the latter being either associated with the laying on of hands, or identified with it. The two elements had been clearly distinguished by Cyril of Jerusalem: Ambrose goes further, and tries to distinguish the action of the Holy Spirit in the two sacramental acts: the gift of a new birth in baptism, and the equipment of the initiate with the seven gifts in the subsequent consignation. It was this notion of a bestowal of the plenitude of spiritual strength which led to the use of the term *confirmatio*, 'strengthening', to describe the consignation, and in the Western Church the newer appellation generally displaced the earlier title.

In his teaching on the Eucharist Ambrose normally employs the language of symbolism—the bread and wine are a 'type' or 'figure' of the Lord's body and blood: they 'signify' that which they convey to the faithful receiver 'by way of a resemblance'. This was the usual language of the Western Church. But on other occasions Ambrose uses the language of 'conversion' which had become current in the East: the elements are 'changed', 'transfigured': the consecration is a miracle which 'alters their nature'. His study of the Greek Fathers makes him in this respect the transmitter to the West of the Eastern conception of a quasi-physical change in the sacramental species.

Jerome

Jerome was born between 340 and 350 of a wealthy family in Dalmatia, and was sent to Rome in boyhood to receive the customary education in the *trivium*—grammar, rhetoric, and dialectic. Modern scholars have been inclined to discount his later castigation of the wildness of his student days: it may be that he denounced the peccadillos of his youthful self with the same acrimony which he vented on the errors of his opponents. After completing those studies he went to Gaul, and decided to devote his life to the service of Christ. He had already been baptized at Rome; and the catacombs there had fired his imagination with the thought of heroic discipleship; and examples of Gallic monasticism probably led him to join a group of friends at Aquileia who practised an austere rule of life. In 373 he set out on pilgrimage to Jerusalem, and when illness compelled a long sojourn at Antioch he employed the time in acquiring a mastery of Greek: and he became a competent Hebraist during three years of retirement in the desert near Antioch. Ordained priest in 379, he soon proceeded to Constantinople, where he heard Gregory of Nazianzus and studied, with admiration, the exegetical writings of Origen. In 382 he returned to Rome, on the invitation of Pope Damasus, and spent three years as his secretary. It was at the bidding of Damasus that Jerome began his revision of the Latin versions of the Bible, which eventually bore fruit in the publication of the Vulgate. In 385 he left Rome for Palestine, and finally settled in Bethlehem as the superior of a monastery founded by Paula, a wealthy Roman widow who had belonged to a group of Roman aristocrats who had been observing an ascetic regimen under Jerome's direction. Here he remained till his death, probably in 420, engaged in his studies and writings, but involved from time to time in bitter controversy, for which he seems to have had an almost Swiftian relish. His saintliness was not of a kind which exercises much attraction today; yet few saints have been more often portrayed in Christian art; and he is one of the Church's greatest scholars, whose prodigious labours in the translation of the Bible put the Western Church incalculably in his debt.

Jerome was more a scholar than a thinker, and he makes no great contribution to the development of doctrine. One might expect his biblical preoccupations to have made him a notable exegete: in fact it must be confessed that his commentaries offer little of interest. Though he stresses the plenary inspiration of Scripture, and holds that every passage is full of meaning in every syllable, he has no clear theory of inspiration, nor any consistent principle of interpretation. He soon lost his first enthusiasm for Origen's allegorical exegesis (and he became a bitter opponent of 'Origenism' in theology) but he continued to employ it whenever the literal sense of Scripture seemed self-contradictory or unedifying.

Jerome became deeply involved in the dispute with Pelagius over the question of free will and grace: but here again one can discern no consistent position. In some passages the initiative seems to lie with man: 'To begin belongs to us; to perfect belongs to God'. But elsewhere he asserts the necessity for prevenient grace for the initial motion of our will.

Augustine of Hippo

The greatest of the 'Doctors' of the Western Church was the son of an official of the Numidian town of Thagaste. His mother Monica was a devout member of the Church: but his father deferred baptism until shortly before his death. Born in 354, Augustine was educated for a rhetorical career in a local school, and later at Carthage. He tells us that in his student days he regarded Christianity as intellectually beneath contempt. At the age of twenty he conceived an interest in philosophy, and in search of some explanatory and guiding principle he attached himself to the Manichean sect.[1] In 375 he set up as teacher of literature and rhetoric at his native town—estranged from his mother because of his rejection of her faith. In 383 he went to Rome, and in the next year to Milan, as professor of rhetoric. By now he was disillusioned about the Manichean system, and relapsed for a time into complete scepticism. At Milan he listened to Ambrose interpreting the Old Testament allegorically, and was attracted by the Neoplatonic strain in the bishop's teaching, which owed something to Plotinus. About this time Augustine began to study Plotinus in the course of his profession, and a priest named Simplicianus, who was to succeed Ambrose in the bishopric, explained to him the congruity between the best in Neoplatonism and the Christian Logos doctrine; he also urged Augustine to study the teachings of St. Paul. From Paul Augustine learned that salvation could not come through philosophy, but only through God's grace: and his spiritual struggle was finally resolved when in his garden he heard a child's voice saying *Tolle, lege*; he took up Paul's epistles, opened the volume at random, and his eye fell on Romans 13, 13, '. . . not in sensuality and self-

[1] Cf. p. 85, n. 2.

indulgence . . .' He realized that it was moral reluctance rather than intellectual doubt that had been holding him back from committing himself finally. All the barriers now fell. In 385 he resigned his post and retired to Cassiacum, a friend's villa near Milan, to prepare for baptism, which he received from Ambrose in 387. Soon after he set out, with his mother, for Africa: but Monica died at Ostia, and Augustine stayed at Rome for nearly a year, engaged in writing. In 388 he arrived at Thagaste, where he lived for three years in retirement, in a quasi-monastic community with a few friends. He did not seek ordination: but in 391 he consented to be ordained at the pressing request of Valerius, bishop of Hippo: and in 395 he was consecrated bishop, to assist Valerius, whom he soon succeeded. As bishop he continued the community life, in company with his clergy, devoting much of his prodigious energy to writing the immense corpus of books which bear his name, while never, we are assured, neglecting his pastoral duties to his flock. He died in 430, when the Vandals were at the gates of his city.

No one could dispute that Augustine is the greatest formulative influence in the shaping of the thought and life of the Western Church; in fact the whole of medieval Christendom, we may say, would have been very different without him. It would be the merest impertinence to attempt even a sketch of his contribution in a few pages: it is more proper to confine our remarks to the characteristic teaching which is usually understood when one speaks of 'Augustinianism': the teaching which earned him the title of *Doctor Gratiae*.

This doctrine was developed in the course of controversy with Pelagius and his followers: it did not arise from it. For Augustine was already speaking of mankind as a *massa peccati*, utterly helpless without the grace of God, when the British teacher arrived at Rome (about 400) with an anthropology which gave a more comforting sound. In fact, the clash between the two opposing views of man did not come until Pelagius and his follower Celestius arrived in Africa in 409, fleeing before the invasion of Alaric. Pelagius had achieved a considerable reputation in Rome as a moral teacher, and as a moralist we are told that he was shocked by the prayer in Augustine's *Confessions*, 'Grant what thou dost command, and command what thou wilt', which seemed to remove from man all freedom, and therefore all responsibility. Pelagius certainly thought that man needs God's grace: but by grace he meant man's power to choose the good, and God's revelation of that good in the Law, the prophets, and, above all, in Christ. Each soul, he taught, comes into being in the same condition as did Adam: there is no inherited guilt, no *damnosa hereditas* of weakness.

For Augustine the reality of original sin was clearly laid down in Scripture; the Church affirmed it in its teaching, and in the practice of infant baptism; and men found it true in their experience. There was inherited guilt because the whole human race was identified with its first parents in the first act of disobedience; in Augustine's text of the Bible St. Paul seemed to confirm this in Romans 5. 12; for the Old Latin Version translated ἐφ᾽ ᾧ ('seeing that') by *in quo*, '*in whom* all have sinned'. This doctrine was no novelty: even the Greek Fathers, without benefit of mistranslation, had often spoken of the solidarity of the human race in Adam; but they had not pressed on with Augustine's ruthlessness. There was also, in Augustine's view, an inherited weakness and corruption in man's nature, which continued even when the guilt of sin was removed in baptism; a corruption which showed itself most clearly in man's concupiscence, though not to be identified with it (even if Augustine seems often very near to making the equation). And man, through Adam's sin, has lost his freedom. Adam was endowed with freedom in the sense of the ability to avoid sin (*posse non peccare*). He lost this liberty when he misused his free choice. Augustine maintains that this *liberum arbitrium* still remains to man: but he is perplexed in his attempts to give any real content to it, after asserting the loss of the 'liberty not to sin'. Man, he seems to be saying, is responsible for his sin, and yet he cannot help sinning.

Man's only hope is in the free gift of God's grace. Here again Augustine is reiterating an essential part of the Christian tradition; but no teacher before had developed it so relentlessly. Before man can even respond to God's offer of grace God must already have begun his gracious work in him. Augustine is the originator of the technical term 'prevenient grace', from the Latin of Psalm 59, 'His mercy will *go before* me'. This must be followed by 'co-operant grace'; in which Augustine sometimes distinguishes 'sufficient' and 'efficient' assistance (terms somewhat confusing, since the latter corresponds to the 'sufficient cause'—*adiutorium quo*—and the former to the 'necessary cause'—*adiutorium sine quo non*). 'Sufficient grace' is the gift of *posse non peccare*; 'efficient grace' the gift of *non posse peccare*, attained by the elect in virtue of the 'gift of perseverance'. But since God's grace is irresistible, and is given solely to those on whom he wills to have mercy, it is clear that these 'kinds' of grace can only be stages in a predestinated process. Though Augustine dwells chiefly on the mercy which destines the elect to final bliss, he does not shrink from speaking of predestination to eternal damnation. How could he, since he is convinced that the number of elect is limited to the number required to fill the gaps left by the fallen angels, and that Scripture defines that number? 'God wills that all men should be saved' can only mean that God has chosen a certain number of men, of all kinds. We are left with the assertion of God's 'inscrutable justice'.

Here was the first sustained attempt to grapple with the problems of grace and freedom, of predestination and responsibility. The conclusions were sombre enough; and though the Church as a whole did not accept all the affirmations of Augustine, especially the doctrines of irresistible grace and double predestination (to bliss and to damnation), his general doctrine prevailed over the well-meant but somewhat shallow optimism of Pelagius, especially as that was carried further by his follower Julian of Eclanum, whose teaching seemed to make man so independent of God as to have no need of him. Pelagianism was condemned at several African Councils, most emphatically at the last of them at Carthage in 418; in 431 it suffered the censure of an Oecumenical Council of Ephesus and the modified Augustinianism formulated at the Council of Orange in 529 became the standard doctrine on these topics for the Western Church. The problems had not received a satisfactory philosophical solution. How could they? But the concept of freedom had been examined, and the primacy of God asserted, 'whose service is perfect freedom'.

Cyril of Alexandria

Theophilus, the patriarch of Alexandria who so bitterly opposed John Chrysostom, died in 412, and his nephew Cyril was elected to succeed him. We know little of his early life, and the first date we can fix in his career is the year 403 when he took part, with his uncle, in the 'Synod of the Oak' which deposed Chrysostom. He took over from Theophilus, with the see, the inveteracy against the saintly patriarch, which he continued for ten years after John's death: for it was not until 417 that Cyril allowed his name to be restored to the diptychs of the departed (the list of names to be commemorated) in the Eucharist of the Alexandrian Church. In other ways Cyril reproduced much of the vehement ruthlessness which had marked the administration of Theophilus. Jews and Novatians were hounded, in spite of the protests of Orestes, the imperial prefect. And his vigorous efforts to extirpate all traces of paganism lent colour to the accusation, which must be dismissed as non-proven, that he was at least partly responsible for the lynching of the philosopher Hypatia by a mob of Christian fanatics: and one is tempted to suspect that he found some satisfaction in attacking the see of Constantinople in the person of Nestorius, the Antiochene who succeeded to the patriarchate in 428. The Christological controversy which arose from the teaching of Nestorius was Cyril's main preoccupation for the rest of his life: and it was not only a theological contest between the Alexandrian and Antiochene schools; it was also a struggle between the rival sees of Alexandria and Constantinople. Cyril obtained the condemnation of Nestorius at a synod at Rome in 430: he launched twelve anathemas against the new teaching and threatened excommunication. Theodosius II, anxious to avoid an open split in the Eastern Church, summoned a general council at Ephesus, at which Cyril presided, as representative of Pope Celestine I. Nestorius was condemned, deposed, and excommunicated, and Cyril's Christology was confirmed by what became recognized as the Third Oecumenical Council. But there was more than a hint of sharp practice in Cyril's conduct of the Council: certainly he had taken care that it should meet, and conclude its main deliberations, before the 'Antiochene' bishops from Syria could arrive, even before the arrival of the delegates of the pope. The Syrians, in fact, reached Ephesus four days after the conclusion of the first sitting of the council: John of Antioch held a counter-synod with his bishops, which deposed Cyril. Theodosius, with a sweeping gesture of Mercutio-like impartiality, confirmed both councils, and deposed and imprisoned both Cyril and Nestorius. But Cyril was released after a few weeks, and returned to his city in triumph: Nestorius retired to a monastery. A reconciliation between the sees of Alexandria and Antioch was effected in 433: John agreed to the condemnation of Nestorius; Cyril to a compromise profession of faith drawn up, it seems likely, by Theodoret of Cyrus. But the controversy was not finally settled, and Cyril had to explain and defend his position many times. He died in 444.

In his early writings Cyril expounded the traditional Christology of Alexandria which went back to Athanasius, the 'Word–flesh' interpretation of Christ's person, which paid no theological attention to the human soul in the Redeemer. The sufferings are referred simply to the flesh; at the same time it is the flesh which is glorified. It was the challenge of Nestorius which led Cyril to develop his doctrine. Nestorius had been educated at Antioch, and it is likely that he studied under Theodore of Mopsuestia: certainly he was greatly influenced by Theodore's teaching: and soon after his election as patriarch he gave a provocative explanation of the Word–man line of interpretation characteristic of Antioch, when he questioned the applicability to our Lady of the title 'Mother of God' (Θεοτόκος). This title was a corollary of the doctrine of the *communicatio idiomatum*, and had been generally accepted, even at Antioch. Nestorius argued that it was, at best, dangerous, because God could not have a mother: Mary bore the man Jesus who was the habitation of the divine Christ. *Theotokos*, he protested, suggested Arianism or Apollinarianism: that the Son was created, or that the manhood was incomplete. To Cyril, and others of the Alexandrian school, Nestorius seemed to postulate two Sons, the divine Word and the human Jesus, connected by some kind of moral union; and he was accused of reviving the heresy of Paul of Samosata. On such grounds his doctrine was condemned by the church at Ephesus in 431. Nestorius himself maintained to the end that what was condemned was a travesty of his teaching, and towards the end of his life he wrote a defence of his teaching which was discovered at the end of the last century and published in 1910, the English version bearing the curious title, *The Bazaar of Heraclides*. The study of this apologia has led many scholars to hold that Nestorius was not a 'Nestorian', but essentially an orthodox Chalcedonian, even if some of his phraseology was, by Chalcedonian standards, inadequate. He was certainly concerned to preserve the Antiochene doctrine of the two natures, and the genuine human experiences of Christ; and he was shocked by the freedom with which Cyril, and the Alexandrians in general, made use of the *communicatio idiomatum* to ascribe suffering and death to the divinity. He repeatedly denies any intention of teaching 'two Sons', or any 'adoptionist' doctrine: in fact he becomes tedious in his repeated denials. But he has difficulty in stating the unity of Christ's person, because for him a 'nature' must have a *prosopon* and an *hypostasis*, a recognizable aspect, and an objective reality.

Such language was bound to suggest two distinct entities, however strongly Nestorius insisted that the historical Jesus Christ formed 'the *prosopon* of union'. And he thought to avoid the notion of a mixture of the natures by using the term *synapheia* ('conjunction') in preference to *henosis* ('joining in one'); and 'conjunction', however qualified by such adjectives as 'continuous', 'complete', 'perfect', was bound to suggest an external link.

Cyril, as an Alexandrian, thought in terms of a 'Word–flesh' relation. The Word, remaining as he was, 'took the form of a servant' and became incarnate. And he summed up his doctrine in a formula which he believed to belong to Athanasius, but which was in fact Apollinarian: 'one incarnate nature of God the Word'. It must be remembered that in the general use of Alexandria 'nature' was practically identical with *hypostasis*. Cyril insisted on the reality of the two natures—even speaking of two *hypostases*. Christ was 'one out of two', by a 'coming together'; and he described this union as 'physical' (κατὰ φύσιν), or 'hypostatic' (καθ᾽ ὑπόστασιν), the human nature becoming an *hypostasis* (or 'nature') in the *hypostasis* of the divine Word. At the same time Cyril repudiated any notion of confusion, mixture, or alteration resulting from the indissoluble union; the union preserved the differences of the 'natural properties' (a phrase he preferred to 'natures', because of the Alexandrian usage), while it excluded any division of persons. And, in his later writings, the human soul of Christ is essential to Cyril's soteriology.

Theodoret of Cyrus

The last of the great Antiochene theologians was born at Antioch about 393. After a monastic education he was in 423 elected bishop of Cyrus, a small town near Antioch, and administered the diocese for thirty-five years, showing concern alike for the spiritual and the temporal welfare of his flock; for he was as active in the building of public works as in the defence of the faith against pagan and heretic. He supported Nestorius against Cyril, and just before the Council of Ephesus he put out a *Refutation of the Twelve Anathemas* of Cyril, which has not survived. At Ephesus he naturally took the side of John of Antioch, maintaining his position after the decisions of the Council, and publishing a weighty criticism of these decisions, and of Cyril's teaching. It seems likely that the Formula of Union of 433 was drawn up by Theodoret, but he refused to adhere to the reconciliation until the demand for a recognition of the condemnation of Nestorius ceased to be one of the conditions.

Soon after this he was involved in the controversy over the teaching of Eutyches, which represented the extreme form of 'Alexandrian' theology, as Nestorianism had represented the far 'left' of Antiochene teaching. Cyril's successor, Dioscorus, who had all Cyril's ruthlessness and none of Cyril's theological perception, supported Eutyches, and secured the deposition and exile of Theodoret at the 'Robber Council' of Ephesus in 449. Theodoret appealed to Pope Leo I, and the pope declared the council null and void: it was he who called it the 'Robber Council', 'no *concilium*, but rather a *latrocinium*'. At Chalcedon, in 451, Theodoret was at length induced, much against his will, to anathematize the teaching of Nestorius and 'all who do not acknowledge the Blessed Virgin as Mother of God, and who divide into two the only Son'. He was then reinstated and certified as an 'orthodox teacher'. He returned to administer his diocese for seven years more, and died about 466. But in 553 the Second Council of Constantinople (the Fifth General Council) condemned his writings against Cyril, and his criticisms of the Council of Ephesus.

Although Theodoret championed Nestorius against Cyril, his Christology avoided Nestorian extremes, and stated the moderate Antiochene teaching along 'Word–man' lines. He affirmed the distinction between the two natures in Christ, while asserting their union in one *prosopon*: and he criticized Cyril's 'hypostatic ("natural") union', partly because it suggested a necessary development rather than a free act of love on the part of the divine Word; and he repudiated the Alexandrian's liberal facility with the *communicatio idiomatum* which seemed to compromise the distinction between the humanity and the divinity. But his insistence on the reality of the union (*henosis*) sufficiently clears him of any taint of 'Nestorianism', as the Council of Ephesus interpreted and condemned it.

Leo the Great

We have scarcely any information about the early life of the pope who
in the day when heaven was falling,
The hour when earth's foundations fled,

in the general catastrophe of the barbarian invasions and the collapse of the Roman Empire in the West, 'held the sky suspended' over the Church's power and influence, claiming jurisdiction in Gaul, Africa, and Spain, and laying the foundations of the political influence of the papacy in medieval Christendom. Leo had been an important member of the papal councils for ten years before he was elected pope in 440; Valentinian III recognized his claim to supremacy in the Western Church by granting him jurisdiction over the Western provinces; and the famous encounter with Attila in 452, when at Mantua he achieved the withdrawal of the Huns to behind the Danube, and the authority which won from Gaiseric a mitigation of the worst horrors of a sack when Rome was taken by the Vandals in 452, led to an enormous increase in the prestige of the Roman see. In the Church his support was sought by the conflicting parties in every dispute, even in the East, which did not recognize his claim to a superior jurisdiction; and that support was sought especially in the Eutychian controversy. His representatives presided over the Council of Chalcedon, and his dogmatic letter to Flavian of Constantinople, later called the *Tome of Leo*, was adopted as the standard statement of orthodox Christology. Leo contributed nothing original to theology: but he gave a clear and vigorous statement of the doctrine of the West, in answer to the uncontrolled 'Alexandrianism' of Eutyches and his supporters, who were bent on overthrowing the Formula of Union of 433.

Eutyches had no claim to intellectual distinction, and it is difficult to discover whether he said what he meant or meant what he said: but as the venerable archimandrite of an important monastery at Constantinople he won favour and influence at court. In 448 he was accused of heresy by Eusebius of Dorylaeum, who had been one of the first to denounce Nestorius. His doctrine was examined at the local synod of Constantinople, at which the patriarch Flavian put forward a statement which points towards the Chalcedonian definition: 'We acknowledge Christ to be of two natures after the incarnation; we acknowledge one Christ, one Son, one Lord, in one *hypostasis* and one *prosopon*.' The synod condemned and deposed Eutyches: and Eutychianism became the name for the extreme form of monophysitism which taught that Christ was indeed 'of two natures', as Flavian maintained; but that after the incarnation the humanity was totally absorbed by the divinity, so that one nature only remained. That such teaching was very much in the air at this period is shown by the attack of Theodoret in *Eranistes* which, without naming Eutyches, is aimed at doctrine of this kind. It is, in fact, difficult to discover precisely what doctrine Eutyches held: he was, as Leo said, a muddle-headed illiterate in theology (*multum imprudens et nimis imperitus*). While rejecting the two natures he asserted that Christ was both truly God and truly man, and that he took human flesh of the Virgin; yet he refused to confess that Christ was 'of the same substance' as the rest of mankind. A horror of Nestorian 'dualism', and the Alexandrian understanding of 'nature' as virtually equivalent to *hypostasis*; these were the sources of his teaching: and amid all his confusions and inconsistencies he reiterated his principal assertion: 'two natures before incarnation; one after'.

Against such teaching Leo affirmed that the Word was the *persona* of him who was God and man. Like Hilary, he maintained that the 'employing' of the incarnation did not entail the abandonment of his essential power and glory. In this one person each nature keeps its own characteristics (*proprietates*), without confusion, while the two natures always act in harmony: 'Each nature carries out its characteristic activity in fellowship with the other; the Word performs what pertains to the Word, the flesh what pertains to the flesh'. And the unity of person justifies the *communicatio idiomatum*.

Such a statement of the Rule of Faith solved no difficulties: but it stated clearly the data which any attempted solution had to recognize. And the Chalcedonian Definition did no more than that.

Note on References, etc.

The translations throughout are the Editor's.

References to the works of the Fathers are given according to the customary titles, Latin ones being used where there are no standard English titles. See also List of Works Cited, pp. 281 ff.

. . . indicates the omission of some words of the original.

. . . [Isa. 53. 1–12]: biblical references given thus indicate that the omitted words reproduce, wholly or substantially, the passage of Scripture referred to.

LXX = Septuagint (i.e. the earliest Greek version of the Jewish Scriptures). Unless otherwise stated it may be assumed that quotations from the O.T. and Apocryphal books are from the LXX; the symbol is inserted only to explain the use of a text different from that of current English versions (A.V., R.V., &c.) based on the Hebrew.

Ps. 21 (22), &c., indicates a quotation from a Psalm in the LXX where the numbering differs from the current English versions (e.g. Ps. 21 (LXX) = Ps. 22 (Heb., B.C.P., A.V., &c.)); but these double references are given only when there is a difference of text between LXX and current versions.

Cyril of Jerusalem

I. Man and the Fall

Before the soul comes into this world it has not sinned at all: we come
into this world sinless, and then we sin through our own choice . . .

The soul has free will: and though the devil can tempt the soul he
has not the power to compel it against its will. He suggests to you the
idea of fornication; the acceptance or rejection of the suggestion
depends on your decision.   *cat.* 4. 19, 21

Through the devil our forefather Adam was expelled, because of
disobedience; and he exchanged a paradise which produced wonderful
fruits of its own accord for an earth which produced thorns. 'Well
then', someone will say, 'we have been deceived and ruined: is there
no chance now of salvation? We have fallen: is there no hope of rising?
We have been blinded: is there no way of recovering our sight? We
are dead: is there no resurrection?' Will not he who awoke Lazarus
raise you? . . . He who shed his precious blood for us will rescue us from
sin. . . . Thorny ground is changed to fertile by good cultivation: is
salvation irrecoverable for us? Nature then admits of salvation: what
is needed is our decision.   *cat.* 2. 4

II. The Person of Christ

Believe also in the Son of God, that one and only Son, our Lord
Jesus Christ: God begotten of God, Life begotten of Life, Light
begotten of Light, like to his begetter in all respects: who did not
begin his existence in time, but has been before all ages eternally and
incomprehensibly begotten of the Father; who is the Wisdom and
Power of God and his Righteousness in personal subsistence; who sits
at the right hand of the Father before all ages.   *cat.* 4. 7

Believe also that he, the only begotten Son of God, for our sins came
down to earth from heaven, assuming a manhood subject to the same
feelings as ours, and being born of a holy virgin and the Holy Spirit:
and this not in appearance or in imagination, but in reality. He did not
pass through the Virgin as through a channel, but truly took flesh and

was truly fed with milk from her. He truly ate as we eat, and drank as we drink. For if the incarnation was a figment then our salvation was a figment. Christ was twofold; he was man, in what was visible; he was God, in what was invisible. He ate, as being really man like us (for he had the feelings of the flesh just as we have); but he fed the five thousand with five loaves, as being God. He died, as being really man; but as God he raised the body four days dead.   *cat.* 4. 9

Religion does not allow us to worship the mere man: and it is not true reverence to speak of him as God only, separate from his manhood. For if Christ is God (as he truly is) but did not take manhood, we are aliens from salvation. Let him then be worshipped as God, but let it be believed that he also became man. For it is of no avail to call him man, without his divinity; and we do not receive salvation if we fail to acknowledge his manhood together with his Godhead.   *cat.* 12.1

III. The Work of Christ

(a) The Defeat of the Devil

The devil had used the flesh as an instrument against us ... [Rom. 7. 23]. Thus we were saved by the very weapons with which the devil fought against us. The Lord took from us a likeness to us, that we might save human nature. He took our likeness so that he might give greater grace to that which lacked; that sinful human nature might become partaker of God. 'For where sin abounded, grace abounded overwhelmingly.'[1] The Lord had to suffer for us: but if the devil had recognized him, he would not have dared to approach him. 'For had they known, they would not have crucified the Lord of glory.'[2] His body therefore became a bait for death, so that the dragon, hoping to swallow him, might vomit up also those whom he had swallowed. 'For death growing strong has swallowed us up, and yet God has removed every tear from every face.'[3]   *cat.* 12. 15

(b) The Ransom

Do not be amazed at the statement that the whole world was ransomed. For it was no mere man, but the only begotten Son of God, who died

[1] Rom. 5. 20.   [2] 1 Cor. 2. 8.   [3] Isa. 25. 8 [LXX].

for the world. The sin of one man, Adam, had the power to bring death to the world. But if by one man's fall death reigned over the world, then surely all the more will life 'reign by the righteousness of one man'.[1] And if they were then cast out of paradise because of the tree from which they ate, will it not be easier for believers to enter paradise because of the tree of Jesus? If the first man, fashioned from earth, brought universal death, does not he who fashioned him out of earth bring eternal life; since he himself is the Life? If Phineas stopped the anger of God by slaying the wrong-doer in righteous wrath,[2] does not Jesus, who did not slay another man, but 'gave himself up as a ransom',[3] remove God's anger against man? *cat.* 13. 2

(c) *The Sacrifice*

The Saviour endured these things, 'making peace, through the blood of the cross, for things in heaven and things on earth'.[4] For we were enemies of God through sin, and God had ordained death for the sinner. Then one of two things had to happen: either God might be consistent and destroy all men, or he might show compassion and cancel the sentence. But observe the wisdom of God. He preserved consistency in the sentence, but allowed compassion to operate. Christ 'took up our sins on to the Cross in his own body so that we might cease to live for sins and might live for righteousness'.[5] And he who died for us was of no small account. It was not a literal lamb that was killed; it was not a mere man, nor just an angel: it was God made man. The lawlessness of sinners was not as great as the righteousness of him who died for them. Our sins are not comparable with the righteous action of him who laid down his life for us. *cat.* 13. 33

IV. The Holy Spirit

(a) *Personality*

There is only one Holy Spirit, the Paraclete. And as there is one God the Father, and no second Father; and as there is one only begotten Son and Word of God, who has no brother; so there is only one Holy Spirit, and no second spirit, equal in honour to him. The Holy Spirit is a most mighty power, a being divine and unsearchable. He is a living, intelligent being, the sanctifying power of all things made by God through Christ. *cat.* 16. 3

---

[1] Rom. 5. 17.　[2] Cf. Num. 25. 5-11.　[3] 1 Tim. 2. 6.　[4] Col. 1. 20.　[5] 1 Pet. 2. 24.

There is one life in the Father and the Son and the Holy Ghost. We do not proclaim three Gods; let the Marcionites[1] be put to silence. We proclaim one God, through one Son, with the Holy Spirit. Our faith is indivisible, our worship is inseparable. We do not, like some, divide the Holy Trinity; nor do we confuse the Persons as does Sabellius.[2]

cat. 16. 4

(b) The Life-giver

Why did he [in John 4. 14] refer to the grace of the Spirit under the name of water? Because through water all things have subsistence. Because water produces vegetables and animals. Because the water of rain comes down from heaven. Because it comes down in one form, but its effects take many forms. For one spring watered all Paradise and the same rain comes down on the whole world. Yet it becomes white in the lily, red in the rose, purple in the violet . . . it adapts itself to each recipient. So also the Holy Ghost, being one, of one nature, indivisible, 'distributes to each his grace as he wills'.[3] And as the dry tree puts out shoots when it partakes of water, so the sinful soul, when through repentance it has been granted the Holy Spirit, brings forth clusters of righteousness. Though one in nature, the Spirit produces many excellencies by the will of God, and in the name of Christ.

cat. 16. 12

(c) In the Trinity

The Father gives to the Son; and the Son communicates to the Holy Spirit . . . [Matt. 11. 27; John 16. 13, 14]. The Father through the Son, with the Holy Spirit, confers all his gifts; the gifts of the Father are none other than those of the Son and those of the Holy Spirit. For there is one salvation, one power, one faith; one God, the Father; one Lord, his only begotten Son; one Holy Spirit, the Paraclete. It is enough for us to know these things; do not be curious about the Spirit's nature or *hypostasis*. If it had been explained in Scripture I should have spoken of it: let me not venture on what has not been revealed. It is enough for salvation to know that there is a Father, a Son, and a Holy Spirit.

cat. 16. 24

---

[1] See n. 3 on p. 85
[2] S. taught that the Son and the Spirit were successive modes of God's activity.
[3] 1 Cor. 12. 11.

V. The Church

The Church is called 'Catholic' because it extends through all the world, from one end of the earth to another. Also because it teaches universally and without omission all the doctrines which ought to come to man's knowledge, about things both visible and invisible, heavenly and earthly; and because it brings under the sway of true religion all classes of men, rulers and subjects, learned and ignorant; and because it universally treats and cures every type of sin, committed by means of soul and body, and possesses in itself every kind of virtue which can be named, in deeds and words, and spiritual gifts of every kind.

It is appropriately called the Church (ἐκκλησία), because it calls out (ἐκκαλεῖσθαι) all men and assembles them together . . .

When you are staying in any city, do not inquire simply where the Lord's House is (for the sects of the impious attempt to call their dens 'houses of the Lord'). And do not ask simply where the Church is, but say, 'Where is the Catholic Church?'. For that is the special name of this holy Church which is the mother of all. *cat.* 18. 23, 24, 26

VI. The Sacraments

(a) Baptism

(i) *The Necessity of Baptism*

Man is a being with a twofold nature, since he consists of body and soul; and his purification is twofold: immaterial purification for the immaterial element, material for the body. The water cleanses his body, the Spirit seals his soul. . . . Therefore, when you are about to descend into the water, do not think merely of the actual water, but look for its saving power through the effective operation of the Holy Spirit; for without both of these you cannot be made perfect . . . [John 3. 5]. If anyone has been baptized with water, without being counted worthy of the Spirit, he does not have the grace in its completeness; while no one will go into the Kingdom of Heaven, however virtuous in his actions he may prove to be, if he does not receive the seal given by means of water. . . . [*In the case of Cornelius*] the Scripture tells us that, after the grace of the Spirit had been given, Peter 'commanded them to be baptized in the name of Jesus Christ';[1] that after the regeneration of the soul through their faith, the body also might share the grace, by means of the water.   *cat.* 3. 4

(ii) *Enrolment*

You are already in the entrance-hall of the King's palace . . . you have had your names registered, you have been called up for military service . . . (4) We, as Christ's ministers, have admitted each of you, and, being appointed as it were to the office of doorkeepers, we have left the door open. . . . You have entered, you have been admitted, your name has been registered. Observe the dignified organization of the Church. Notice her order and discipline: the reading of the Scriptures, the presence of the clergy, the course of training. You should be impressed by these surroundings and instructed by what is presented to your eyes. . . . Put off fornication and uncleanness, and put on the shining garment of self-control. I give you this command, before Jesus, the bridegroom of souls, comes in and sees your garments.[2] You have ample notice; you have forty days for penitence.   *procat.* 1

(iii) *Preparation*

You were given the title of 'Catechumen', one who is 'lectured'—from outside; hearing of hope, yet not acquainted with it; hearing of mysteries without understanding them; hearing Scripture without knowing its deeper meaning. Now you are no longer 'lectured to' from outside; you are instructed within. For the Spirit dwells within you, and from henceforth fashions your mind into a house of God . . . Do not count it a light thing that you are receiving: you, a pitiable human being, are receiving a title which belongs to God. Paul says: 'God is faithful.'[3] And another too says: 'He is faithful and just.'[4] The psalmist foresaw this when, he said, speaking in the person of God: 'I said, You are gods, and you are all sons of the Highest.'[5] The psalmist said this because, though men, they were to receive a title belonging to God. Beware lest while you have the title of 'faithful' your moral behaviour may be unfaithful.   *procat.* 6

Let your feet be swift to attend the instructions [catechizings]; receive the exorcisms with eagerness. When you are breathed on,[6] when you

---

[1] Acts 10. 48. [2] Cf. Matt. 22. 11. [3] 1 Thess. 5. 24. [4] 1 John 1. 9. [5] Ps. 82. 6.
'Exsufflation' was one of the ceremonies of exorcism; 'insufflation' ('breathing on') is more generally used of the ceremony symbolizing the gift of the Spirit.

are exorcized, the action is for your salvation. . . . Without exorcisms the soul cannot be purified. Your face has been veiled, so that from now on your thoughts may be undistracted; so that a roving eye may not cause a roving heart. But though your eyes have been veiled, your ears are not hindered from receiving what is for your salvation. The goldsmith applies wind to the fire by means of ingenious mechanisms, and blows on the gold which is hidden in the crucible, stimulating the flame around it, and thus he finds what he seeks. In the same kind of way the exorcizers, inspiring fear by a divine breath [spirit], heat up the soul, as it were, in the crucible of the body: thus the enemy, the evil spirit, flees, while salvation remains, and so does the hope of eternal life. And henceforth the soul, being purified from its sins, possesses salvation.

Attend carefully to the course of instruction; even if our discourse is long drawn out, do not let your attention slip. For you are receiving your armour against the activity of the enemy, against heresies, against Jews, Samaritans and Gentiles.   *procat.* 9, 10

When an instruction is given, if a catechumen inquires what the instructors have said, do not tell anything to an outsider. For we are entrusting to you a mystery, the hope of the life to come. . . . If a catechumen is told of these mysteries by one of the faithful . . . he does not understand what he is told, and he criticizes and jeers: and the faithful is condemned for treachery. You are now standing on the frontier: take care not to let slip a word: not because what you might say is unworthy of utterance, but because the hearer is not worthy to receive it. You yourself were once a catechumen, and then I did not tell you what was to come in future instruction.   *procat.* 12

When exorcism is performed, let the men be with the men, the women with the women, until all the rest of those being exorcized have arrived. Here Noah's ark supplies me with a useful illustration. In the ark were Noah and his sons; and, separately, his wife and his sons' wives. There was just one ark and the door was shut; but everything was carefully organized. And though the Church is shut, and we are all inside, still there must be a separation, men staying with men, women with women. Do not let the ground of your salvation be an occasion for your ruin. Even if there is good reason for their sitting next to one another, all improper emotions must be banished. Again, let the men, as they sit there, have some profitable book; and let one of them read aloud and another listen. If there is no book available, let one pray, and another give some profitable discourse. And let the gathering of young women be so arranged that they may be either singing hymns or reading quietly, so that their lips may be speaking but others may not hear ('I do not allow a woman to speak in church'[1]). And let a married woman copy the same example: let her pray, with her lips moving but her voice inaudible.   *procat.* 1

(iv) *The Creed*

Since all cannot read the Scriptures, some being prevented by illiteracy, others by lack of leisure, we comprise the whole teaching of the faith in those few articles, so that the soul may not perish from ignorance. I want you to commit this to memory, word for word; and to recite it very carefully among yourselves: not writing it down on paper, but inscribing it by memory on your heart. Be careful while you are rehearsing it, and do not let any of the catechumens overhear what has been entrusted to you.   *cat.* 5. 12

(v) *The Rite*

You have been admitted to the divine life-giving baptism, and are now capable of receiving the more sacred mysteries. . . . Let us now instruct you in detail, so that you may know the meaning for you of what happened on the evening of your baptism.

First you entered into the vestibule of the baptistery, and as you stood facing west, you heard the command to stretch out your hand; and you renounced Satan, as if he were present.

                                   cat. 19. [*cat. myst.* 1] 1, 2

I want to tell you why you stand facing west. This is necessary because the west is the region of visible darkness, and Satan is darkness and has his dominion in darkness. . . . And what did you say as you stood there? 'I renounce thee, Satan' . . .

Then in the second formula you are instructed to say, 'and all thy works' . . .

And then, 'and all thy pomp' (such as the mania for shows, and horse-racing, hunting, and all such frivolity) . . .

And after this you say, 'And all thy service' . . . [*All idolatry and superstition*].   *cat.* 19. [*cat. myst.* 1] 4–6, 8

[1] 1 Tim. 2. 11 f.; 1 Cor. 12. 34.

Then, when you renounce Satan, utterly cancelling every covenant with him, the ancient alliance with hell,[1] there is opened to you the paradise of God, which he planted towards the east,[2] whence our first ancestor was expelled. To symbolize this, you turned from the west to the east, the region of light. And you were told to say, 'I believe in the Father, and in the Son, and in the Holy Ghost, and in one baptism of repentance' . . .

All this took place in the outer chamber. But when, God willing, we have entered the Holy of Holies in the succeeding explanation of the mysteries, we shall then understand the symbolism of the rites performed there.   *cat.* 19. [*cat. myst.* 1] 9, 11

As soon as you entered, you took off your clothes: this was a symbol of stripping off the old man with his behaviour.[3] And after undressing, you were naked, thus imitating the naked Christ on the cross . . . And you bore the likeness of the first-formed Adam, who was naked in the garden without feeling shame.[4]

Then, after stripping, you were anointed with exorcized oil, from the hairs on top of your head to your feet, and were thus connected with the good olive tree, Jesus Christ. You were cut off from the wild olive and grafted on the good one[5] . . . the oil symbolized participation in the richness of Christ, a remedy to drive away all trace of the hostile power . . .

After this you were led by the hand to the holy pool of divine baptism, as Christ was taken from the cross to the appointed sepulchre. And each of you was asked if he believed in the Name of the Father, and of the Son, and of the Holy Ghost. And you made that saving confession; you descended into the water and came up again three times; thus alluding symbolically to the three days burial of Christ . . . In the very same moment you died and were born; and that water of salvation became both your grave and your mother.   *cat.* 20. [*cat. myst.* 2] 2–4

You were made 'christs'[6] when you received the symbol of the Holy Ghost, and all that was done representationally, for you are representations of Christ. After his baptism in the river Jordan, when he imparted some tincture of his divinity to the waters, he came up from them: and the Holy Ghost came upon him in substantial form, like resting

---

[1] Cp. Isa. 28. 15.   [2] Gen. 2. 8.
[3] Col. 3. 9.   [4] Gen. 2. 25.   [5] Rom. 11. 24.   [6] 'anointed ones'.

on like. Similarly, when you came up from the pool of the holy streams, chrism was given you, an emblem of the anointing of Christ. This is the Holy Spirit . . .

Christ was not anointed by men with oil or material ointment; but when the Father appointed him as Saviour of the whole world he anointed him with the Holy Ghost, as Peter says . . . [Acts 10. 38] Christ was anointed with the spiritual 'oil of gladness;'[1] the Holy Spirit who is called the oil of gladness because he is the cause of spiritual gladness. And so you are anointed with ointment, being made partakers and 'fellows'[1] of Christ.

Beware of supposing that this is merely ointment. For as the bread of the Eucharist, after the invocation of the Holy Spirit, is no longer simply bread, but the Body of Christ; so also this holy ointment is no longer merely ointment, not what one might call ordinary ointment, after the invocation; it is the gift of Christ, and by the presence of the Holy Spirit it conveys the power of his divinity. It is applied symbolically to the forehead and the other organs of sense; and while the body is anointed with the visible ointment, the soul is sanctified by the holy and life-giving Spirit.

And you were anointed first on the forehead, that you might be freed from shame. . . . Next, on your ears, so that you might have ears ready to hear the divine mysteries. . . . Then on your nostrils, that you might say . . . 'We are to God a sweet fragrance'[2]. . . . Then on your breast; that you might 'put on the breastplate of righteousness and withstand the devices of the devil'[3] . . .

When you have been granted this chrism you are called Christians, verifying the name by your new birth. Before you were admitted to this grace you had no genuine right to the title, but you were advancing along the way to becoming Christians.   cat. 21. [cat. myst. 3] 1-5

(b) The Eucharist

(i) The Doctrine

The teaching of blessed Paul is in itself sufficient to give you complete assurance about the divine mysteries, the admission to which makes us 'of the same body'[4] and blood with Christ. For he proclaimed, with emphasis and precision, 'That our Lord Jesus Christ . . . took bread . . . and said: "This is my body:"' and, taking the cup, he gave thanks, and

[1] Ps. 45. 7.   [2] 2 Cor. 2. 15.   [3] Eph. 6. 14, 11.   [4] Eph. 3. 6.

said, . . . "This is my blood".[1] Since Christ himself in his own words asserted of the bread, 'This is my body', who will dare any longer to have doubts? And since in his own words he insisted, 'This is my blood', who will have any doubts or say that it is not his blood?

Once, in Cana of Galilee, he changed water into wine (and wine is akin to blood); is it incredible that he should change wine into blood? . . . Therefore with complete assurance let us partake of those elements as being the body and blood of Christ. For in the symbol of bread his body is given to you, and in the symbol of wine his blood; so that by partaking of the body and blood of Christ you may be made of the same body and blood with him. For in this way we become Christ-bearers, since his body and blood is distributed in the parts of our body. Thus, as blessed Peter says, we 'become partakers of the divine nature'.[2]

Christ once said in conversation with the Jews: 'If you do not eat my flesh and drink my blood you have no life in you.'[3] They did not take the meaning spiritually and were shocked: they withdrew themselves, supposing that he was urging a literal eating of flesh.

Even under the old covenant there was shewbread; but this came to an end, as belonging to the old covenant. But in the new covenant there is the bread of heaven[4] and the cup of salvation,[5] sanctifying both soul and body; for as the bread is adapted to our body, so the Word is appropriate to our soul. Therefore think of the bread and wine not as merely that, for they are in fact, according to the Lord's express statement, the body and blood of Christ. For though sense suggests the mere elements, let faith assure you otherwise. Do not judge the matter from taste, but from faith be assured, without hesitation, that you have been granted the body and blood of Christ.   *cat.* 22. [*cat. myst.* 4] 1–6

You have been instructed and assured that what appears as bread is not (mere) bread (though it is thus perceived by taste) but the body of Christ; and that what seems wine is not (mere) wine (though the taste will have it to be so) but the blood of Christ; and that David of old referred to this when he sang, 'And bread strengthens the heart of man, to gladden his face with oil'.[6] Therefore 'strengthen your heart' and 'gladden the face' of your soul, by partaking of this as spiritual.

cat. 22. [*cat. myst.* 4] 9

[1] 1 Cor. 11. 23 f. [2] 2 Pet. 1. 4. [3] Cf. John 6. 53. [4] Ps. 78. 24; John 6. 31 etc. [5] Ps. 116. 13.
[6] Ps. 104. 15.

(ii) *The Rite*

Then after sanctifying ourselves with those spiritual hymns [*viz. the Preface and Sanctus*], we call upon the compassionate God to send out his Holy Spirit on the gifts that are set out; that he may make the bread the body of Christ, and the wine the blood of Christ. For whatever the Holy Spirit has touched is assuredly sanctified and changed.

Then when the spiritual sacrifice, the bloodless act of worship is complete, we beseech God, on the ground of that sacrifice of propitiation, for the common peace of the churches; for the stability of the world; for kings; for our soldiers and allies; for the sick and afflicted; in fact, we pray for all who need help, and for them we offer this sacrifice. Next we remember those who have fallen asleep before us; first the Patriarchs, Apostles, Martyrs; that by their prayers and intercessions God may receive our supplication. After that we pray for the holy Fathers and bishops who have already fallen asleep; and, in short, for all the departed, believing that it will be the greatest advantage for the souls of those for whom this supplication is offered when the holy and awful sacrifice is set before God.

We offer up Christ, sacrificed for our sins, propitiating our compassionate God on their behalf, and on our own.   *cat. 23. [cat. myst. 5]* 7–10

'Give us today our "super-substantial"[1] bread.' Our ordinary bread is not super-substantial, but this holy bread is super-substantial, which means that it is 'applied to the substance'[2] of the soul. This bread does not 'pass into the stomach and out into the sewer[3]' but is distributed through the whole system for the benefit of body and soul.

cat. 23. [cat. myst. 5] 15

After this, [*i.e. after the priest has said 'Holy things for holy people'*] you hear the cantor inviting you with sacred melody to participate in the holy mysteries, in these words: 'Taste and see that the Lord is good.'[4] Do not trust your palate to form the judgement; trust unhesitating faith. For those who taste are not bidden to taste bread and wine, but the body and blood of Christ thus symbolized.

When you approach, therefore, do not come forward with wrists outstretched, or with fingers spread open. Make your left hand, as it were, a throne for the right, since it is about to receive a king; and

---

[1] ἐπι-ούσιον—*super-substantial.*   [2] ἐπὶ τὴν οὐσίαν.   [3] Matt. 15. 17.   [4] Ps. 34. 8.

hollow your palm, and receive the body of Christ, adding your 'Amen'. Then, after you have carefully hallowed your eyes by the touch of the holy body, partake of it. Take care to lose none of it . . .

After partaking of the body of Christ, approach the cup of his blood also. Do not stretch up your hands, but bow down and say, in a manner of worship and reverence, 'Amen'; and be sanctified by partaking also of Christ's blood. And while the moisture is still on your lips, touch them with your hands, and sanctify your eyes and forehead and the rest of your organs of sense. Then wait for the prayer, and give thanks to God who has counted you worthy of admission to those great mysteries. *cat.* 23. [*cat. myst.* 5] 20-2

Hilary of Poitiers

I. The Trinity

'Homoousion' and 'Homoiousion'

The term *homoousios* (of one substance) may express a grasp of the true faith; but it lends itself to deception. If we apply it to a combination of distinction and likeness of nature, to insist that the 'likeness' asserts not a likeness in mere externals [*speciem*] but in underlying reality [*genus*], then our teaching accords with the truth of our religion: providing that we take 'one substance' as meaning a likeness of distinct entities, so that unity means not numerical singularity but equality. . . . If 'Father and Son of one substance' is taken as implying a single entity, though signified by two names, we may confess the Son in name, but we do not acknowledge him in thought, if by confessing 'one substance' we are asserting that one single being is himself both Father and Son. Again, there is a foothold for the error which supposes the Father to have divided himself, to have cut off a part of himself to be his Son. . . . There is also a third error, which takes 'Father and Son of one substance' to indicate a prior substance, which the two share equally. The orthodox will assert 'one substance of Father and Son'; but he must not *start* from that: nor must he hold this as the chief truth, as if there could be no true faith without it. He will assert 'one substance' without danger, when he has first said, 'The Father is ingenerate; the Son has his origin and existence from the Father; he is like the Father in goodness, honour, and nature.' He is subject to his Father, as the origin of his being. . . . He does not come from nothing; he is generate. He is not unborn; but he shares in timelessness. He is not the Father, but the Son derived from him. He is not a portion, he is a whole: not the Creator himself, but his image; the image of God, born of God, from God: he is not a creature; he is God. But he is not another God in underlying substance, but one God though essence of undiffering substance. God is one, not in person, but in nature.

de syn. 67–9

I know, dearest Brethren, that some acknowledge the likeness, while denying equality. . . . If they say that there is a difference between likeness and equality, I ask what is the basis of equality. For if the Son is

like the Father in essence and goodness and glory and time, I ask in
what way does he appear not to be equal. . . . If the Father has given to
the Son, whom he has generated impassibly, a nature that was not
other than his own, nor different from his own, it must have been his
own nature that he gave. Thus 'like' means 'his own'; and that entails
equality, the absence of difference. Things which show no difference
are one; not by unity of person, but by equality of nature.

de syn. 74

II. The Person of Christ

(a) *The Two Natures*

Anyone who fails to see Christ Jesus as at once truly God and truly
man is blind to his own life: to deny Christ Jesus, or God the Spirit, or
our own flesh, is equally perilous. 'If anyone acknowledges me before
men, I shall acknowledge him before my Father who is in heaven.
But if anyone denies me before men, I shall deny him before my
Father, who is in heaven'[1]. . . . Christ has been appointed as in himself
the Mediator, for the salvation of the Church, and in that mystery
[*sacramentum*] of meditation between God and mankind he is one
being, yet he is both God and man: by the union of the two natures
he is one entity comprising both natures; but in such a way that in
either capacity be lacked nothing of the other, so that he did not cease
to be God by being born as man, or fail to be man by remaining God.
This is the true faith of human blessedness, to proclaim God and man,
to acknowledge Word and flesh; not to fail to recognize God because
he is man, nor to fail to see the flesh because he is the Word.

He is born as man, while remaining God: this is in contradiction of
our natural understanding. That he should remain God, though born
as man, does not contradict our natural hope. For the birth of a higher
nature into a lower state gives us confidence that a lower nature can
be born into a higher condition. But on the analogy of the familiar
ordering of things in the physical world, the fulfilment of our hopes
is more readily comprehended than the working of the divine mystery
of the incarnation. For in all that comes into being, the world has the
power to increase; there is no possibility of diminution. Consider trees,

[1] Matt. 10. 32–3.

crops, and cattle. Observe mankind, the rational creation. Man always advances by increase: he does not contract by diminution; but his increase does not mean that he ceases to be himself. For even if he fails through advancing years, or is cut off by death, though he suffers a change in respect of time, or comes to an end in respect of his mode of life; yet it is beyond his power to cease to be what he is, so as to to create a new self by decrease, that is, by dwindling from an old man into an infant. The law of the physical world necessitates the advance of our nature towards increase: therefore it is reasonable to look for development to a higher order of nature. Increase is according to nature, decrease is against nature. So it was appropriate for God to be other than what he continued to be, while not ceasing to be what he had always been: for God to be born in human nature, and yet not cease to be God; to contract himself even to conception, to the cradle, to infancy; without departing from the power of God. This mystery [*sacramentum*] is not for his own sake, but for ours. The assumption of our manhood was not an advancement for God; but the willing acceptance of his humiliation is our advantage. He does not lose the status of God, while he acquires divinity for man.   *de trin.* 9. 3, 4

Jesus Christ is man and God: his existence as God does not begin with his birth as man; nor does he cease to be God when he becomes man; and after his human life there is the whole of manhood and the whole of Godhead in his divinity.... There is a distinction between the three states: God, before his human life; then God-and-man; and thereafter wholly God and wholly man.   *de trin.* 9. 6

I had briefly to establish these points so that we should remember that in the Lord Jesus Christ a person of both natures is encountered; for he who remained in the form of God took the form of a servant, through which he was obedient even to death.[1] For the obedience of death is not in the form of God, just as the form of God is not in the form of a servant. But through the mystery [*sacramentum*] of the gospel dispensation, he who is in the form of a servant is the same as he who is in the form of God. To take the form of a servant and to remain in the form of God are not the same thing: and he who remained in the form of God could not have taken the form of a servant except

[1] Phil. 2. 8.

by his self-emptying [*evacuatio*], since the combination of both forms is inconsistent. But he who emptied himself is the same as he who took the form of a servant. If he ceased to exist he could not have 'taken': to take entails the existence of the taker. Thus the self-emptying of the form is not the abolition of the nature; since he who emptied himself did not cease to exist, and he who took continued to be. The identity of 'emptier' and 'taker' involves a mystery [*sacramentum*], but not a ceasing to be [*interitus*]. . . . Christ was one and the same, when he changed his outward fashion [*habitus*], and when he reassumed it.

de trin. 9. 14

Jesus Christ is both Son of God and Son of Man. . . . The Son of Man is the same person as the Son of God; he who is in the form of God is the same as he who was born as complete man in the form of a servant. Just as, by the nature determined for us by God when man was first created, man is born as a creature of body and soul, so Jesus Christ through his own divine power was man and God, compounded of body and soul. He had in himself the whole reality of manhood, and the whole reality of godhead.

de trin. 10. 19

(b) The Heavenly Body

The Lord himself, when expounding the mystery of his nativity, said, 'I am the living bread, I who came down from heaven . . .'[1]. He calls himself bread, for he himself is the origin of his own body. So that it should not be thought the power and nature of the Word left him when he became flesh, he spoke again of his bread; so that by 'the bread that comes down from heaven' it might be understood that his body does not derive from human conception, being shown to be heavenly. It is 'his bread', and this proclaims the assumption of a body by the Word; for he added, 'Unless you eat the flesh of the Son of Man, and drink his blood, you will not have life in you.'[2] He is the Son of Man, and he himself descended as the bread from heaven. Thus by his 'bread which comes down from heaven', and by 'the flesh and blood of the Son of Man' is understood the assumption of flesh conceived by the Holy Spirit and born of a virgin.

de trin. 10. 18

[1] John 6. 51.   [2] John 6. 53.

(c) The Sufferings of Christ

The man Jesus Christ, only-begotten God, through flesh and the Word, both Son of Man and Son of God, assumed true humanity, in the likeness of our human nature, without departing from his godhead. Though blows fell on his human body, and wounds were inflicted on it; though it was lashed with the scourge and lifted up on the cross; all these brought the onslaught of suffering, but they did not convey its pain. When a weapon pierces water, or probes fire, or slashes the air, it inflicts all these 'sufferings' which belong to its nature—it pierces, probes, slashes; but the 'suffering' inflicted does not retain its nature in those subjects, since it is not in the nature of water to be pierced, fire to be probed, air to be slashed. . . . So the Lord Jesus Christ suffered when he was flogged, hung, crucified, died. But the suffering which assailed the Lord's body, though it *was* suffering, still it did not convey the nature of suffering. . . . If the nature of the Lord's body was unique in that by its own power, by its own spirit, it was borne on the water, and walked on the waves, and passed through solid obstacles, why do we think of the flesh conceived by the Spirit in terms of nature of an ordinary human body? That flesh (the bread, that is) is from heaven: and that manhood is from God. The body was capable of 'suffering'; but it had not a nature susceptible of pain. That body had its own unique nature, which on the mountain of the Transfiguration was conformed to heavenly glory, which put to flight fevers by its contact, which by its spittle gave men sight.   *de trin.* 10. 23

(d) The Human Soul in Christ

Further, what a great mystery [*sacramentum*], connected with his words and acts, is the fact of Christ's weeping, and shedding tears through anguish of heart![1] How could there be such weakness in his soul, that the pain of sadness should wring tears from his body? What harshness of circumstances, and what intolerable grief dissolved into tears the Son of Man who came down from heaven? What was it, in fact, which wept in him? Was it the Word of God, or the soul of his own body? For though the act of weeping is the responsibility of the body, still it is a kind of grief of mind which brings those tears through the functioning of the body. What then made him weep? Did he pay a due tribute of tears to impious and murderous Jerusalem, which was to suffer nothing adequate to match the slaughter of such

[1] Luke 19. 41.

great prophets and apostles, and the putting to death of its own Lord himself? Is it as the calamities of human deaths are wept for, that he mourns for the tragic case of this lost and hopeless race? What, I ask, is the mystery [*sacramentum*] of his weeping? The soul is sad, and weeps. But was it this soul which sent the prophets? Was it the soul which so often wished to 'overshadow the chickens with the covering of wings'.[1] Grief does not come within the experience of the Word of God, nor tears within that of the Spirit. And the soul cannot act before it is united with the body. Yet there is no doubt that Jesus Christ really wept. *de trin.* 10. 55

If, besides the mystery of weeping, thirst, and hunger, the flesh, that is the whole man, was assumed, the flesh was subject to natural 'passions'; but not so subject as to be overwhelmed by the hurt of 'sufferings'. . . . The ordinary behaviour of the body was accepted to show the reality of his body. . . . When he took drink and food, he did not submit himself to bodily necessity, but to customary bodily behaviour.

He had a body, but one appropriate to its origin; not owing its being to the faults of human conception, but existing in the form of our body by his divine power. He bore the form of a servant, but he was free from the sins and weaknesses of a human body; so that we might be in him through his birth from a virgin, but that our weaknesses should not be in him in virtue of the divine power of his origin from himself. *de trin.* 10. 24, 25

III. The Work of Christ

(a) Redemption by Participation

The Son of God was born of a virgin and the Holy Spirit for the sake of mankind. . . . He was made man of a virgin so that he might receive into himself the nature of flesh; that the body of mankind as a whole might be sanctified by association with this mixture.

He, through whom man was created, did not need to be made man. It was we who needed that God should be made flesh and dwell in us, that is, should dwell within all flesh, in its entirety, by taking our flesh to himself. His humility is our ennoblement: his shame is our honour. He who is God co-existed with us in flesh, and thus we have been restored from the flesh to the divine nature. *de trin.* 2. 24, 25

[1] Matt. 23. 37.

(b) The Defeat of the Devil

'I shall give you the nations as an inheritance'[1]. . . . This is his inheritance, that he may give eternal life to all flesh; that all nations, baptized and instructed, may be re-born to life . . . and transferred to God's eternal kingdom, removed from the authority of the power who dominated them unjustly, sinfully, and perversely . . .   *tract. in Ps.* 2. 31

[*On* Ps. 68 (69) 6, 7. *Christ is assumed as the speaker*] . . . 'Thou, O God, knowest my folly, and my crimes are not hidden from thee'.[2] . . . Without cause and without justice he is tormented, as a sinner and a fool, even to the folly of the cross. But he took upon himself the folly and the crimes on account of our wisdom, so that he might judge the prince of the world, and, as a sacrifice for sin, might condemn sin in the flesh.[3] No trace of sin could be found in him, that is in the flesh of his body; as he says, 'The prince of the world will come, and he will find nothing in me.'[4] The prince of the world did come; and though he found nothing, still he exacted the penalty of sin, the punishment of death: and by this the author of man's death is judged, because he contrived the death of the author of life, who 'knew no sin'.[5]

tract. in Ps. 69. 8

(c) Sacrifice and Reconciliation

The Lord was smitten, taking our sins upon himself, and suffering on our behalf, so that in him, who was smitten as far as the weakness of crucifixion and death, health might be restored to us through his resurrection from the dead. . . . God 'did not spare his own Son'[6]. . . . He did not spare the first Adam, made from the mud of the earth, whom he expelled from paradise after his guilt, lest he should lay hands on the tree of life and continue for an eternity of punishment. His purpose was that the second Adam, coming from heaven, should assume a bodily nature, and be smitten by a similar death, and should thus recall that nature to eternal life, now freed from eternity of punishment.   *tract. in Ps.* 68. 23

He offered himself to the death of the accursed, to remove the curse of the Law[7] by offering himself of his own free will to God the Father

---

[1] Ps. 2. 8.   [2] Ps. 68 (69). 5.   [3] Cf. John 16. 11; Rom. 8. 3.   [4] John 14. 30.
[5] 1 Pet. 2. 22.   [6] Rom. 8. 32.   [7] Gal. 3. 13.

as a sacrifice.[1] . . . God the Father spurned the sacrifices of the Law; therefore he offered the acceptable sacrifice of the body he had taken. . . . He was to purchase the complete salvation of mankind by the offering of this holy and perfect sacrifice. *tract. in Ps. 53. 13*

IV. The Holy Spirit

Relation to the Father and the Son

The Advocate will come, and the Son will send him from the Father, and he is the Spirit of truth, who proceeds from the Father.[2] . . . How are we to understand that which the Son sends from the Father? As received, or sent out, or begotten? For he must mean one of these modes of sending that which he is to send from the Father. Receiving is ruled out, since proceeding is clearly indicated. It remains to make sure of our decision on the question whether we are to think of the coming forth of a co-existent being, or the proceeding of one begotten. He receives from the Son, since he is both sent by the Son and also proceeds from the Father. I ask whether to receive from the Son is the same as to proceed from the Father. If there is believed to be a difference . . . it will certainly be supposed that to receive from the Son is one and the same thing as to receive from the Father. For the Lord himself says: 'Since he will receive of what is mine and will announce it to you. All that the Father has is mine . . .'[3] *de trin. 8. 19, 20*

Christ dwells in us: and when Christ thus dwells, God dwells. And the Spirit of Christ dwells; and it is not another Spirit than the Spirit of God who dwells. But if Christ is understood to be in us through the Holy Spirit, we must recognize this as both the Spirit of God and the Spirit of Christ. *de trin. 8. 26*

For my part I cannot be satisfied with denying . . . that Jesus Christ is a creature. I cannot allow that this name of creature can be attached to thy Holy Spirit. . . . And, because I know that thou alone art ingenerate, and that the Only-begotten is born of thee, I would not refuse to say that the Holy Spirit is begotten; I will never assert that he was ever created. I fear that the disrespect implied by that term (which I share

[1] Cf. Ps. 40. 6.　[2] John 15. 26.　[3] John 16. 14 f.

with all things brought into existence by thee) may extend even to thee. . . . Shall I express, or rather dishonour, by the title of 'creature' the power of the nature that dwells in me, derived from thee through thy Only-begotten? As in the case of the generation of thy Only-begotten before everlasting time, when our ambiguous speech fails and the struggles of our understanding find their limit, there remains only the fact that he is generated; so I hold fast to the consciousness that thy Holy Spirit is from thee, through him, though I cannot perceive it with my intellect. . . . I will not venture beyond the grasp of my intelligence; nor will I say anything else about thy Only-begotten but that he is generate: similarly, I will not venture beyond the reach of human thought; I will make no statement about the Holy Spirit, except that he is thy Spirit. Let me not engage on the fruitless strife of words, but let me hold to the constant profession of unwavering faith.

de trin. 12. 55, 56

Let us make use of those generous gifts and seek to avail ourselves of this most essential boon. . . . 'We have received the Spirit which comes from God, so that we may know the gifts which have been generously given to us by God.'[1] The Spirit, then, is received to give us knowledge. For as the natural human body will be useless if the necessary conditions of its functions fail . . . [*e.g. eyes without light, ears without sound*], so the human mind, unless it has by faith appropriated the gifts of the Spirit, will have the natural faculty of apprehending God, but it will not have the light of knowledge. That gift, which is in Christ, is available to all alike: it is nowhere withheld, but is given to each in proportion to his willingness to accept it: it remains with him in proportion to his willingness to be worthy of it. It continues with us to the final consummation of history; it is the solace of our waiting; in the working of its gifts it is the pledge of our hope for the future, the light of our minds, the radiance shed on our hearts.

de trin. 2. 35

There is one Author of all things. For God the Father is one, from whom are all things; and our Lord Jesus Christ is one, through whom are all things; and the Spirit is one, who is God's gift in all things. All things therefore are set in order with their own powers and excellences. There is one power, from whom are all things; one offspring, through

[1] 1 Cor. 2. 12.

whom are all things; one gift of perfect hope. Nothing can be found lacking to that unity of perfection, which comprises, in Father, Son, and Holy Spirit, infinity in the Eternal, his likeness in his Image, his availability in the Gift. *de trin.* 2. 1

V. The Church and the Eucharist

'They were united in soul and heart.'[1] Did this unity come through faith in God? Certainly it did. . . . If then all were a unity through the nature of one faith, how is it that you do not recognize a natural unity in those who are one through the nature of one faith? For they were all reborn to innocence, to immortality, to the knowledge of God, to hopeful faith. There can be no diversity here, since the hope is one, and God is one, and the Lord is one, and the baptism of regeneration is one. If these are a 'unity of agreement' rather than a unity of nature, then you may attribute a 'unity of will' to those who are thus reborn. But if they are reborn to the nature of one life and one eternity, and it is in virtue of this that they are 'one in soul and heart', 'unity of agreement' does not apply to those who are one in being reborn to the same nature. *de trin.* 8. 7

If the Word was truly made flesh, and we truly take the Word-flesh by means of the Lord's food; surely we must think that he naturally remains in us, seeing that by being born as man he assumed the nature of our flesh as now inseparable from himself, and has mingled the nature of his flesh with the nature of eternity under the sacrament of the flesh which is to be communicated to us. *de trin.* 8. 13

Christ himself gives evidence of the nature of our life in him through the sacrament of the flesh and blood imparted to us, when he says . . . 'Since I live, you also will live; since I am in my Father, and you are in me, and I am in you'.[2] If he means a unity merely of will, why did he describe a kind of order of ascent in the establishment of that unity? His purpose surely was that we should believe that he was in the Father by nature, as being divine; whereas we are in him in virtue of his birth in the flesh, and he is in us through the mystery of the sacraments: and

[1] Acts 4. 32. [2] John 14. 19 f.

that thus we should have a doctrine of a unity consummated through
the Mediator, since, while we abide in him, he would abide in the
Father, and, thus abiding, should abide in us; and thus we should
advance to unity with the Father. He is in the Father naturally, because
of his generation: so we also should be in him naturally, while he
naturally abides in us.

Christ also gives evidence of this natural unity in us: 'He who eats
my flesh, and drinks my blood, dwells in me, and I dwell in him'.[1]
For no one will be in Christ, unless Christ is in him, unless he has taken
into himself the flesh of Christ, who took man's flesh. . . . He lives
'through the Father': and as he lives through the Father, so we live
through his flesh.[2] . . . This is the cause of our life, that we have Christ
dwelling in our fleshly nature, in virtue of his flesh, and we shall live
through him in the same way as he lives through the Father. We live
through him by nature, according to the flesh, that is, having acquired
the nature of his flesh. Then surely he has the Father in himself according to the Spirit, since he lives through the Father.

The mystery of the real and natural unity is to be proclaimed in
terms of the honour granted to us by the Son, and the Son's dwelling
in us through his flesh, while we are united to him bodily and
inseparably.   *de trin.* 8. 15, 16, 17

[1] John 6. 56.   [2] Cf. John 6. 57.

Basil of Caesarea

I. Authority

Scripture and Tradition

[*The use of the phrase* 'with *the Holy Spirit*' *in the doxology has been attacked as an unwarranted substitution for the scriptural* 'in the Holy Spirit'.]

Of the beliefs and practices preserved in the church, whether by tacit sanction, or by public decree,[1] we have some derived from written teaching; others we have received as delivered to us 'in a mystery'[2] from the tradition of the Apostles; and both classes have the same force, for true piety. No one will dispute these; no one, at any rate, who has even the slightest experience of the institutions of the Church. If we tried to depreciate the customs lacking written authority, on the ground that they have but little validity, we should find ourselves unwittingly inflicting vital injury on the Gospel: or rather reducing official definition to a mere form of words. For example, to mention the first and commonest instance—who has given us written instructions to sign, with the sign of the cross, those who have set their hope on the name of the Lord Jesus? What written instructions have we for turning to the east in prayer? Which of the saints has left to us, in writing, the words of the invocation at the displaying[3] of the bread of the Eucharist, and the cup of blessing? For to be sure, we are not content with the record of the Apostle and the Gospel, but we add, by way of preface and conclusion,[4] other elements which we have received from the unwritten teaching, and we regard them as having great importance for the performance of the sacrament. We bless the water of baptism, and the oil of the chrism, and moreover we bless the person who is being baptized. On whose written instructions? Is it not on the authority of silent and secret tradition? And what of the anointing with oil itself? What written word rejoined that? And whence comes the custom of triple immersion? And with regard to the other rites of baptism, from what scripture do we obtain the renunciation of Satan and his angels?

---

[1] τῶν πεφυλαγμένων δογμάτων καὶ κηρυγμάτων. B. observes what seems to be a private distinction between δόγματα, doctrines, and practices tacitly accepted, and κηρύγματα, official definitions and prescribed ritual. [2] i.e. a secret design of God, now revealed to believers; 1 Cor. 2. 7. [3] i.e. apparently, the consecration. The Liturgy of St. Basil thus concludes the Invocation: 'bless, hallow, and *display* these gifts'. [4] *Sursum corda* and *Sanctus* before the consecration: after it, the Oblation and Invocation of the Spirit (Epiclesis).

Does not this come from this unpublished and secret teaching? Our
fathers, by silence, preserved this teaching from inquisitive meddlers,
having been well instructed to safeguard, by silence, the awful
solemnity of these mysteries. It was scarcely likely that a public display,
in the shape of written documents, should be made of teaching about
things at which the uninitiated are not even allowed to look . . .
[*Moses excluded people from parts of the Tabernacle*.] Moses had
the wisdom to know that contempt readily falls on the trite and the
easily accessible, while eager interest tends naturally to attach to the
remote and the unusual. In the same way the Apostles and Fathers, who
at the beginning laid down ordinances concerning the Church, were
concerned to safeguard the solemnity of the mysteries, by secrecy
and reticence; for what is published for the casual hearing of the general
public is no mystery at all. This is the reason for the tradition of
unwritten matters, that the knowledge of dogmas may not be slighted
and despised by the multitude, through familiarity? 'Dogma' and
'Kerygma' are two different things. We keep silent about 'Dogma':
'Kerygma' is published'.   *de sp. sanct.* 66

II. The Condition of Man

Freedom and Sin

It is not God who is responsible for the sufferings in Hades; it is we
ourselves. For the source and root of sin is our self-determining free
will. It was in our power to abstain from evil and therefore to suffer
no harm: but we were enticed into sin by pleasure. What plausible
reason can we adduce, to excuse us for the responsibility for those
sufferings? There is a distinction between evil as felt by our senses, and
evil in its own nature. What is evil by nature derives from us,
unrighteousness, lasciviousness [*etc.*] . . . On the other hand we apply
the name of evil to what brings us physical pain and discomfort, bodily
disease and physical affliction, poverty, disgrace, loss of memory,
bereavement. But each of these is brought upon us for our good, by a
wise and beneficent Master . . . [*Physical disasters are punitive and
remedial*.] The absolute evil is sin, and it is sin which really deserves
the name of evil. All sin derives from our free choice; it is in our
power to abstain from wickedness, or to be evil . . . [*Other 'evils' are
challenges or remedies*]. Do not on any account suppose God responsible
for the existence of evil: and do not imagine that evil has any substan-

tive existence[1] of its own. Wickedness does not exist as if it were a kind of living creature: we cannot produce its essence in real subsistence.[2] For evil is the privation of good . . . as blindness supervenes on destruction of the eyes, so evil, having no independent existence, supervenes upon mutilations of the soul. It is not ingenerate, as they impiously assert who put the nature of wickedness on an equal footing with that of good, in making both equally underived and independent of generation. Nor is it brought into being. For if all things derive from God, how can evil come from good? . . . 'All was good, exceedingly good'.[3] And yet evil does exist, and its activity shows it diffused throughout the whole of life. How then does it come to be, asks an objector, if it is neither independent nor created? . . .

[*Bodily disorders arise from departure from the natural state.*] God made the body; he did not create disease: he made the soul; he did not create sin. The soul deteriorated when it was perverted from its natural state. What was the soul's supreme good? Attachment to God and conjunction with him through love. When it failed in this, the soul deteriorated because of weaknesses of many various kinds. But why was it at all capable of evil? Because of its self-determined impulse, an endowment specially appropriate to rational nature. Freed from all constraint and endowed by the Creator with self-determining life, because made in God's image, it had the conception of the good, and experienced the enjoyment of the good. And it had the right and power to preserve its natural state of life, by persevering in the contemplation of the good, and the enjoyment of spiritual pleasure. It had also the power to turn away from the good. And this it is that happened when, sated with this blessed delight, and weighed down as it were with drowsiness, it slipped from the higher sphere, and was mingled with the flesh, for the sake of the enjoyment of base satisfactions.

Adam lived on high, not locally, but in the decision of his will, when he had just received the gift of life, and, looking up to heaven, he rejoiced in what he saw, and was full of love for his benefactor, who had bestowed on him the enjoyment of eternal life, and had made him to take his ease among the delights of paradise. He had given him a dominion like that of the angels; he had made him share the life of archangels, and to hear the divine voice. Besides all this, he was protected under God's shield and enjoyed the good things of God. But he quickly became satiated with all this, and by satiety he grew as

[1] ἰδία ὑπόστασις. [2] οὐσία ἐνυποστατός. [3] Gen. 1. 31.

it were insolent, and preferred, to the spiritual beauty, that which appeared pleasant to the eyes of flesh, and set greater store by the satisfaction of his belly than by spiritual joys. Thus he was straightaway expelled from paradise and that blessed manner of life, and became evil, not because of compulsion but as the result of folly. Therefore he swerved because of a perverted will, and he died because of sin. . . . God did not create death: we have drawn death upon ourselves[1] as the result of our evil intention. He certainly did not prevent our dissolution, lest by so doing he should preserve our weakness for ever; as a potter would not allow a clay vessel to be put in the kiln in a state of collapse, but would first remedy the fault by remoulding. But why, comes the objection, were we not so equipped as to be incapable of sin, so that we had not the ability to sin, even if we wished? For the same reason that you do not regard your servants as loyal when you keep them under constraint, but only when they voluntarily perform their duties. God is not blessed with forced service, but with service which springs from virtue; and virtue derives from decision, not from compulsion. And decision implies self-determination.

[*The devil is an angel fallen because of perverted will, and he was jealous of man's primal bliss.*] Why then was that tree in paradise, which was to be the means of the devil's success in his attempt on us? . . . Because there had to be a command to test our obedience; and the tree produced plenty of fine fruit, so that by abstinence from indulgence we might display the virtue of self-control and be justly qualified for crowns as a reward for endurance. . . . Thus the devil has been set up as our adversary on account of the fall which happened to us long ago as the result of arrogance; for the Lord planned our struggle against him, so as to restore us again through the obedience (of Christ)[2] and to give us the crown of *victory* over our opponent.

hom. 9 [*quod Deus non est auctor malorum*]. 3, 5, 6, 7, 9

III. The Status and Person of Christ

(a) Of One Substance with the Father

[*B. has been strongly, and rather unjustly, criticizing Dionysius of Alexandria for using expressions of an Arian tendency in combating Sabellius.*][3]

If I must express my own personal opinion, I am prepared to accept the phrase 'like in substance',[4] provided that 'without any difference' is added. I accept it as conveying the same meaning as 'consubstantial'.[1] according to the sound interpretation of that word. This was the opinion of the Fathers at Nicaea, when they gave to the Only-begotten such appellations as 'Light from Light', 'True God from true God', and added 'consubstantial' as a corollary. Thus no difference can possibly be conceived between light and light, truth and truth, or between the substance of the Only-begotten and the substance of the Father. As I said, I admit the phrase 'of like substance', if it is taken in this sense. But if the qualification 'without any difference' is cut out, which is what happened at Constantinople,[2] then I suspect the phrase, as diminishing the glory of the 'Only-begotten'. For we frequently employ the notion of similarity in cases of obscure resemblance, where the similitude is far inferior to the original. *ep. 9. 3*

We are the heirs of those who at Nicaea issued the great proclamation of true religion. Their doctrine has been generally received without cavil, but the word 'consubstantial', reluctantly accepted by some, is still not universally admitted. One may be justified in blaming those who reject it, while at the same time acknowledging that they may have some excuse. Their refusal to follow the Fathers and to regard their pronouncement of higher authority than their own opinion is deserving of censure for its excessive arrogance. On the other hand, their suspicion of a word impugned by others does to some extent seem to clear them of this charge. For it is true that the members of a synod,[3] dealing with Paul of Samosata,[4] reprobated this word, as having the wrong kind of sound. For they said that 'consubstantial' suggested the notion of a physical substance, and the things made out of it; the parcelling out of a substance into particular things giving the appellation 'consubstantial' to the things into which it has been divided. Such a notion is appropriate in the case of bronze and the coins made from that substance; but in the case of God the Father and God the Son there can be no thought of a substance prior or superior to the two particulars: it would be the extreme of impiety to entertain or to express such an idea. What could be prior to the Unbegotten? And such a blasphemous notion would destroy our faith in the Father and the Son; for it is a fraternal relation which unites those things which derive their subsistence from one source. And because there were still some who asserted that the Son was produced from nothing, the

[1] *homoousios*; cf. p. 2.   [2] In 360; cf. p. 2.   [3] At Antioch in 268.   [4] Cf. p. 12.

Nicene fathers added the phrase 'of the same substance' to rule out this irreverence. For the conjunction of the Son with the Father is timeless and continuous. The preceding words prove that this was the meaning of the Fathers. For after the assertions, 'light from light', 'begotten of the Father's substance, not made', they added the phrase 'of the same substance'. In this they showed that the meaning attached to 'light', when applied to the Father, holds good when applied to the Son. The very notion of light makes impossible any difference between one true light and another. Then since the Father is unoriginated light, and the Son is begotten light, but each is light, the Fathers were right to use the term 'of the same substance', in order to establish the equal dignity of their nature. 'Of the same substance' does not, as some have supposed, describe entities connected by a fraternal relation. The term is used when the source, and that which derives its being from the source, are identical in nature.

This expression also corrects the perversion of Sabellius, for it removes the idea of identity of subsistences,[1] and introduces the full conception of persons.[2] Thus the expression is sound and reverent, since it establishes the distinctive marks of the subsistences, while asserting the absence of difference in nature. But when we are told that the Son is 'of the substance of the Father; begotten not made', we must beware of lapsing into ideas of some kind of physical process. There is no division of substance, as if it were taken from the Father and given to the Son: nor did the substance generate by a process of flux; or by production, like a plant bearing fruit. The mode of divine generation is ineffable and inconceivable by human thought.   *ep. 52. 1–3*

(b) The Meaning of 'Consubstantial'.
(i) A Letter to Apollinarius

[The correspondence between Basil and Apollinarius has widely been regarded as spurious. But its authenticity has been defended by G. L. Prestige (*St. Bas. the Gr. and Ap. of Laodicea*, 1956) and others.]

Those who bring all things into confusion, and have filled the whole world with their arguments and questions, have refused to admit the term *ousia* [substance], on the ground that it finds no place in the inspired scriptures. Will you be so good as to tell me how the Fathers used this term, and whether you have failed to find it embedded in Scripture? They reject the evidence of such phrases as *epiousios artos*

---

[1] ὑποστάσεις.   [2] πρόσωπα.

[*daily bread*], and *laos periousios* [*a people for his possession*], as having no relevance. And then will you please let me have a more extended treatment of the term *homoousios* [*consubstantial*]; for I suppose that those who make a thorough-going attack on *ousia* are doing so with a view to leaving no place for *homoousios*. Please explain its meaning and show how it may be employed in cases where there is no question of a superior common genus, nor any pre-existent material substrate, nor a distribution of the former into the latter. How ought one to call the Son *homoousios* with the Father, without involving oneself in any of these notions? Will you please explain this more fully? I have taken it that whatever we assume the Father's *ousia* to be, we are bound, *ex hypothosi* to assume the same of the *ousia* of the Son. So that if one speaks of the Father's *ousia* as intellectual light, eternal, ingenerate, one must speak of the Son's *ousia* as intellectual light, eternal, ingenerate. In view of this conception, it seems to me that the phrase 'like without difference' is more appropriate than *homoousios*. If a light shows no difference of degree from another light, I conceive that one would not be right in calling it 'the same' as the other, since each light exists in the individuality of its *ousia*; but one would rightly describe it as 'precisely similar in respect of *ousia*, without difference.'   *ep.* 361

(ii) *The Reply of Apollinarius*

'One *ousia*' is a phrase used not only of numerical unity, of one individuality; it also properly applies to two men, or two of anything else, united in genus. So that, on this principle, two or more things are identical in respect of *ousia*, as all of us men are Adam, since we are one, and the son of David is David, in that he is identical with him. Just so you rightly say that the Son, in respect of *ousia*, is what the Father is. Otherwise the Son would not be God, since the Father is confessedly the one and only God; in the same way, Adam, the source of the human race, is one, and David, the first ancestor of the royal line, is one. On this principle, to be sure, the notion of one antecedent genus, or one material substance, in the case of the Father and the Son, will be obviated, when we compare the original individuality of the first source, and the generations derived from the originals, with the only-begotten offspring of the one Source (for the examples suggest 'similarity'). Just as there is no antecedent genus including Adam, as created by God, and us, as begotten by man, but Adam himself is the source of mankind; neither is there a common material shared

by him and us; but he himself is the substrate of all mankind. . . .
But the analogy breaks down, in that there are other mutual relations
shared by all mankind, as for instance, of brothers. There is nothing of
this kind in the case of the Father and the Son; the Father is completely
the source, and the Son is from the source. Thus there is no distribution
of the former into the latter, as in material things, but simply derivation
by way of generation. The Father's individuality is not as it were
distributed into the Son, but the Son's individuality is manifested from
the Father: there is identity in diversity, and diversity in identity; as
the Son is said to be in the Father, and the Father in the Son.[1] For mere
difference will not safeguard the reality of the sonship; while identity
will not preserve the indivisibility of the *hypostasis*. Each is interwoven
and unitary; identical with difference; different in identity. One has to
strain language, which is inadequate for an explanation of the reality.
The Lord confirms our conception, by presenting the Father as greater
in a state of equality, while the Son, in subordination, enjoys equality.[2]
He taught us to think of the Son under the image of light of the same
kind, but lesser in degree, not by supposing a change of *ousia*, but
by considering identity in superior and inferior status. Those who
admit no identity of *ousia* attribute to the Son a merely extrinsic likeness:
a likeness which extends also to men, when they are made like to
God. Those who recognize that likeness is appropriate to created beings
connect the Son with the Father in identity, but in an inferior identity,
to avoid thinking of the Son as the Father himself, or as part of the
Father. This is emphasized by saying, 'The Son is other than the
Father'; he is God, not as being the Father, but as being *from* the Father:
he is not the prototype but the copy. He is *homoousios* in a completely
unique and special sense; not as members of the same genus are
homoousia, or as parts of the same whole; but as being from one genus
and form of godhead, the one and only offspring, by an inseparable and
incorporeal progression, in course of which, uniquely, the begetter,
remaining in his individuality as begetting, has issued into the individuality of the begotten.   *ep.* 362

(c) Ingenerate and Generate

The difference between ingenerate and generate is not one of greater
and less, like that between the greater and the lesser light: it is the
difference that separates attributes which cannot possibly co-exist in

[1] Cf. John. 14. 11.   [2] Cf. John 14. 28.

the same subject. It is inconceivable that a subject possessing one of these characters should change to the opposite character—the ingenerate becoming generate, or vice versa. . . . There is here a diametrical opposition. Therefore those who suppose generacy and ingeneracy to be within the category of substance [ousia], find themselves in absurdities. For these will be a begetting of contrary from contrary; and instead of the natural affinity, an inevitable discord will appear between them in respect of substance itself. This shows more folly than impiety, to say, in respect of anything whatsoever, that its substance is self-contradictory; since it has long been the accepted doctrine even among non-Christian philosophers (whose teachings our opponents treat as of no account when they do not find them supporting their blasphemies) that contradiction cannot conceivably exist within substance. But anyone who accepts the truth that generacy and ingeneracy are certain distinctive properties observed in the substance, which lead to the clear and unconfused conception of the Father and the Son, will escape the danger of this impiety; and, at the same time, will preserve consistency in his reasoning. For those special properties, which are observed in the substance, like characters or forms, make a distinction within the common nature by these individualizing characters, while they do not split up the unity of nature. The godhead is common: fatherhood and sonship are, as it were, individual properties. As a result of the interweaving of the two, the common and the particular, the apprehension of the truth comes, arises in us. And so, when we hear of 'ingenerate light', we think of the Father; while 'generate light' conveys to us the notion of the Son. In respect that both are light there exists no contrariety in them: in respect that one is generate, the other ingenerate, a contrast is observed. It is the nature of special properties to display a difference within the identity of the substance, and it frequently happens that these special properties are mutually contrary and utterly distinct, without destroying the unity of the substance. Thus . . . [in the case of animals] we have the special properties of winged and pedestrian, aquatic and terrestrial, rational and irrational: there is one underlying substance, and these special properties do not alter that substance; nor do they produce disunity.   c. Eunom. 11. 28

(d) The Subordination of the Son
[The letter from which this passage comes is now thought by many to be the work of Evagrius Ponticus.]

'My father is greater than I.'[1] This text is much employed by those ungrateful wretches, the devil's brood. But I am confident that even in this saying the consubstantiality of the Son with the Father is demonstrated. For I know that comparison can only properly be made in respect of things of the same nature. We speak of an angel as greater than an angel, a man more righteous than a man, a bird swifter than a bird. If these comparisons are made between things of the same species, and the Father is said to be greater than the Son, it follows that the Son is consubstantial with the Father. But there is another meaning contained in the saying. Is there anything extraordinary in his admission that his Father is greater? He is the Word, and has been 'made flesh';[2] and he was seen as inferior to the angels in glory, and inferior to men in beauty. 'Thou hast made him a little lower than the angels.'[3] 'We saw him, and he had neither grace nor beauty; he was lacking in beauty in comparison with all the rest of mankind.'[4] All this he endured because of his great compassion towards his handiwork, that he might rescue the lost sheep and bring it back safe to the flock,[5] and restore safe and sound to his own land the man who went down from Jerusalem to Jericho, and so fell into the hands of robbers.[6] Will the heretic also taunt him with the manger, though it was by means of this that he himself, when devoid of reason, was nourished by the Word? Will he reproach the poverty of the carpenter's son who was not furnished with a bed? That is why the Son is inferior to the Father; because for your sake he became dead, to free you from mortality and make you partake of the heavenly life. It is just as if one should find fault with a physician for bending down to sickness, and breathing its stench, in order that he may heal the sufferers.

It is also on your account that he 'does not know the hour and the day'[7] of judgement: although nothing is outside the knowledge of the true Wisdom, for 'all things came into being through him',[8] and even among men no one is ever ignorant of what he had made. But this is part of his dispensation, because of your weakness, so that sinners should not be plunged into despair, by the narrow limits of the appointed time, thinking that no space for repentance is left them: while, on the other hand, those who are fighting a long campaign against the opposing force should not leave their post because the time is protracted.

ep. 8. 5, 6

---

[1] John 14. 28.   [2] John 1. 14.   [3] Ps. 8. 5; Heb. 2. 7, 9.   [4] Isa. 53. 2, 3.   [5] Cf. Luke 15. 4.
[6] Cf. Luke 10. 30.   [7] Matt. 24. 36.   [8] John 1. 3.

(e) The Human Ignorance of Christ

[On the text 'No one knows the day or hour.' Mark 13. 32.] I can give the explanation which I heard from our Fathers in boyhood, which I received without question. . . . 'No one' is apparently a universal term, admitting of no exception, not even of a single person; but this is not its use in Scripture, as I have observed in the saying 'no one is good save one, namely, God'.[1] For even in this passage the Son does not mean to exclude himself from the nature of the good. But, since the Father is the First Good, I believe that 'no one' was said with the understood addition of 'first'. And in the saying 'no one knows the Son, save the Father,'[2] there is no charge of ignorance against the Spirit, but simply a testimony that knowledge of the Son's own nature belongs first to the Father. Similarly, I suppose that 'no one knows the day or hour' refers the first knowledge of present and future to the Father, and in general, points out to men the first cause. Otherwise, how can this saying fit in with the rest of the scriptural evidence? How can it be harmonized with the generally accepted belief that the Only-begotten is the image of the invisible God? That is, not a representation in physical shape, but the image of the very Godhead, and of the mighty properties ascribed to the substance of God; the image of his power, the image of his wisdom, since Christ is called 'the power of God, and the wisdom of God?[3]   *ep.* 236. I

(f) The Human Weakness of Christ

It is the property of flesh to suffer division, diminution, dissolution; of animal flesh to experience weariness, pain, hunger and thirst, and to be overcome by sleep; of a soul making use of a body to feel grief, care, anxiety, and the like. Some of these experiences are natural and inevitable for any living being; others arise from perverse choice, brought on by a life without discipline, without training in virtue. Hence it is clear that the Lord accepted the natural experiences to establish that his incarnation was real and not a mere semblance; but the experiences which arise from wickedness, which defile the purity of our life, he rejected as incompatible with his unsullied Godhead. Therefore he is said to have been 'born in the likeness of flesh of sin',[4] not, as these men suppose, 'in the likeness of flesh', but 'the likeness of flesh *of sin*'. So that he assumed our flesh with its natural experiences,

[1] Luke 18. 19.   [2] Matt. 11. 27.   [3] 1 Cor. 1. 24.   [4] Rom. 8. 3.

but 'he did no sin'.[1] Just as the death which is in the flesh, having been transmitted to us through Adam, was swallowed up by the godhead,[2] so the sinfulness was annulled by the righteousness which is in Christ Jesus; so that in the resurrection we receive back the flesh neither subject to death, nor liable to sin.   *ep.* 261. 3

IV. The Work of Christ

Expiation and Ransom

Every human soul has submitted to the evil yoke of slavery; slavery to the common enemy of all: mankind has been despoiled of the liberty which was the gift of the Creator, and has been brought into captivity through sin. Now, for any captive to recover his liberty, a ransom is required: nor is it possible for a brother to ransom his brother,[3] nor for each to ransom himself; for the ransomer must be far superior to the conquered slave. Man is utterly powerless to make atonement to God for the sinner, since every man is charged with sin. . . . Therefore do not seek a brother to effect your ransom. But there is one superior to our nature; not a mere man, but one who is man and God, Jesus Christ, who alone is able to make atonement for us all, because 'God appointed him as the expiation, through faith, by his blood'.[4]

What can a man find of such value that he may give it for the ransoming of his son? One thing has been found of such worth as to pay the price for all mankind; the holy and most precious blood of our Lord Jesus Christ, which he poured out on our behalf for us all. Therefore we were 'bought with a price'[5]. . . . If a man cannot ransom us, he who ransomed us was not a mere man.   *in Ps.* 48. 3

If the Lord did not come to dwell in our flesh, then the ransom did not pay the fine due to death on our behalf, nor did he destroy through himself the reign of death. For if the Lord did not assume that over which death reigned, death would not have been stopped from effecting his purpose, nor would the suffering of the God-bearing flesh have become our gain: he would not have slain sin in the flesh. We, who were dead in Adam, would not have been restored in Christ . . . that

[1] I Pet. 2. 22.   [2] Cf. I Cor. 15. 22, 24.   [3] Ps. 49. 7.   [4] Rom. 3. 25.   [5] I Cor. 6. 20.

which was alienated from God by the serpent would not have been
brought back by him.   *ep.* 261. 2

V. The Holy Spirit

(a) *His Nature*

Can anyone fail to have his mind lifted up, when he hears the titles
of the Spirit? Can he fail to raise his thoughts to the Supreme Nature?
The Spirit is called 'God's Spirit', 'Spirit of Truth proceeding from the
Father', 'Right Spirit', 'Leading Spirit'.[1] But his proper and peculiar
appellation is 'Holy Spirit', which is a name specially applicable to
everything that is incorporeal, purely immaterial, and indivisible.
Thus when the Lord was instructing the woman who thought that
God was to be worshipped in a particular place, he told her that the
incorporeal is not spatially limited and said, 'God is Spirit'.[2] When we
hear the title 'Spirit', we cannot picture a nature circumscribed, or
subject to change and variation, or in any way resembling created
beings. It is inevitable that our imagination should proceed to the
highest point, so that we should conceive an intellectual substance
[*ousia*], of infinite power, of unlimited magnitude, not measurable
by times or ages, unstinting of its good gifts; a being to which all turn
when needing sanctification . . . simple in substance [*ousia*], manifold
in powers; present entirely in each individual while existing in entirety
everywhere; divided without suffering diminution, shared without
loss of completeness; after the likeness of the sun's beam, which gracious
gift comes to each who enjoys it as if it came to him alone, yet shines
on land and sea and mingles with the air. So the Spirit comes to each
of these who receive him, as though given to him alone; yet he sends
out to all his grace, sufficient and complete, and all who partake in him
receive benefit in proportion to the capacity, not of his power, but
of their nature.

When the sun's ray falls on bright and transparent objects, they
themselves become radiant and from themselves shed a further shining
beam: so the souls inhabited by the Spirit, and illuminated by the Spirit,
themselves are rendered wholly spiritual and send out their grace to
others. From this source comes foreknowledge of the future, the
understanding of mysteries, the apprehension of things hidden, the
partaking of spiritual gifts, the heavenly citizenship, a place in

[1] John 14. 17; John 15. 26; Ps. 51. 10; Ps. 50 (51). 14.   [2] John 4. 24.

the choir of angels, unending joy, the power to abide in God, to become like God, and, highest of all ends to which we can aspire, to become divine.[1]   *de sp. sanct.* 9. 22, 23

It is asserted[2] that the Holy Spirit is not to be placed in the same category with the Father and the Son, since he is alien to them in nature, and inferior in dignity. We are justified in replying with the statement of the apostles, 'We must obey God rather than men.'[3] For when the Lord entrusted his disciples with the baptism of salvation, he unambiguously commanded them to 'baptize all the nations with the name of Father, Son, and Holy Spirit',[4] not disdaining fellowship with him, and yet those men say that we must not rank him with Father and Son; is it not obvious that they are openly resisting the injunction of God?[5] If they deny that this collocation is proof of a fellowship and conjunction, let them tell us why they feel obliged to hold this opinion. What more intimate mode of conjunction have they in mind?   *de sp. sanct.* 10. 24

(b) His Divinity

[The authorship of this passage is uncertain. See note on p. 67.]

Let us contemplate the divine powers of the Holy Spirit from the following point of view especially. We find three creations mentioned in Scripture. The first is the bringing into existence from non-existence; the second is the change from worse to better; the third is the resurrection of the dead. In all these you will find the Holy Spirit, co-operating with the Father and the Son. The heavens are brought into being: and what does David say? 'By the word of the Lord the heavens were set fast, and by the Spirit [breath] of his mouth all the power of them.'[6] Man is created again through baptism, for 'if a man is in Christ, there is a new creation'.[7] And why does the Saviour say to his disciples, 'Go and make disciples in all nations, baptizing them in the name of the Father and the Son and the Holy Spirit'?[8] Here also you see the Holy Spirit present with the Father and the Son. Again, at the resurrection of the dead, when we have 'passed away and returned again to our dust'[9] (for 'we are earth and shall return to the earth'[10]) 'he will send the Holy Spirit [breath] and create us, and will renew the face of the earth'.[11] What St. Paul calls resurrection, David describes as

[1] Cf. John 16. 13; 1 Cor. 13. 2 and Matt. 13. 11; 1 Cor. 12. 4; Phil. 3. 20; Heb. 12. 22; Rom. 14. 17; John 14. 23, etc.; 1 John 3. 2; 2 Pet. 1. 4.   [2] By Eunomius and other 'Anomoians'.   [3] Acts 5. 29.   [4] Matt. 28. 19.   [5] Cf. Rom. 13. 2.   [6] Ps. 32. (33). 6.   [7] 2 Cor. 5. 17.   [8] Matt. 28. 19.   [9] Ps. 103 (104). 29.   [10] Cf. Gen. 3. 19.   [11] Ps. 103. (104). 30.

renewal. . . . If they object to the word 'God', let them learn the significance of the word. God is called *Theos* either because he placed [*tetheikenai*] all things, or because he beholds [*theasthai*] all things. If then God is so named because of 'placing' or 'beholding' all things, while the spirit 'knows all the things of God, as the spirit in us knows our things',[1] then the Holy Spirit is God. Again, if 'the sword of the Spirit is the word of God',[2] then the Holy Spirit is God; for the sword belongs to him of whom it is called the word. He is called 'the Father's right hand' ('the right hand of the Lord did mightily', 'Thy right hand, O Lord, shattered the enemy':[3] and the Holy Spirit is God's finger, since 'if I by the finger of God cast out devils' appears in another Gospel as 'if by God's Spirit'[4]). It follows that the Holy Spirit is of the same nature as the Father and the Son.   *ep.* 8. 11

The question which now crops up, owing to those who are always endeavouring to introduce novelties, was passed over in silence by earlier generations, because the teaching had never been controverted, and thus it had been left without authoritative explanation: I refer to the doctrine of the Holy Spirit. I will therefore add a statement on this subject, keeping close to the sense of Scripture. As we are baptized, so we believe: as we believe, so also we give praise. Baptism has been given to us by the Saviour, 'into the name of the Father and of the Son and of the Holy Spirit'.[5] Therefore we present our confession of faith in accordance with our baptism, and our offering of praise in accordance with our faith. We glorify the Holy Spirit together with the Father and the Son, in the conviction that the Spirit is not alien to the divine nature: for that which is alien by nature does not share in the same honours. We pity those who speak of the Holy Spirit as a creature, because by such a statement they fall into the unpardonable calamity of blasphemy against the Spirit.[6] For those who are even slightly instructed in the Scripture, it needs no argument that the creation is distinct from the godhead. Creation is a slave; the Spirit sets free. Creation stands in need of life; the Spirit is the life-giver. Creation needs instruction; the Spirit is the teacher. Creation is sanctified; the Spirit is the sanctifier.[7] If you speak of angels, or archangels, or all the supernal powers, they receive their sanctification through the Spirit;

[1] 1 Cor. 2. 10, 11.   [2] Eph. 6. 17.   [3] Ps. 117 (118). 16.   [4] Luke 11. 20; Matt. 12. 28.
[5] Matt. 28. 19.   [6] Cf. Matt. 12. 31.   [7] Cf. Rom. 8. 2; John 6. 63; cf. John 14. 26; cf. Rom. 15. 16.

but the Spirit himself has his holiness by nature, not receiving it by favour, but having it as something inherent in his being. Hence he has been given the distinctive title of 'Holy'. Since then he is by nature holy, as the Father is holy by nature, and so is the Son, we do not allow him to be separated and divided from the divine and blessed Trinity, and we repudiate those who ignorantly count him as part of creation.   *ep.* 159. 2

In relation to contingent beings the Spirit is said to be in them 'in various measures and in various ways'.[1] In relation to Father and Son it is more in keeping with true reverence to say that he is *with* them rather than *in* them. . . . His eternal pre-existence and his unceasing abiding with Father and Son cannot be thought of without postulating the titles which describe everlasting conjunction. . . . When we consider the proper dignity of the Spirit we contemplate him as being *with* Father and Son; when we have in mind the grace which comes from him in its operation on those who participate, then we say that the Spirit is *in* us.

Just as the Father is seen in the Son, so the Son is seen in the Spirit. . . . By means of the illumination of the Spirit we behold 'the radiance of the glory'[2] of God: by means of the 'impression'[2] we are led up to him of whom he is the impression, exactly reproduced on the seal.

de sp. sanct. 26. 63, 64

VI. The Trinity

(a) Three and One

[The authorship of this passage is uncertain. See note on p. 67.]

But you, my friends, godly and best-beloved, beware of the shepherds of the Philistines [*sc. the Arians*], lest they secretly choke your wells,[3] and befoul the purity of your knowledge of the faith. This is always their concern, not to teach simple souls from the Holy Scriptures, but to falsify the truth by heathen philosophy. When a man introduces the terms 'unbegotten' and 'begotten' into our faith, and asserts a formula that the everlasting 'once was not'[4]; that he who is Father by nature and from eternity became Father, and that the Holy Spirit is not eternal; is not such a one a downright Philistine? He casts the evil eye on our

[1] Heb. 1. 1.   [2] Heb. 1. 3.   [3] Cf. Gen. 26. 15.   [4] The Arian formula, ἦν ὅτε οὐκ ἦν.

patriarch's sheep, so that they may not drink of the pure 'water leaping up for eternal life',[1] but may bring upon themselves the prophet's saying; 'They have forsaken me, the spring of living water, and have dug for themselves broken cisterns, which will not hold water.'[2] When they ought to confess that the Father is God, the Son is God, the Holy Spirit is God, according to the teaching of the inspired sayings, and of those who have more deeply understood those sayings. In reply to those who taunt us with tritheism, let this be our answer: we confess that God is one, but one in nature, not in number. For not everything which is called one numerically is one absolutely, nor is it simple in nature: but God is universally admitted to be simple and incomposite. Therefore it is not in number that God is one. What I mean is this. We say that the world is one, numerically, but not one in nature, not simple; for we divide it into its constituent elements, fire, water, air, and earth. Again, a man is called one, numerically; we frequently speak of 'one man'. But he is not simple: he is compounded of body and soul. Similarly we would speak of an angel as one, numerically, but not one in nature, and not simple: for we conceive of the subsistence [hypostasis] of an angel as substance [ousia] combined with sanctification. If, therefore, not everything which is one in number is one in nature, and that which is one and simple in nature is not one in number; and if we call God one in nature; how can they bring number as a charge against us, when we completely exclude it from that blessed and immaterial nature? Number refers to quantity, and quantity is connected with material nature: thus number refers to material nature. But we believe our Lord to be the creator of material bodies. Therefore every number signifies these things which have been given a material and circumscribed nature. Monad and unity, on the other hand, signify a simple and unlimited being. Whoever then confesses that the Son of God or the Holy Spirit is a number or a creature introduces unawares the notion of material and circumscribed nature. And by circumscribed I mean not only locally limited, but comprehended also by the foreknowledge of him who is about to produce it from non-existence, and capable of comprehension by human knowledge. Every holy thing, therefore, which is by nature circumscribed, and whose holiness is acquired, is not incapable of evil. But the Son and the Holy Spirit are the source of sanctification, whence every rational creature is sanctified in proportion to its virtue.   *ep.* 8. 2

[1] John 4. 14. [2] Jer. 2. 13.

When the Lord enjoined the use of the formula 'Father, Son, and Holy Spirit', he did not add any numerical qualification. He did not say 'into first, second, and third', nor 'into one, two, and three'; but by means of holy names he graciously bestowed the knowledge of the faith that leads to salvation. . . . Nothing else suffers any change as a result of the addition of number; and yet these opponents pay especial respect to number in regard to the divine nature, lest they should exceed the measure of honour owed to the Paraclete. . . . Either let ineffable things be honoured by silence, or let proper reverence be observed when number is applied to holy things. There is one God and Father, one only-begotten Son, one Holy Spirit. We proclaim each of the persons [hypostases] singly: and when we must count them together, we are not carried away by an ignorant arithmetic to the notion of a plurality of Gods.

We do not count by addition, making the increase from unity to plurality, and saying 'one, two, three', nor 'first, second, third'. For 'I am God, the first, and I am what follows.'[1] And we have never yet, to this day, heard of a second God. As we worship God from God we also confess the individuality of the person [hypostasis] while we abide by the monarchy. We do not scatter our theology into a divided plurality, because the one form, so to speak, is contemplated in God the Father and God the Only-begotten, united by the invariableness of the godhead. For the Son is in the Father, the Father in the Son, since the Father is such as the Son is, the Son such as the Father, and herein is the unity. And so in respect of the individuality of the persons we have one and one; in respect of the community of nature the two are one. How then are there not two Gods, if we have one and one? Because we speak of a king and the king's portrait, not of two kings. The authority is not split, nor the glory divided. The sovereign power that rules us is one, and the worship we offer is not plural, but one, because the honour paid to the portrait passes over to the original. In this case the portrait is by way of imitation, but in the other case the Son is the Father's image by nature. As in works of art the likeness is in respect of the form, in the case of the divine incomposite nature, the unity consists in the sharing of the godhead. The Holy Spirit also is one, and we proclaim him singly, attached to the one Father through the one Son, through himself completing the worshipful and blessed Trinity. *de sp. sanct.* 44, 45

[1] Isa. 44. 6 [LXX].

[B. could never bring himself to assert that the Spirit is 'of one substance' with the Father and the Son, though his teaching implies it. He is clear that the Spirit proceeds 'from the Father through the Son': and sometimes states this in terms approaching Arian subordinationism. Eunomius asserted that 'the Holy Spirit is third in rank and order; so we have believed him to be third in nature' (*Lib. Apol.* 25). Basil was prepared to say: 'It may be that the traditonal teaching of true religion is that the Spirit is second in rank to the Son ... but even if (to make the utmost concession) he is subordinate in degree and rank, it clearly does not follow that he is alien in nature' (*c. Eunom.* 2, 1). This was traditional in the sense that earlier writers had used such language: Tertullian in *adv. Prax.* 3 and 8, and Origen in *de principiis*, 1, 3. But Athanasius had maintained the full divinity of the Spirit in his letters to Serapion, some five years before Basil wrote those words in 365: and he and Greg. Naz. attributed Basil's hesitation to a pastoral tact ('economy'), in view of waverers who might be driven into Arianism if the divinity of the Spirit were taught in terms which seemed to go beyond the evidence of Scripture.]

(b) Substance and Persons

If I must give my own opinion in a brief statement, I shall say that substance [*ousia*] is related to subsistence [*hypostasis*] as the general to the particular. Each one of us partakes of existence because he shares in *ousia* while because of his individual properties he is A or B. So, in the case in question, *ousia* refers to the general conception, like goodness, godhead, or such notions; while *hypostasis* is observed in the special properties of fatherhood, sonship, sanctifying power. If then they speak of persons without *hypostasis* they are talking nonsense, *ex hypothesi*; but if they admit that the persons exist in real *hypostasis*, as they do acknowledge, let them so number them as to preserve the principles of the *homoousion* in the unity of the godhead, and proclaim their reverent acknowledgement of Father, Son, and Holy Spirit, in the complete and perfect *hypostasis* of each person so named.

ep. 214. 4

The distinction between *ousia* and *hypostasis* is the same as the distinction between the general and the particular; for example, 'animal' and 'the man X'. Therefore in respect of the godhead we acknowledge one *ousia*, so as not to give a different account of being; but we also confess the particular *hypostasis* so that we may have an unconfused and clear conception of Father, Son, and Holy Spirit. If we have no distinct idea of the distinctive marks of each, fatherhood, sonship, and sanctification, and confess our belief in God on the basis of the general notion of being, then we are at a loss to give a sound account of our faith. We must therefore confess our faith by adding the particular to the general. The godhead is general; the fatherhood is particular. We must bring them together then by saying, 'I believe in God the Father.' Again, in our confession of the Son we must follow a like course, joining the particular to the general, and saying 'I believe in God the Son.' Similarly, in respect of the Holy Spirit we must make our statement conform to this type of pronouncement, and say, 'I believe in the divine[1] Spirit, the holy one'. Thus the unity is entirely preserved in the confession of one identical godhead, while the individual character of the persons is acknowledged by the distinction of the particular properties contemplated in each of them. But those who identify *ousia* with *hypostasis* are compelled to confess merely three different characters, and in their reluctance to speak of three *hypostases* they evidently fail to avoid the disaster of Sabellius; for even Sabellius himself, while in many places confirming the conception, attempts to distinguish the characters in saying that the same *hypostasis* changes its form to meet the need of each occasion.   *ep. 236. 6*

[This letter 'to Greg. Nyss'. is thought by some to have been written by G.N.]

The word *hypostasis* is used to indicate that which is spoken of in respect of some special distinction. When we say 'man' the effect on the hearer is a vague, dispersed notion because of the indefinite meaning of the word. It succeeds in indicating the general nature, but it does not signify what subsists, and what is particularly referred to. If we say 'Paul' we indicate the nature as it subsists, by referring to the particular instance to which the name applies. This then is the *hypostasis*, or sub-sistence (under-standing); not the indefinite notion of *ousia*, which finds no *standing* because of its generality of meaning, but the notion which gives *standing* and circumscription to what is general and uncircumscribed in any instance, by reference to the particular elements revealed in it. . . . When Job is about to narrate his life-story, he begins by mentioning the general, 'There was a *man*,' and immediately proceeds to particularize by adding 'a certain'.[2] He says nothing more to describe the *ousia*, since this has no bearing on the subject of his narrative; but he distinguishes the 'certain man' by his particular

---

[1] εἰς τὸ θεῖον Πνεῦμα τὸ ἅγιον. Another reading is εἰς τὸν Θεόν 'God, the Spirit'. But Basil seems to have avoided the direct application of 'God' to the Holy Spirit. He avoids it in *de sp. sanct.*   [2] Job 1. 1–3.

characteristics, mentioning his dwelling-place, his distinctive points of character, and all the external qualifications which in combination separate him and individualize him from the general notion of 'man'. . . . The account of the general *ousia*, would have been identical in the case of Bildad and Zophar, and in every individual mentioned in the book.

You will not go wrong if you transfer to theological doctrine this principle of distinction between *ousia* and *hypostasis* which you recognize on the human level. Whatever your thought suggests about the mode of being of the Father (and it is useless to attempt to confine the soul to the contemplation of a closely defined conception; for we are convinced that God's mode of being is beyond all conception) you will refer the same notion to the Son, and likewise to the Holy Spirit. For the principle of uncreatedness and incomprehensibility is precisely the same in the case of the Father, and the Son, and the Holy Spirit; there are no higher or lower degrees of uncreatedness and incomprehensibility. And since, in the case of the Trinity, it is essential to keep the distinction unconfused, by means of the marks of differentiation, we shall direct our inquiry only to means by which the conception of each particular entity will be clearly and distinctly separated from that which is presented to thought as the common character.

Now it seems to me that the best way to advance our investigation is as follows. We say that every good thing that comes to us from God's power is due to the activity of the grace which effects all things in all men. The Apostle says, 'But all these things come from the activity of the one same Spirit, distributing to each one individually as he wills.'[1] But when we ask whether the supply of good things has its origin in the Holy Spirit alone and thus reaches those who deserve it, we are led by Scripture to the belief that it is the Only-begotten God who is the originator and cause of the supply of the good things which are effected in us through the Spirit. For we are taught by the Holy Scripture that, 'All things have come into being through him, and are held together by him.'[2] But further, when we have been lifted up to this conception, we are led on, by this divinely inspired guidance, to learn that while it is by this power that all things are brought from non-existence into being, it is not by this power as an uncaused cause. But there is a power which subsists without generation and without cause, which is the cause of the cause, of all that exists. For the Son

[1] 1 Cor. 12. 11. [2] Col. 1. 17.

derives from the Father, and through the Son all things have being, and with him the Holy Spirit is at all times inseparably connected in our thought. For it is impossible for anyone to conceive of the Son unless he has first been enlightened by the Spirit. Thus the Holy Spirit, the source from which the supply of good things is bestowed on creation, is attached to the Son, and is apprehended inseparably with him, and at the same time he has his being in dependence on the Father, as cause, and from him he also proceeds. In this the Spirit shows the character by which his particular *hypostasis* is distinguished; he is known after the Son and with the Son, and has his *hypostasis* from the Father. The Son makes known the Spirit who proceeds from the Father through himself and with himself; whereas he has shone out, alone and as only-begotten, a light from the unbegotten light. In respect of his particular distinguishing characteristics he has nothing in common with the Father, or with the Holy Spirit. He alone is distinguished by these aforesaid marks. While God who is over all things has his one mark of differentiation which characterizes his subsistence; and this is that he alone is Father, he alone has his *hypostasis* underived from any cause. Through this distinguishing quality, his particular being is recognized. For this reason we assert that in the sharing of the *ousia* there is no coalescence or sharing of the distinctive properties which are observed in the Trinity. . . . We discover the distinction between the *hypostases*; but in respect of such attributes as infinite, incomprehensible, uncreated, unconfined, there is no variation in the life-giving nature; the nature, that is, of the Father, the Son, and the Holy Spirit. In them is observed a kind of continuous and indivisible community of nature. By means of certain ideas, one may conceive the majesty of any one of the Beings whom faith contemplates in the Holy Trinity; and by the same considerations, one may pass on without variation to behold the glory in the Father, the Son, and the Holy Spirit, while there is no empty interval separating them, for the mind to traverse. There is nothing inserted between them; nothing subsisting besides the divine nature, as to be able to divide that nature from itself, by the interposition of alien matter; nor any interval of vacuum, without subsistence, such as to make a gap in the internal harmony of the divine substance, and break the continuity by the interpolation of a void. He who has a conception of the Father conceives him as he is in himself, and at the same time includes the Son in his mental picture; and when he thus apprehends the Son, he does not

separate the Spirit from the Son; but he has formed an image of the
faith which is a combination in his mind of the three Beings, regarded
in sequence in respect of order, in conjunction in respect of nature. . . .
If we speak of the Spirit alone, we include in this statement him of whom
he is the Spirit. And since the Spirit is Christ's, and derives from God,
as Paul says,[1] then just as a man who takes hold of one end of a chain
pulls the other end to him, so the man who, in the words of the prophet,
'draws the Spirit',[2] draws through him the Father and the Son to
himself. And if anyone truly receives the Son, he will have him on both
sides, since the Son brings with him his own Father on one side, his
own Spirit on the other. For he who is always 'in the Father' can never
be severed from him, nor can he who 'effects all things' in the Spirit
ever be disjoined from him. Similarly, he who receives the Father
receives, with his power, the Son and the Spirit; for it is not possible to
conceive of severance or division in any way, so that the Son should be
thought of without the Father, or the Spirit disjoined from the Son.
There is apprehended in this a kind of inexpressible and unimaginable
community and at the same time a distinction. The difference of the
hypostasis does not tear apart the continuity of nature, nor does the
community in respect of *ousia* confuse the individual characteristics.

ep. 38. 3, 4

Eunomius says: 'We cannot say that, while both share the same substance, one has precedence in rank and by reason of temporal priority.'
Now if by community of *ousia* he understands a pre-existing matter
which is distributed and divided between those who derive from it,
then we ourselves could not accept such a notion. Most emphatically
not; and we declare that those who make this assertion, if there are
such, are no less irreverent than those who allege dissimilarity. But
if community of *ousia* is taken to mean that both are regarded as having
an identical principle of being, then it is confessed that light is also the
substance of the Only-begotten, and whatever principle of being one
ascribes to the Father is attributed also to the Son: if that is taken to be
the meaning of community of substance, then we accept the doctrine.

c. Eunom. 1. 19

When I speak of one *ousia*, beware of thinking of one divided into two.
Think of the Son as having existence from the Father, as source, not of

[1] Rom. 8. 9; 1 Cor. 2. 12.   [2] Cf. Ps. 118 (119). 131, 'I drew breath'.

the Father and Son, emerging from one pre-existent *ousia*. We are not speaking of brothers; we are acknowledging Father and Son. There is identity of *ousia*, since the Son derives from the Father, not made by a command, but begotten from his nature: not separated from the Father by division, but shining forth entire, while the Father remains entire. And please do not . . . say, 'He preaches two Gods; he teaches polytheism.' There are not two Gods; there are not two Fathers. It is the man who introduces two sources who preaches two Gods. Such is Marcion.[1] . . . And anyone who speaks of the begotten, as of different *ousia* from the begetter; he also speaks of two Gods, for he introduces polytheism because of the unlikeness of *ousia*. If there is one begotten Godhead, another unbegotten, then it is you who are preaching polytheism . . . if ingeneracy is the *ousia* of the Father, generacy of the Son. . . . There is one source, and one being derived from that source; one archetype, and one image. Thus the principle of unity is preserved. The Son exists as begotten from the Father, and in himself naturally representing the Father: as the Father's image, he shows a perfect likeness; as an offspring, he safeguards the *homoousion*. Suppose a man looks at a king's portrait in the forum, and says, 'That is the king.' He is not admitting the existence of two kings, the portrait, and the original of the portrait. Nor does he deprive the original of his royal title: he rather confirms his honour by this statement. For if the portrait is called king, then clearly the original cause of the portrait is all the more king. . . . Thus this analogy of the portrait, understood in a way appropriate to God, displays the unity of the Godhead. Thus the two are united, because there is no difference between them, nor is the Son thought of as being of a different form or alien character. Therefore I repeat, there is one and another, but the nature is undivided, perfect, and entire. Thus God is one, since by means of the two one form is observed, shown in entirety in both . . .

About the Holy Spirit we assert the same as we have been asserting about the Son, namely, that we must acknowledge his individual personality. The Scripture says, 'God is Spirit';[2] it does not therefore follow that the Spirit is identical with the Father; nor because it says 'if anyone has not the Spirit of Christ, he does not belong to Christ: but Christ is in you'[3] does it follow that the Son and the Spirit are one person [*prosôpon*]. These passages have misled some people into supposing that the Spirit is identical with Christ. What then do we assert?

[1] Cf. p. 85 n. 3.   [2] John 4. 24.   [3] Rom. 8. 9, 10.

That these sayings demonstrate the conjunction of nature between them, but not the confusion of persons. For the Father exists, having his being complete and lacking nothing, the root and source of the Son and the Holy Spirit: the Son exists in full Godhead as the living Word, the offspring of the Father, lacking nothing: and the Spirit exists in fullness, not as part of another, but complete and entire, considered in himself. The Son inseparably conjoined with the Father: the Spirit conjoined with the Son. There is nothing to separate them, nothing to sunder this eternal conjunction. No period of time intervenes between them: our mind cannot imagine any separation, such that the Only-begotten should ever cease to exist with the Father, and the Holy Spirit with the Son.   *hom.* (24) *c. Sabell., Ar., Anom.* 3. 4

What are the activities of the Holy Spirit? 'By the word of the Lord the heavens were set fast, and by the Spirit [*breath*] of his mouth all the power of them.'[1] As therefore God the Word is the creator of the heavens, so the Holy Spirit imparts to the heavenly powers the quality of firmness and stability. And Job says, 'the Spirit of God, which made me';[2] where he is not, I think, speaking about creation but about fulfilment in respect of human excellence. Again, Isaiah speaks in the person of the Lord (in respect, that is, of his humanity) and says, 'The Lord has sent me, and his Spirit'.[3] Furthermore, the psalmist declares that the power of the Spirit pervades the whole universe: 'Whither shall I go from thy Spirit, and whither shall I flee from thy face?'[4] Then consider the nature and extent of the benefits which come to us from the Holy Spirit. As the Lord himself 'gave to those who received him the power to become the children of God,'[5] so also the Holy Spirit is the 'Spirit of adoption'.[6] . . . As the Father is said to distribute the activites among those who are working to receive them, and the Son is said to distribute the responsibilities, so the Holy Spirit, by the same testimony, distributes the gifts.[7] . . . Do you observe how the activity of the Holy Spirit is conjoined with the activity of the Father and the Son? There follows a passage which even more emphatically declares the divine nature of the Holy Spirit: 'All this is the activity of one and the same Spirit, distributing to each one individually as he wills.'[8] This evidence attributes to the Spirit absolute and complete authority.
                                                      c. Eunom. 3. 4

[1] Ps. 32 (33). 6.   [2] Job 33. 4.   [3] Isa. 48. 16.   [4] Ps. 139. 7.   [5] John 1. 12.   [6] Rom. 8. 15.
[7] 1 Cor. 12. 4–6.   [8] 1 Cor. 12. 11.

The Spirit is said to be 'from God' not in the same sense in which 'all things are from God',[1] but as proceeding from God, not by way of generation, like the Son, but as the 'breath (Spirit) of his mouth'.[2] . . . The Spirit is a living *ousia*, having the power to sanctify. Thus his close relationship to God is revealed, while the manner of his being is preserved as an ineffable secret. He is also called 'Spirit of Christ', as being by nature closely related to him. . . . As Paraclete he expresses in himself the goodness of the Paraclete[3] who sent him, and in his own dignity he displays the majesty of him from whom he proceeded.

'No one knows the Father, except the Son;' similarly, 'no one can say 'Jesus is Lord' except in the Holy Spirit'.[4] . . . Thus the way to the knowledge of God is from one Spirit, through the one Son, to the one Father: conversely, the natural goodness and the natural power to sanctify, and the royal dignity, pass from the Father through the Only-begotten, to reach the Spirit. Thus the *hypostases* are acknowledged, and the reverent dogma of the monarchy is not abandoned. Those who bring in 'subnumeration', by speaking of first, second, and third, must be made to realize that they are importing the Greek error of polytheism into the pure theology of Christians. For the effect of this wicked device of 'subnumeration' . . . is the recognition of a first, a second, and a third God.   *de sp. sanct.* 46. 47

VII. The Sacraments

(a) Validity—Schismatic and Heretical Baptism

Canon 1. With regard to your question about the Cathari[5] it has already been said (as you rightly remind me) that we ought to follow the custom of each particular region, because those who, at the time, gave rulings about these matters were divided in their decisions about their baptism. But in my judgement the baptism of the Pepuzenes[6] has no validity: and I am amazed that this escaped the great Dionysius,[7]

---

[1] 1 Cor. 11. 12. Applied to the Son by George of Laodicea: 'He may be said to be from God in the sense in which "all things are from God".' [2] Ps. 33. 6. [3] John 2. 1. παράκλητός is here rendered 'advocate' in A.V. and R.V.; 'comforter' when used of the Spirit. [4] Matt. 11. 27; 1 Cor. 12. 3. [5] The followers of Novatian, who led a rigorist schism in Rome *c.* 250. The schism persisted in places for more than two centuries. [6] The Montanists, a sect (latter half of second century) of apocalyptic enthusiasts claiming special inspiration of the Spirit, in particular for such prophets as Montanus and Priscilla. 'Pepuzenes' from Pepuza in Phrygia, where, according to M. the descent of the Heavenly Jerusalem was to be expected. [7] Dionysius of Alexandria (d. *c.* 264) agreed with Stephen of Rome, against Cyprian, in accepting the validity of heretic and schismatic baptism.

versed as he was in the canons. Earlier generations decided to accept a baptism which in no way swerves from the faith. Thus they applied the names *heresies*, *schisms*, and *illicit assemblies* to the various groups. *Heresies* referred to those who had completely broken away, alienated in respect of the faith itself: *schisms*, to those who had separated from the rest for some reasons of Church policy and questions capable of adjustment: *irregular assemblies* was a term applied to congregations gathered by rebellious presbyters, or bishops, or uninstructed laymen. For instance, if a man convicted of a crime and debarred from the exercise of his ministry refuses to submit to canonical authority and arrogates to himself episcopal and ministerial functions, and other persons leave the Catholic Church to go off with him, this constitutes *irregular assembly*. To differ from members of the Church on the question of penitence is *schism*. While examples of *heresy* are seen in the Manicheans,[1] the Valentinians,[2] the Marcionites,[3] and these Pepuzenes; for in these cases there is from the start a disagreement touching the actual faith in God. It was therefore decided, in primitive times, to reject the baptism of *heretics*, while accepting that of schismatics, because the latter still have some link with the Church; those attached to *irregular assemblies* were to be reunited with the Church after amendment by adequate repentance and reformation, and consequently, in many cases, when men holding office had detached themselves to join the rebels, were received back into the same station, on repentance.

The Pepuzenes are clearly *heretical*, for they give to Montanus and Priscilla the title of Paraclete. . . . How could one justify accepting as valid the baptism of those who baptize into Father, Son, and Montanus (or Priscilla)? . . .

The Cathari are *schismatic*: but earlier authorities—including Cyprian,[4] and our own predecessor Firmilianus[5]—decided to reject, under one inclusive condemnation, Cathari, Encratites,[6] and Hydroparastatae,[7]

---

[1] Followers of the Persian Manes (third century), who taught a Light–Darkness, Spirit–Matter dualism, like that of many Gnostics. More a rival religion than a heresy. [2] Followers of the Gnostic Valentinus (second century), who interposed an elaborate system of 'aeons' between the 'ideal' and the 'phenomenal' world, and taught redemption through 'gnosis' (knowledge) brought by the 'aeon', Christ, through the man Jesus. [3] Marcion (*c.* 150) contrasted the Creator (Demiurge) of the O.T., the God of Law, with the God of Love revealed by Jesus. This heresy was not numerous or influential after the third century, but small pockets continued. [4] Bishop of Carthage 247–58. Rejected heretical and schismatic baptism as invalid. [5] Bishop of Caesarea 230–68. Supported Cyprian against Stephen. [6] A name applied to various ascetic groups. [7] A sect which used water in the Eucharist, instead of wine. Also called 'Aquarians'.

on the ground that the origin of separation arose from schism, and that those who apostatized from the Church no longer had upon them the grace of the Holy Spirit, since the gift ceased to be imparted when the continuity was interrupted. The original separatists had received ordination from the Fathers, and possessed the spiritual gift through the laying on of their hands. But those who break away become laymen, lacking authority either to baptize or to ordain, because they cannot confer on others a gift of the Holy Spirit from which they have defected. Therefore those who had been baptized by them were bidden, on the ground that they had been baptized by laymen, to come to the Church to be purified again. However, since some of those in Asia have definitely taken the line that their baptism should be accepted to make it possible for them to deal with the majority, let it be accepted. We must notice the intolerable behaviour of the Encratites. In order to make themselves incapable of being received back by the Church, they have undertaken to anticipate baptism by a peculiar baptismal rite of their own, an action involving the cancelling of their own habitual practice.[1] My opinion is that, since no clear pronouncement has been made about them, their baptism should be rejected; and if a man has received baptism at their hands and then comes to the Church, he should be baptized. But if this threatens to be an impediment to the general order of the Church, we shall have to fall back on custom and follow the practice of the Fathers who here provided precedents for our guidance. For I am apprehensive lest in our attempt to discourage them for baptizing we may, through the severity of our ruling, offer an obstacle to those who are being saved. The fact that they accept our baptism must not be allowed to disquiet us; we are under no obligation to reciprocate this favour, but we *are* bound to a strict observance of the canons. In any event, it must be decreed that those who come to us from their baptism are to be anointed (at the hands of the faithful, obviously) and on this condition are to approach the mysteries. I am, however, well aware that I have received the brothers, Zois and Saturninus[2] into the episcopal chair, and they belonged to that community. I am therefore prevented from excluding from the Church those who have been attached to their company, since by my acceptance of the bishops, I have as it were promulgated a canon of communion with them.

ep. 188 [*ad Amphilochium*]

---

[1] The nature of these innovations is not known.   [2] Nothing is known of these brothers.

Whence is it that we are Christians? 'Through our faith,' would be the universal reply. How are we saved? Clearly by being reborn in the baptism of grace. How else could it be? Then after recognizing that this salvation is made secure through Father, Son, and Holy Spirit, are we going to let slip that 'form of teaching'[1] which we received? . . . Whether a man has departed this life without partaking of baptism, or has received the rite deficient in some of the elements of the tradition,[2] his loss is the same. . . . If my baptism was for me the beginning of life and that day of rebirth the first of days, then clearly the most precious of all utterances is the statement made at the moment of the grace of adoption. . . . I pray that I may depart to the Lord with this confession, and I counsel these opponents[3] to preserve the faith intact until the day of Christ, to guard against separating the Spirit from Father and Son, and to hold to the doctrine taught at baptism, in the confession of their faith and in the performance of their offering of praise. *de sp. sanct.* 10. 26

(b) Baptism: The Threefold Name

Let no one be misled by the fact that the Apostle often omits the name of the Father and the Holy Spirit, when he mentions baptism: let no one therefore assume that the invocation of the names was not observed. He says, 'All of you who were baptized into Christ have put on Christ', and again, 'All of you who were baptized into Christ were baptized into his death.' For the use of the name of Christ [*The Anointed One*] is the confession of the whole, since it points to the God who anointed, the Son who was anointed, and the Spirit who is the unction. . . . Faith and baptism are two kindred and inseparable ways of salvation: faith is perfected by baptism; baptism is established by faith, and both are completed by the use of the same names. As we believe in Father, Son, and Holy Spirit, so we are baptized into the name of Father, Son, and Holy Spirit. Confession leads the way and brings us to salvation; baptism follows, setting the seal on our assent. *de sp. sanct.* 28

[The Baptismal Formula

Athanasius argued that Arian baptism was void, despite the use of the threefold

---

[1] Cf. 2 Tim. 1. 13.   [2] i.e. the baptismal formula.   [3] Those who deny the equality of the Spirit with the Father and Son.

name, because of the lack of Trinitarian faith. 'The Arians do not baptize into Father and Son, but into Creator and creature, Maker and handiwork. As a creature is very different from the Son, so the baptism supposedly given by them is something other than the reality, even though they claim to use the names of the Father and the Son on account of what is written in Scripture. For baptism is not bestowed by one who merely says "Lord", but only by one who accompanies the name with the right faith.' *or.* 2. 42. Cf. Bas. *c. Eunom.* 3. 5: 'Baptism is the seal of our faith, and our faith is the affirmation of the Godhead. We must first believe, and then receive the seal of baptism. And our baptism, according to the tradition of the Lord, is into the name of Father, Son, and Holy Spirit; and the Spirit is no creature, nor a servant attached to Father and Son, for the Godhead has its fulfilment in Trinity.'

Cyprian, in controversy with Stephen, bishop of Rome, held that heretical baptism was invalid. But Stephen's view, that the 'majesty of the Name', when the correct formula was employed, conveyed the full reality of the sacrament, prevailed in the W. It was laid down in the 7th canon of the Council of Arles (314); 'Concerning the Africans, because they employ their peculiar custom of baptizing, our decision is that if anyone comes into the Church from heresy, they should ask him to recite the creed: and if they find that he was baptized with the Father, the Son, and the Holy Spirit, he should receive only the laying on of hands, that he may receive the Holy Spirit. But if on interrogation he does not respond with the Trinity, let him be baptized.' So St. Augustine: 'If Marcion baptized in the words of the Gospel, in the name of the Father, the Son and the Holy Spirit, the sacrament was perfect; even though his faith was imperfect, since what he meant by the words was different from the teaching of Catholic truth, being polluted with fables and falsehoods.' (*de bapt. c. Don.* 3. 19). The attitude of the Council of Nicaea is uncertain. Canon xix prescribes re-baptism for the followers of Paul of Samosata, and according to Athanasius they used the Trinitarian formula in baptism. And the so-called 7th canon of Constantinople regards as void the baptism of Eunomians (with a single immersion), Montanists, and Sabellians, despite the use of the evangelical formula, though it recognizes the validity of Arian baptism.]

(c) The Eucharist
(i) Spiritual Food

[The authorship of this passage is uncertain. See note on p. 67.]

'He who eats me,' he says, 'shall live because of me',[1] For we eat his flesh, and drink his blood, by becoming, through his incarnation and his visible life, partakers of his word and his wisdom. For by 'flesh' and

[1] John 6. 57.

'blood' he referred to the whole of his mystical dwelling among us, and he also indicated his teaching; teaching about conduct, about the world, about God. For by his teaching our soul is nourished, while it is made ready for the contemplation of reality. This is perhaps the meaning of the saying. *ep.* 8. 4

(ii) *Frequent Communion and Reservation*

Daily communion and participation in the holy body and blood of Christ is a good and helpful practice. He clearly says, 'The man who eats my flesh and drinks my blood, has eternal life.'[1] Who doubts that to partake of life continually is really to have life in abundance? For myself, I communicate four times a week, on the Lord's day, on Wednesday, Friday, and Saturday, and on the other days if there is a commemoration of a martyr. If in times of persecution individuals, under this compulsion, give themselves communion with their own hands, without the presence of priest or minister, this raises no difficulty. In fact there is no need to point this out, since long-established custom has sanctioned the practice under pressure of circumstances. All the hermits in the desert, when there is no priest, keep the communion at home and give it to themselves. And in Alexandria and Egypt it is the general rule for each member of the laity to keep the communion at his own house. For when once the priest has completed the sacrifice, and has given the sacrament, he who has received it as one entire portion is bound to believe, as he participates day by day, that he rightly partakes of it and receives it from him who gave it. Even in the church the priest gives the portion and the recipient retains it, with complete power to do what he will, and he brings it to his mouth with his own hand. It makes no difference to validity whether one portion is received from the priest or several portions at the same time.

ep. 93

VIII. The Last Things

(a) *Judgement*

'Why am I afraid in the evil day? The lawlessness of my heel will surround me.'[2] He calls the day of judgement evil and of this day it is said that 'the Day of the Lord is irremediable'[3] against all nations.

---

[1] John 6. 54.   [2] Ps. 48 (49). 6.   [3] Isa. 13. 9 (LXX), 'The Day of the Lord comes irremediable . . . to make the whole world desolate.'

The prophet says that on this day each man's own decisions will surround him: and therefore at that time I 'am not afraid of the evil day', when nothing lawless has been done by me, in my journey through life, for the 'lawlessness of my heel' will not surround me. The evidence of my sins will not stand round me, nor will they encircle me to prove me guilty by their silent accusation. For no other accuser will stand up against you: only your own actions, each facing you in its own proper shape, . . . each sin will confront you with its own particular marks of recognition, to recall the act vividly to your memory.

in Ps. 48. 2

[Ps. 33. 6 (34. 5): '*Come to God and be enlightened, and your faces will not be ashamed.*'] Blessed is the man who in the day of God's just judgement, when the Lord comes to 'throw light on the hidden things, of the darkness, and to reveal the intentions of men's hearts', submits boldly to that testing light, and comes out unashamed because his conscience is unpolluted by evil actions. While those who have acted wickedly will 'rise to reproach and shame', for they will see in themselves their disgrace, and the marks of their sins. And perhaps the shame in which the sinners are destined to live for ever is more horrible than the darkness and the eternal fire: for they will have always before their eyes the evidence of their sins committed in the flesh, like some indelible stain, which will endure in the memory of their souls, for all eternity.

in Ps. 33. 4

(b) Heaven

'Blessed are the pure in heart, for they shall see God.'[1] Brethren, think of the kingdom of heaven as just this, the genuine contemplation of realities. This is what the inspired Scriptures call blessedness: for 'the kingdom of heaven is within you'.[2] Now the inner man consists simply of contemplation: it follows that the kingdom of heaven must be contemplation. Now we behold 'as in a glass'[3] the shadows of things, the archetypes of which we shall behold later, when we are set free from this earthly body and have put on an incorruptible and immortal body.[4] Then we shall see, that is, if we steer our life's course towards the right, and if we take heed of the right faith; for otherwise

---

[1] Matt. 5. 8. [2] Luke 17. 21. [3] 1 Cor. 13. 12. [4] Cf. 1 Cor. 15. 54.

no one will see the Lord.[1] . . . Let no one object that I am disregarding
what is in front of my eyes and philosophizing to them about incorporeal and completely immaterial being. I regard it as absurd that we
should allow the senses unhindered satisfaction in their own material
things, while we prevent only the mind from enjoying its proper activity. For just as the senses can apprehend sensible objects, so the mind
apprehends intelligible objects. . . . As the senses, if they are impaired
in any way, readily recover their proper activity after the necessary
treatment, so the mind, fettered to the flesh, and filled with the imagi-
nations that arise from the flesh, needs faith and a right regimen, which
'equip its feet like the feet of a deer, and make it stand on the high
places'.[2]   *ep.* 8. 12[8]

[*On Ps.* 33. 17 (34. 16): '*The face of the Lord is over those who do evil, that
he may destroy their memory from the earth.*'] No *man* will see God's face
and live; it is the *angels* of the 'little ones' in the Church, who 'continually behold the face of the Father in heaven.'[3] Thus it is impossible
for us now to be capable of the sight of his glorious appearance, because we are 'encompassed by the weakness'[4] of the flesh: but the
angels, having no covering like our flesh, have nothing to hinder them
from gazing at the face of God's glory. And so we also, when we become sons of the resurrection, shall be counted worthy to know God
face to face. Then the righteous will be counted worthy of the 'joy of
the sight of his countenance'.[5]   *in Ps.* 33. 11

If ever a kind of light has fallen upon your heart, arousing a multitude
of thoughts about God, if it has shone upon your soul, so that you have
felt love towards God, and contempt for the world and all material
things, then you can realize what is the whole condition of the righteous
who attain to constant and uninterrupted delight in God. This rejoicing
falls to your lot, by the design of God, so that it may remind you, by
this brief taste, of the joys of which you have been deprived. But the
righteous has this divine and heavenly delight continually, because the
Spirit abides in him for ever.[6] And the first-fruit of the Spirit is love,
joy, peace. 'Rejoice *in the Lord*, you righteous ones.'[7] The Lord is, as
it were, a place to receive the righteous; and one who is in this place

[1] Cf. Heb. 12. 14.   [2] Ps. 17 (18). 33.   [3] Matt. 18. 10.   [4] Heb. 5. 2.   [5] Cf. Acts 2. 28;
Ps. 15 (16). 11.   [6] John 14. 16.   [7] Ps. 33. 1.   [8] Authorship uncertain: see note on p. 67.

cannot help but be filled with happiness and delight. And the righteous;
is a place for the Lord, for he welcomes the Lord into himself.

in Ps. 32. 1

(c) Eternal Punishment

[*The Lord speaks of eternal punishment and eternal fire.* Matt. 25. 46;
Mark 9. 48.]
Many men have forgotten such important sayings and declarations of
the Lord, and fix for themselves a time-limit to punishment, so that
they may sin with greater confidence. This is the result of the devil's
trickery. For if there is any time-limit for eternal punishment, it follows
that there will be a time-limit for eternal life. If we cannot bring ourselves to suppose this with regard to eternal life, what plausibility is
there in ascribing a limit to eternal punishment? The adjective 'eternal'
is applied equally to both. . . . [*The 'many and few stripes' of* Lk. 12. 47
refer to intensity of punishment, not to its duration.[1]] The 'unquenchable fire'
may burn freely or violently, the 'undying worm' may inflict gentler
or fiercer torture, according to desert; hell surely has different kinds of
chastisement; one man is consigned to outer darkness, where for some
there is only weeping, while for others there is the gnashing of teeth.
And outer darkness inevitably suggests an inner darkness.

reg. br. 267

Those who have grieved the Holy Spirit . . . will, according to one of
the Evangelists, be completely 'cut asunder',[2] which means utter
separation from the Spirit . . . the eternal alienation of the soul from the
Spirit. . . . Thus 'in hell there is no one who confesses, no one in death
who remembers God',[3] because the help of the Spirit is no longer
available.   *de sp. sanct.* 40

IX. Discipline

(a) Penance

[Three 'Canonical Letters' were addressed to Amphilochius, bishop of Iconium.
They contain detailed regulations for penitential discipline, and attained
canonical authority in the Eastern Church.]

[1] Augustine makes the same point; cf. p. 249.   [2] Matt. 24. 51.   [3] Cf. Ps. 6. 6 (LXX).

Those guilty of sodomy or bestiality, and also murderers, sorcerers, adulterers, and idolaters, all deserve the same penalty. . . . We ought to receive those who have repented for the space of thirty years: ignorance, voluntary confession, and the long lapse of time, give ground for forgiveness.   *ep.* 188 [*ad Amphil.*] *can.* 7.

An intentional homicide, on repentance, will be excommunicated for twenty years, appointed as follows; for four years he must weep, standing outside the door of the house of prayer, beseeching the faithful as they enter to pray for him, and confessing his sin. After four years he will be admitted among the 'hearers' and for four years will go out with them. For seven years he will go out with the 'kneelers'. For four years he will merely stand with the faithful, not partaking of the oblation. On the completion of this period he will be admitted to partake of the sacrament.

The unintentional homicide will be excommunicated for ten years . . . [2 *as* 'weeper', 3 *as* 'hearer', 4 *as* 'kneeler', 1 *as* 'stander'].

Adulterer; fifteen years [divided, as above, 4. 5. 4. 2]. Fornicators; seven years[1] [2. 2. 2. 1].

He who has denied Christ ought to weep for the whole of his life, and must remain in penitence, being granted the sacrament only in the hour of death.   *ep.* 217 [*ad Amphil.*] *can.* 56-8, 73

Heretics are to be received on a death-bed repentance. *ep.* 188, *can.* 5

(b) Divorce

The declaration of the Lord, that it is not permitted to withdraw from marriage 'except for the cause of fornication',[2] applies to men and women equally according to the logic of the argument. But custom does not so hold . . . but enjoins that adulterous and promiscuous husbands be retained by their wives. And so I am not certain whether a woman who lives with a man who has been dismissed can be termed an adulteress. For in this case the guilt attaches to the woman who has divorced her husband, and it depends on the cause for which she withdraws from marriage. If she was beaten and refused to submit to this treatment, she ought to have endured it rather than be separated

---

[1] But *ep.* 199. 22 gives four years.   [2] Matt. 5. 32.

from her husband: if she refused to submit to financial loss, even this would not be an adequate pretext. If her reason was her husband's promiscuity, this is not a custom observed in the Church: in fact a wife is enjoined not to be separated even from an unbelieving husband . . . [1 Cor. 7. 16]. In these cases, then, the wife is an adulteress if she leaves her husband and then goes to another man. But a deserted husband is to be pardoned, and the woman living with him is not condemned. But if the man who has left his wife goes to another woman, he himself is an adulterer, because he makes her commit adultery, and the woman who lives with him is an adulteress, because she has brought over to herself another woman's husband.   *ep.* 188. 9

(c) Monastic Discipline
(i) Competitive Austerity Forbidden
The Lord said, 'Not to do my own will, but the will of him who sent me'.[1] Therefore every decision of a man's private will is dangerous. . . . Whatever a man does in accordance with his own private will belongs morally to the doer, and is far removed from true piety. . . . To aspire to outdo others in a competitive spirit is to fall a prey to jealousy; it is the result of false pride. . . . If any one imagines that he needs more in the way of fasting, or vigil, or anything else of the kind, he should explain to those who are entrusted with the oversight of the community what are his reasons for supposing that he needs more: and then he must abide by their decision. For often he will have to satisfy his need in some other way, rather than in this.   *reg. br.* 137, 138

(ii) The Life in Community
In the solitary life the powers we have become useless: the power we lack cannot be supplied . . .

The sole purpose of the solitary life is to minister to the needs of the individual: but this is clearly contrary to the laws of love. . . . A number of men living in community can easily perform many of the commandments; which is impossible for a solitary man, since the fulfilment of one prevents the fulfilment of another. When, for example, we are visiting the sick, we cannot be entertaining the stranger.[2] . . . Who would choose the ineffective and unfruitful life in preference to the fruitful life that is lived in fulfilling the Lord's commands? . . .

[1] John 6. 38.   [2] Cf. Matt. 25. 35.

We are 'each one of us, members of one another':[1] but if we are not
united in harmony into one close-knit body in the Holy Spirit, but each
individual chooses solitude, not serving the welfare of the community
in the manner well-pleasing to God, but satisfying the private desires
of self-fulfilment, how, when thus separated and divided, can we
preserve the mutual relation and service of the members, and their
subjection to our head, that is, to Christ? For when our life is thus
divided, how can we 'rejoice with him who is glorified, or suffer with
the sufferers'?[2] It is scarcely possible for the individual to know what
is happening to his neighbour. Then again, no man is capable of
receiving all the spiritual gifts. . . . In the community life, the private
gifts of the individual become the common property of his fellows . . .
the activity of the Holy Spirit in one man extends to all the rest at
once. . . . What scope will a man have for showing humility, if he
has no one before whom to show himself humble? What chance of
showing compassion, when cut off from fellowship with other men?
How practise patience, when there is none to oppose his wishes? . . .
The Lord washed the disciples' feet. Whose feet will you wash? Whom
will you look after? . . . When brethren live together in community,
then there is a stadium for athletic exercise, a method for development,
a combined course of training and practice in the Lord's commands.
And its object is the glory of God . . . [Matt. 5. 16.]   *reg. fus.* 7

(iii) *The Rule of Work*

Our Lord Jesus Christ says, 'The *labourer* deserves his food'[3] (he does
not say that every man without exception deserves it) and the Apostle
commands to 'toil and produce good work with our own hands,
so that we may have something to share with the man who is in need'.[4]
Thus it is immediately evident that it is our duty to work energetically.
For we must not make our aim of piety into an excuse for idleness or
an escape from hard work. . . . Such a manner of life is beneficial to
us not merely because it 'buffets the body',[5] but because it gives an
opportunity for showing love to one's neighbour; so that God through
us may supply the necessities of life to those of our brethren who are
in distress. . . . The Apostle clearly enjoins that a man who will not work
shall not eat.[6] Daily food is a necessity for everyone: no less necessary
is it for everyone to work to the best of his power. . . . Some use

[1] Rom. 12. 5.   [2] Cf. Rom. 12. 15.   [3] Luke 10. 7.   [4] Cf. Eph. 4. 28.   [5] 1 Cor. 9. 27.
[6] Cf. 2 Thess. 3. 10.

prayers and psalmody, as a pretext for exemption from work. But we must remember that, as Ecclesiastes says, 'There is a time for everything',[1] and each particular task has its own particular time. However, every time is appropriate for prayer and psalmody, as for many other things, and so while our hands are busy with our work, we praise God with our tongue, when possible . . . or, if not, in our heart, giving thanks to him, who has given us the strength of hand to work, and the cleverness of brain to understand our craft . . . and we pray that the work of our hands may be directed towards our aim of pleasing God.   *reg. fus.* 37

(iv) *The Hours of Prayer*

However, we must not suppose that because we are commanded to give thanks 'at all times'[2] we should therefore neglect the prescribed times of prayer . . . which are as follows:

[*Prime*]

First, *at dawn*, so that the first activities of soul and mind should be consecrated to God, and that we should not admit any other concern into our thoughts until we have been delighted by thoughts of God . . . [Ps. 88. 13; Ps. 5. 2, 3.]

[*Terce*]

Next *at the third hour* we must arise to prayer, and assemble the brotherhood, even if they happen to be dispersed at their various occupations. Remembering the giving of the Spirit to the Apostles at the third hour, we must all join in united worship so that we too may be made worthy to receive sanctification. . . . Then we resume our work. If any should find themselves too far away to attend, owing to the nature of the work or of the locality, they are under a strict obligation to fulfil the general ordinances where they are, without fail; for 'where two or three are assembled . . .' [Matt. 28. 20.]

[*Sext*]

We have decided that prayer is necessary *at the sixth hour*, following the example of the saints who said, 'At evening and morning and at

¹ Eccles. 3. 1.   ² Ps. 34. 1.

noon, I will tell my tale, I will proclaim, and he will hear my voice';[1] and at the same time the 90th psalm is said that we may be delivered 'from mishap and the mid-day demon'.[2]

[None]

The ninth hour is enjoined on us as a necessary time for prayer by the Apostles themselves, in Acts, where we learn that Peter and John went up to the Temple at the ninth hour of prayer.[3]

[Vespers]

When the day is over there comes thanksgiving for what we have been given during the day and for our achievements; and confession of our failures, our voluntary or involuntary misdeeds, and those perhaps unknown to us, whether in word or deed or in the heart itself, asking God's mercy for all through our prayers. For a review of the past is a great help against falling again into similar faults. Hence the saying, 'What you say in your hearts, feel compunction for upon your beds'.[4]

[Compline]

Then again *at the beginning of night* there comes the petition that our rest may be free from offence and from phantasies,[5] and we are again obliged to recite the 90th psalm.

[Nocturns]

Paul and Silas have set a precedent for observing *midnight* as an obligatory time for prayers . . . [Acts 16. 25; also Ps. 119. 62.]

[Lauds]

And again we have to rise for prayer *before dawn*, to 'anticipate dawn',[6] so that the day does not catch us sleeping in bed . . .

None of these times may be neglected by those who have chosen to live by regular observance to the glory of God and his Christ. And I

---

[1] Ps. 54 (55). 17. [2] Ps. 90 (91). 6. [3] Cf. Acts 3. 1. [4] Ps. 4. 4 (LXX). [5] Cf. the Latin hymn in Compline: Procul recedant somnia/et noctium phantasmata,/hostemque nostrum comprime/ne polluantur corpora. [6] Ps. 118 (119). 148.

think it useful to have diversity and variety in the prayers and psalms at the regular hours, because where there is monotony the soul tends to become weary and distracted: but when there is change and variety in the psalmody and in the pattern of each hour, then the desire of the soul is renewed and concentration is restored.   *reg. fus.* 37

Gregory of Nazianzus

I. Authority

(a) Scripture

[*G. has been speaking of the superficial attractions of pagan literature.*]

We, on the other hand, trace the careful activity of the Spirit even in the details of Scripture; and we will never admit (it would not be reverent) that even the least important narratives of Scripture were carefully committed to writing by the chroniclers without some serious purpose. In fact, they were recorded so that we may have warnings and instructions to guide our decisions in similar situations if the need arises: so that we may know what to shun and what to choose, by following those previous examples, using them as rules and parallels.
                                                                or. 2. 105

(b) Tradition

[*G., writing against Appolinarius and his supporters, asks why some men should seek to introduce novelties in doctrine.*]

Our faith has been proclaimed both in written and in unwritten form, here and in distant parts, in danger and in security. Why then do some men attempt such innovations, while others remain peaceful?
                                                                ep. 101. 1

II. Man's Condition

(a) Grace and Freedom

'It is not all who are capable of receiving this saying; but those to whom it is given.'[1] When you hear 'it is given' do not allow yourself to succumb to any heretical notion: do not bring in various kinds of natures—the earthy, the spiritual, the intermediate.[2] For there are men so perverse as to suppose that some men are of a nature inevitably doomed to perdition; others of a nature destined for salvation; others

---

[1] Matt. 19. 11.   [2] The gnostic Valentinus (second century) divided mankind into three classes: the *pneumatici* ('spiritual'), who were assured of full salvation; the *hylici* ('material'), irretrievably doomed; and the *psychici* ('animate') who might by good works attain a kind of second-class redemption.

whose state is such that their own choice leads them either to the good or to the bad. Now I concede that some men have more natural aptitude than others; but I maintain that mere aptitude is insufficient to bring men to perfection. It is deliberate choice that effects this, as fire is produced from flint when it is struck by steel. When you hear the words, 'to whom it is given', you must add, 'it is given to those who are called, and who respond to the call'. I advise you to understand the same addition when you are told that 'it is not a matter of human decision, or human activity, but of God's mercy'.[1] There are some who are so elated by their virtuous conduct that they give the whole credit to themselves, and no credit to the Creator, the giver of wisdom, the supplier of everything that is good: and that is why Paul teaches them in this passage that God's help is needed if we are to will rightly; or rather, the very choice of what is right is, in a sense, an act of God, a gift of God's kindness. Our salvation must come from God; but it also depends on us. Therefore Paul says, 'It is not a matter of human decision' (that is, not of human decision *only*), 'nor of activity (only); but of God's mercy'. Thus he rightly ascribes the whole matter to God, since from God comes the act of willing. However hard you run and however hard you fight you need him who gives the crown.[2]

[*When Jesus replied to the request of the mother of James and John.*] 'It does not belong to me to give a seat on my right and left; that seat is for those to whom it has been given.'[3] Does this mean that there is no value in the mind, man's governing principle? No value in hard work, or in reason, or in philosophy? Does fasting go for nothing? And vigils, and sleeping on the bare earth, and floods of tears? Are all those nothing? Does all depend on a kind of election by lot? So that Jeremiah is sanctified, others are rejected, 'from the mother's womb'?[4]

I am afraid of the introduction here of a certain ridiculous theory: that the soul has had a life elsewhere, and after that has been attached to this body; and that as a consequence of this life elsewhere some receive the gift of prophecy, while others, those who have previously lived an evil life, are condemned. This supposition is absurd, and it is contrary to the teaching of the Church; let others play with such doctrines; we regard such pastimes as unsafe. In this place also, after 'to whom it has been given', you must understand 'those who are

[1] Rom. 9. 16.   [2] Cf. 2 Tim. 4. 7 f.   [3] Matt. 20. 21, 23.   [4] Jer. 1. 5.

worthy'. And their worthiness is due not only to what they have received from the Father, but also to what they themselves have contributed.   *or.* 37. 13, 14, 15

(b) Creation and Fall

[*The creation of angels—immaterial intelligences; and of the material world apprehended by the senses.*]

Mind and sense,[1] thus distinct from each other, kept themselves within their own bounds, and bore witness in themselves to the greatness of the creative Word, praising the mighty work in silence, and proclaiming it for all to hear.[2] There was not yet any blending of the two, nor any mixture of these contraries, which should manifest a greater wisdom and a greater bounty in the creation of natures; all the riches of goodness were not yet displayed. This was what the Craftsman–Word decided to exhibit, and he produced a single living being formed out of both (I mean the invisible and the visible natures); he produced man. He took the body from already existing matter and put in it a breath taken from himself (which the Word [of Scripture] knows as the intelligent soul and the image of God[3]). This man he set upon the earth as a kind of second world, a microcosm; another kind of angel, a worshipper of blended nature, a full initiate of the visible creation, but a mere neophyte in respect of the intelligible world. He was king of all upon earth, but a subject of Heaven; earthly and heavenly; transient, yet immortal; belonging both to the visible and the intelligible order; midway between greatness and lowliness; combining in the same being spirit and flesh: spirit, because of God's grace; flesh, because raised up from the dust; spirit, so that he may endure, and glorify his benefactor; flesh, that he may suffer, and by suffering may be reminded and chastened when his greatness makes him ambitious. Thus he is a living creature under God's providence here, while in transition to another state, and (this is the consummation of the mystery[4]) in process of deification by reason of his natural tendency towards God.

This man God honoured with the gift of free will, so that the good might belong as much to him who made the choice as to him who provided the seeds:[5] and he placed him in the paradise, whatever that paradise may have been, as the cultivator of immortal plants, that is,

---

[1] i.e. The intelligent creation (angels) and the material world.   [2] Cf. Ps. 19. 3, 4.   [3] Wis. 7. 22 f.; Gen. 1. 27.   [4] i.e. the fulfilment of God's hidden purpose, which has now been revealed.   [5] The potentialities of good.

perhaps, of divine concepts, both the simpler and the more advanced. He was naked in his simplicity and in his primitive way of life, and devoid of any kind of covering or defence: that was the fitting condition for the first-created man. And God gave him a law, to be the material for the exercise of his free will. This law was a commandment telling him which trees he could partake of, and the tree from which he must abstain. This was the Tree of Knowledge. It was not originally planted with evil intent, nor forbidden through jealousy: the enemies of God must not direct their slanders in this direction, taking their cue from the serpent. It was planted to be a source of good, if partaken of at the right time: for, as I expound it, this tree is Contemplation, which is only safe for those to climb who have reached an advanced stage in the development of character: it is not food for those whose appetite outstrips their development: just as adult food is not suitable for those who are still delicate, who need a milk diet. But Adam fell, through the malice of the devil and his insolent deceit of the woman. She was vulnerable because of her pliability, and she involved her husband, because of her powers of persuasion. (Alas for my weakness! For I share that weakness of my first ancestor.) He forgot the commandment which had been given him and was overcome by the taste—a bitter taste for him. And straightway he was banished from the tree of life, from paradise, and from God, because of his wickedness, and was clothed with coats of skins, that is, perhaps, the grosser kind of flesh, which is mortal and rebellious. This first becomes conscious of its shame, and hides from God. Even here some benefit is gained; namely, death and the cutting short of his sin, so that the evil shall not be immortal.

Thus the penalty turns out to be an act of mercy. For this, I am sure, is God's method of punishment.   *or.* 45. 8, 9

(c) 'In Adam'

The sky is the common possession of all men, and so are the sun and the moon in their circuits . . . and one and the same earth is common to all; the earth which is our mother and our grave, from which we were taken, and to which we shall return. No one has more of it than another. More important than these, we have in common the Law and the Prophets, and even the sufferings of Christ, through which we were re-fashioned. All without exception who shared in the same Adam and were misled by the serpent, and brought to death by sin; we were all

restored to salvation through the heavenly Adam, and through the
tree of dishonour were brought back to the Tree of Life, whence we
had fallen. *or.* 33. 9

(d) *Original Sin and Infant Baptism*

Now, since God has not made me a god, but has fashioned my nature
Able to tend either this way or that, he affords me assistance.
Thus at the font he gives grace: for just as the Hebrews of old time
Cleansing the doorposts with unction of blood thus escaped the
   destroyer,
When the firstborn of Egypt were slain; so God our defender
Gives us the seal of the laver: which is, for innocent children,
Naught but a seal; but for men, a seal and a medicine of healing.

poem. dogm. 1. 85

Some have not been able to receive baptism because of their tender
years or because of some completely involuntary accident. . . . They
will receive neither glory nor chastisement, I think, at the hands of the
just Judge; since, while they have not been sealed, they are void of
offence, and they have incurred this defect involuntarily. But it does
not follow that one who does not deserve punishment deserves honour;
nor that one who does not deserve honour deserves punishment.

or. 40. 23

III. The Status of Christ

The Subjection of the Son

[1 Cor. 15. 25 *is used by Eunomius to support the Arian doctrine of the
inferiority of the Son.*]
He who removes the curse from me was called a curse on my account;
he who takes away the sin of the world was called sin.[1] And he
becomes the new Adam to take the place of the old. In the same way
he makes my insubordination his own, since he is the head of the whole
Body. So long as I am unsubjected and rebellious, by my refusal of
God and because of my passions, Christ also is said to be unsubjected
in respect of me. But when he has brought all things into subjection . . .
then he himself has brought his subjection to fulfilment, by bringing
me over to a state of salvation.

    This, as I see it, is the subjection of Christ; the fulfilment of the

[1] Gal. 3. 13; 2 Cor. 5. 21.

Father's will. The Son puts in subjection to the Father, the Father to the Son. The Son acts; the Father approves. Thus he who has made things subject presents to God that which has been subjected, making our condition his own. Such seems to me to be the meaning of the cry, 'My God, my God, have regard to me; why have you forsaken me?'[1] He himself was not forsaken, neither by the Father, nor by his own divinity (as some suppose, as if the divine nature were afraid of the suffering and therefore removed itself from the sufferer).

For who compelled him to be born at all, or to mount the cross? As I have said, he represents, in himself, our condition. For it was we who were formerly forsaken and neglected, but we have now been brought near and saved by the sufferings of the impassible one. Similarly, when he utters the verses which follow in the psalm,[2] he is taking to himself our folly and our wrongdoing: for the twenty-first psalm clearly refers to Christ.

Connected with the same question is the fact that he learned obedience as a result of what he suffered, and the 'shout' and 'tears' and his 'supplications', and that 'he was heard' and his 'reverent fear'.[3] This is a dramatic representation, marvellously constructed for our benefit. For, as the Word, he was neither obedient nor disobedient. Such language applies only to subjects and subordinates; 'obedient' applies to the well-behaved, 'disobedient' to those who deserve punishment.

But in respect of his 'form of a servant',[4] he comes down to join his fellow-servants and assumes a form which is not his own, taking upon himself me and what belongs to me, so that in himself he may consume the evil, as fire consumes wax, or the sun consumes the mist of earth, and that I may share in what belongs to him, by reason of this commixture. Therefore he does honour to obedience in action, and 'has experience of obedience as a result of his suffering'.[3] For the disposition of obedience was not enough, any more than it is for us, unless we proceed to put it into practice; for disposition is demonstrated by action. . . . Thus Christ can know our experience at first hand and take our infirmity into account, along with what we have to endure. . . . For if because of the concealing screen[5] the light which shone in this life's darkness was persecuted by the darkness[6] (the dark-

---

[1] Ps. 21 (22). 1; Matt. 27. 46.   [2] Ps. 21 (22). 2.' . . . far from my salvation are the words of my transgressions; 3. My God, I will cry in the day, and thou wilt not listen: and in the night, and (thou wilt not listen) to my folly.'   [3] Heb. 5. 7, 8.   [4] Phil. 2. 7.   [5] i.e. the flesh which hid his divinity.   [6] John 1. 5.

ness, I mean, of the evil one, the tempter), then what persecution will befall the darkness of men in their weakness? . . .

'God will be all in all' in the time of restoration. This does not mean the Father, with the Son merely absorbed again into him, like a brand snatched out of a great fire and then returned to it (for I hope that the Sabellians[1] will not employ this text to their own destruction). It means the whole Godhead, and tells of the time when we shall no longer be a plurality as we are now because of our motions and passions, having in ourselves scarcely anything of God; but we shall be entirely godlike, capable of receiving all God and nothing but God. This is the consummation to which we are hastening . . . [Col. 3. 11.]

or. 30. 5, 6

IV. The Person of Christ

(a) The Two Natures in Christ

[*Referring to John* 14. 28 '*The Father is greater*' *and John* 20. 17 '*My God and your God*'.]

He could be called the God, not of the Word, but of him who was seen by men. For how could he be the God of him who is himself genuinely God? In the same way he is the Father, not of him who was seen, but of the Word. Thus in regard to the two natures in Christ one title [for God] is properly applied, another title improperly; in regard to us the same is true, but vice versa. For he is properly termed our God, but improperly Father.[2] This is what occasions the error of the heretics, namely the combination of names, the name being interchanged because of the commingling (of the two natures). This is shown by the fact that, when the natures are considered separately, the distinction of nomenclature corresponds with the distinction of the conceptions. Notice how Paul says, 'The God of our Lord Jesus Christ, the Father of glory'.[3] God of Christ; but Father of the glory.[4]— Though both compose a single whole, it is not by unity of nature but by coalescence of those two natures. What could be more intelligible?

or. 30. 8

---

[1] Sabellius and his followers taught that the Son and the Spirit were successive modes of God's activity. [2] 'God', in 'my God and yours', is properly applied in regard to Christ as man, and in regard to us: improperly in regard to Christ as God. 'Father' is properly applied to Christ as God: improperly to Christ as man. [3] Eph. 1. 17. [4] Exegetically fanciful; and theologically precarious. 'Glory' is an epithet of God, not a name for Christ's divine nature.

He was, and he becomes. He was above time, he became subject to time: he was invisible; he becomes visible. 'He was in the beginning, and he was with God, and he was God.'[1] 'Was' is repeated three times, for emphasis. What he was, he laid aside: what he was not, he assumed. He did not become two; but he allowed himself to become a unity composed of two elements. For that which assumed and that which was assumed combine into a divine being. The two natures coalesce into a unity; and there are not two sons, for we must make no mistake about the commixture of the natures.   *or.* 37. 2

He made his appearance as God, with the assumption of human nature, a unity composed of two opposites, flesh and Spirit.[2] The former he deified, the latter was already deified. O strange mixture! O marvellous blending! He who is comes to be; the uncreated is created, the unconfinable is confined, through the mediation of the intellectual soul, the bridge between the divinity and the grossness of the flesh. He who enriches becomes poor: he takes upon himself the poverty of my flesh so that I may receive the riches of his divinity. He who is full is emptied: he is emptied of his own glory for a little while,[3] that I may share in his fullness.[4] What a wealth of goodness![5] What a mystery[6] is this, concerned with me! I had my share in the divine image, and I did not preserve it. He shares in my flesh in order that he may rescue the image and confer immortality on the flesh. He enters upon a second fellowship with us, much more wonderful than the first. Then he imparted an honour; now he shares a humiliation. The latter is a more godlike act, and thoughtful men will find it more sublime.   *or.* 38. 13

There were many marvels at that time: God crucified, the sun obscured, and then again blazing out (for it was right that created things should share the sufferings of their creator); the veil rent asunder; blood and water pouring from his side (the latter showing that he was man; the former, that he was more than man); the earthquake, the rocks broken, the dead arising, to strengthen faith in the final and general resurrection; the signs at the sepulchre, and the signs thereafter. Who can worthily sing their praise? But none of these is to be compared with the marvel of my salvation. A few drops of blood renewed the whole world, and became for mankind what rennet is to milk, the ingredient to bind and compact all men into unity.   *or.* 45. 39

[1] John 1. 1.   [2] 'Spirit' here = deity: cf. John 4. 24.   [3] Heb. 2. 9.   [4] John 1. 16.   [5] Rom. 2. 4.   [6] A revelation of God's secret purpose.

These men [*sc. the followers of Apollinarius*] must not deceive others, or be themselves deceived, into supposing that 'the Man of the Lord'[1] (to use their title for him who more truly is Lord and God) was without a human intellect.[2] For we do not separate the man from the godhead; we teach that he is one and the same. Formerly he was not man, but only God the Son, before all ages, unconnected with a body or anything corporeal; but at last he became man also, assuming manhood for our salvation; passible in the flesh, impassible in the Godhead; limited in the body, unconfined in the spirit; on the earth and at the same time in heaven; belonging to the visible world, and also to the intelligible order of being; comprehensible and also incomprehensible; so that man as a whole, since he had fallen into sin, might be fashioned afresh by one who was wholly man and at the same time God.

Anyone who does not admit that holy Mary is the Mother of God is out of touch with the godhead. Equally remote from God is anyone who says that Christ passed through the Virgin as through a channel, without being formed in her in a manner at once divine and human— divine, because without the agency of a man; human because following the normal process of gestation. A man comes under condemnation if he says that the human being was first formed and then the divinity supervened. This would not be the birth of God, but the avoidance of birth. If anyone introduces two sons, one derived from God the Father, the other from his mother, not being one and the same, then he fails to attain 'the adoption of sons'[3] which is promised to those who rightly believe. There are indeed the two natures, the divine and the human (the human nature comprising soul and body); but not two sons, or two Gods: nor have we here two human beings, even though Paul speaks in this way of the inner and the outer element in human nature.[4]

To sum up the matter: there are two separate elements of which the Saviour is composed (the invisible is not identical with the visible, nor the timeless with the temporal), but there are not two separate beings; emphatically not. Both elements are blended into one, the divinity taking on humanity, the humanity receiving divinity, or however one may phrase it. I say two elements but not two beings; whereas in the Trinity the contrary is true: for here there are distinct beings, so that we may not confuse the persons: but not separate elements, since the three are one and the same in respect of godhead. If anyone says that the

[1] A title found first in Athanasius (once) and in writings attributed to Ath.   [2] Cf. p. 11 f.
[3] Eph. 1. 5.   [4] When he speaks of the 'inner' and 'outer' man: 2 Cor. 4. 16; Eph. 3. 16.

godhead operated in him by grace, as in a prophet, instead of being
joined to the humanity, in a permanent union, in respect of substance,[1]
such a man is himself devoid of such working of God within him; in
fact he is filled with a contrary inspiration . . .

Anyone who has placed his hope in a human being who lacked a
human mind is himself truly mindless, and does not deserve a complete
salvation. For what was not assumed, was not healed.[2] What is saved
is that which has been united with God. If it was half of Adam that
fell, then half might be assumed and saved. But if it was the whole of
Adam that fell, it is united to the whole of him who was begotten,
and gains complete salvation. Then let them not envy us this complete
salvation, nor equip the Saviour only with bones and sinews, with the
mere representation of a man. If his humanity lacked a human soul,[3]
that is what the Arians allege, so that they may attribute suffering to the
divinity, on the grounds that that which gives the body life must share
the body's experience. If his humanity had a soul, then it was either
irrational, or intellectual. If irrational, how would there be true humanity? For man is not a beast without intellect. It would follow that there
was an outward appearance, a façade, of humanity, while the soul was
the soul of a horse, or an ox, or one of the beasts without intellect. It
will be that which is saved; and I have been cheated by the Truth, since
I have been rejoicing, while a different being has received the honour.
Whereas if it was an intellectual soul, then the humanity did not
lack a human mind, and our opponents must stop behaving with
this real mindlessness . . .

You, my good sir, as an Apollinarian, despise my mind so that you
may attach God to the flesh, on the ground that this is the only possible
mode of attachment. You accuse me of 'anthropolatry'; but you incur
the charge of 'sarcolatry'. Your theory 'takes away the middle wall'.[4]
What then is my account of the matter, the account of a man of very
small claim to learning or philosophy? I hold that mind is blended with
mind, as being closer and more congenial; and thus godhead and
humanity are united through the mediation of mind between godhead
and the grossness of the flesh.   *ep.* 101. 4-7, 10

Let us see what, for them, is his purpose in becoming man, or, to use
the phrase they prefer, of his becoming flesh. If the purpose is that God

---

[1] κατ' οὐσίαν συνῆφθαί τε καὶ συνάπτεσθαι.   [2] τὸ ἀπρόσληπτον, ἀθεράπευτον.
[3] i.e. ψυχή, the animating principle.   [4] Eph. 2. 14.

should be confined, who is otherwise unconfined, and that he should move about among men in the flesh, as beneath a screen, then it is a clever disguise, a subtle piece of play-acting which they represent (I need not say that it was in fact possible for him to be in touch with men in other ways, as in the burning bush, and when he appeared in earlier times in human form). But if his purpose was to remove the condemnation of our sins by sanctifying like with like, then, just as he needed to take on flesh because of the condemnation of flesh, and soul because of the soul's condemnation, he must needs have a mind for the same reason. The mind in Adam did not merely stumble into sin; it was primarily affected (as physicians say about illnesses). For that which received the commandment failed to keep it; and in thus failing it dared to commit the transgression; and that which transgressed stood in the greatest need of salvation; and that which needed salvation was also assumed. Therefore mind was assumed.

ep. 101. 11

(b) *Christ's Human Nature and Will*

The seventh [*of the Eunomian arguments from Scripture*]: 'I came down from heaven not to do my own will, but the will of him who sent me'.[1] If this saying did not issue from that which came down, we should have said that the expression took that form as coming from the human nature, not from the Saviour regarded as such (for his will could not be in the least degree opposed to God, since it was wholly deified), but from him considered as man. For the human will did not completely conform to the divine will, but struggled and wrestled against it, as it frequently does. This is the interpretation we have put on, 'Father, if possible, let this cup pass from me. But let not my will, but thine, prevail.'[2] It is not to be supposed that, regarded as Saviour, he did not know whether it was possible or not; or that his will resisted the will of God. But the utterance under discussion issued from him who assumed human nature (for it was the divine nature which 'came down'), and not from the nature which was assumed. Therefore our reply will be that the saying does not imply that the Son has a will of his own, apart from the Father's will, but that he has not. So the meaning of the words will be, 'Not to do my own will, for my will is not distinct from thine; but to perform the will which is common to thee and me, for our will is one, as our Godhead is one'.

[1] John 6. 38. [2] Cf. Matt. 26. 39; Luke 22. 42.

There are many such statements, ambiguous in form, which do not assert, but deny, the existence of the thing mentioned. For example, 'For he does not give the Spirit by measure'.[1] Both the giving and the measuring are denied—God is not measured out by God. 'Neither my sin, nor my wickedness.'[2] This denies the existence of the sin; it does not assert it. 'Not because of the righteous acts which we have performed'[3]—we have not performed them. This interpretation of one passage is clearly right in view of what follows. For what is the Father's will? That everyone who believes in the Son shall be saved, and shall attain the final resurrection, or rather restoration. Well then, is this the Father's will, but in no respect the Son's? Does the Son bring the good news unwillingly? Is it against his will that men believe in him? Who would credit this? Then the saying that 'the word which you hear is not the Son's but the Father's', has the same significance.

or. 30. 12

In my opinion he is called Son because he is identical with the Father in respect of substance: and, besides this, he derives from the Father. He is called 'Only-begotten', not in the sense of being the only Son, of one Father only, and being nothing but a Son, but in the sense of begotten in a unique way, as distinct from the birth of corporeal sons. He is called 'Word', because his relation to the Father is that of word to mind. . . . One might perhaps say also that of definition to *definiendum*, for word (*logos*) has also this meaning. 'He who has understood' (that is what 'seen' means) 'the Son has understood the Father'.[4] The Son is a compendious and intelligible demonstration of the Father's nature. . . . And one could be right in suggesting that another reason for this title is his immanence in things: for everything that exists has *logos*[5] as its constitutive principle

[*The titles of the Lord as incarnate—Son of Man, Christ, Shepherd, High Priest, etc.*]

Here you have the appellations of the Son. Run over them; the exalted titles in a manner befitting the godhead; those that refer to his bodily existence, with sympathy. Or rather keep throughout the attitude that befits the godhead, so that you may become divine by ascending from below because of him who for our sake descended from above. In all, and before all, keep hold of this text, and you will

[1] John 3. 34   [2] Ps. 58. 4 (59. 3).   [3] Tit. 3. 5 combined with Dan. 9. 18.   [4] John 14. 9.
[5] In the sense of 'reason' or 'law'.

not go astray in respect of the exalted or the humble titles: 'Jesus Christ
yesterday and today' in bodily form, but in his spiritual being 'the same,
even for ever'.[1] Amen.   *or*. 30. 20

(c) Christ's Human Ignorance

The tenth [*of the Eunomian arguments from Scripture*] concerns his
ignorance: 'No one except the Father knows the last day and hour, not
even the Son.'[2] Yet how can he be ignorant of anything that is, when
he is Wisdom, the maker of the worlds, who brings all things to fulfilment, and re-creates all things, who is the end of all that has come
into being? . . . Is it not obvious, if one distinguishes the seen from the
unseen, that, as God, he knows; but he professes ignorance, as man?

The fact that the title of 'the Son' is used absolutely, without qualifications, without specifying *whose* son, suggests to us this interpretation;
so that we put the more reverent construction upon the ignorance,
referring it to the human nature, not to the divine.

If this argument is sound, we shall rest upon it and pursue the
inquiry no further. If not, the alternative explanation is to suppose that
the knowledge of the most important matters, just as everything else
which the Son has, is referred back to its original source to do honour
to the Father. It seems to me that even one who did not follow one of
our scholars[3] in this reading of the passage, would see to some extent
that not even the Son knows the day or the hour except in so far as
his knowledge depends on the Father's. What are we to gather from
this? It is clear that the Son knows because the Father knows, for no one
could receive this knowledge except from the primary existence.

or. 30. 15

V. The Work of Christ

The Ransom

We have now to examine a point of doctrine which has been generally
overlooked, though to me it seems to deserve careful inquiry. The
question is: To whom was offered the blood that was shed for us, and
why was it offered, this precious and glorious blood of our God, our
high-priest, our sacrifice? We were held captive by the Evil One, for
we had been 'sold into the bondage of sin',[4] and our wickedness was the

[1] Heb. 13. 8. [2] Matt. 24. 36. [3] Basil, in *ep*. 236. [4] Rom. 7. 14.

price we paid for our pleasure. Now, a ransom is normally paid only
to the captor; and so the question is: To whom was this ransom offered,
and why? To the Evil One? What an outrage! If it is supposed not
merely that the thief received a ransom from God, but that the ransom
is God himself—a payment for his act of arbitrary power so excessive
that it certainly justified his releasing us! If it was paid to the Father,
I ask first, why? We were not held captive by him. Secondly, what
reason can be given why the blood of the Only-begotten should be
pleasing to the Father? For he did not accept even Isaac when he was
offered by his father, but he gave a substitute for the sacrifice, a lamb
to take the place of the rational victim. Is it not clear that the Father
accepts the sacrifice, not because he demanded or needed it, but because
this was part of the divine plan,[1] since man had to be sanctified by the
humanity of God; so that he might rescue us by overcoming the
tyrant by force, and bring us back to himself through the mediation
of the Son, who carried out this divine plan[1] to the honour of the
Father, to whom he clearly delivers up all things.[2] We have said just
so much about Christ. There are many more things which must be
passed over in reverent silence. The serpent of brass[3] hung up as a
remedy against the bites of snakes is not a type of Christ in his sufferings
on our behalf, but an antitype:[4] and it saves those who see it, not
because it is believed to be alive, but because it has been done to death,
and brings to death its subordinate powers when it meets with the
extinction it deserves. And what may we quote as a fitting epitaph?
It is this. 'Where is your sting, O death? Where is your victory, O
grave?'[5] You have been laid low by the cross, put to death by the life-
giver. You are dead, motionless, inert, and (to keep the picture of the
snake) you are hung on high on a pillar.   *or*. 45. 22

VI. The Holy Spirit

(a) The Divinity of the Spirit

Those Greek thinkers who were interested in theology, and who came
close to the Christian position, had an inkling of the Holy Spirit, but

---

[1] 'Economy'; cf. p. 134. [2] Cf. Phil. 2. 11 and 1 Cor. 15. 24. [3] Num. 21. 8; cf. John
3. 14. [4] Here meaning 'contrast', 'parallel'. The (dead) bronze serpent on the pillar
brought death to other snakes: Christ's death on the cross brought life to other men.
[5] 1 Cor. 15. 55.

they differed about the title, calling him by such names as 'the mind of the universe',[1] 'the mind outside us'.[2] Some members of our own intelligentsia suppose the Holy Spirit to be an 'activity', others a 'creature'; others think of him as God; yet others fail to come to a decision, allegedly through reverence for the Scriptures, on the ground that they give no clear revelation on the question. The result is that they neither reverence the Spirit, nor dishonour him, but take up a kind of neutral position—or rather a pitiable position—with regard to him. Further, of those who suppose him divine, some are reverent towards him in thought, but no further; others go so far as to reverence him with their lips also. Others, even cleverer, I have heard measuring out the godhead:[3] they admit that we have a union of three existences, but they put such a distance between them as to make the first unlimited in substance and power, the second unlimited in power, but not in substance, while the third they represent as circumscribed in both substance and power. In this they imitate, in a different form, those who use the names Demiurge, Fellow-worker, and Minister,[4] and suppose that the relative rank and honour of the names indicates gradation in the realities they denote.   *or.* 31. 5

(b) The Procession of the Spirit

[The *Pneumatomachi*[5] argued that if the Spirit is begotten of the Father, then there are two sons; if of the Son, then he is a grandson of the Father.]

We do not admit your dilemma, which allows of no mean between unbegotten and begotten. Therefore your 'brothers' and 'grandsons' immediately disappear, with the disappearance of your imposing dilemma. . . . Now tell me, what place will you assign to that which 'proceeds'? For this clearly provides an escape from your dilemma, and it derives from a theologian above your standard, in fact from our Saviour himself. Unless, to suit your 'Third Testament', you have removed from your gospels this saying: 'The Holy Spirit, who proceeds from the Father'.

He is not a creature, in that he proceeds from such a source; he is not a son, in that he is not begotten: he is God, in that his status is a mean between unbegotten and begotten. Thus he escapes the toils of

---

[1] The reference is doubtless to Plato, who has the thought, though not the actual phrase; this may well have been used by Neoplatonists, although it does not seem to have been found in any extant work.   [2] This occurs in Aristotle *de Gen. An.* 2. 3.   [3] The reference is not known.   [4] Presumably the Arians.   [5] Cf. p. 8 f.

your syllogisms and is revealed as God, being too strong for your dilemmas. What then is 'procession'? Well, if you will explain the Father's 'ingeneracy', I will give you a scientific account of the 'generation' of the Son, and the 'procession' of the Spirit; and thus let us both go crazy through peering into the mysteries of God. Who are we to pry into such matters? We cannot understand what is in front of our noses; we cannot count the sands of the sea-shore, the drops of rain, the days of endless time. Still less can we penetrate the depths of God, and give an account of his nature, which is so ineffable, which surpasses our powers of reason.

'Then in what respect does the Spirit come short of being a son? For if he did not come short, he would be a son.' He does not 'come short'. There is no deficiency in God. But the difference of their coming into being, so to say, and the difference in their mutual relation, results in the difference of their designation. For the Son does not 'come short' of being the Father—sonship is not a deficiency: but that does not mean he is identical with the Father. Otherwise the Father will 'fall short' of being the Son: for the Father is not a son. Those relationships do not entail a deficiency in any direction, nor any inferiority in substance. 'Ingeneracy', 'generation', 'procession' proclaimed them to be respectively Father, Son, and Holy Spirit, so that the distinction of the three subsistent persons [*hypostases*] may be preserved without confusion, within the single nature and rank of the Godhead. For the Son is not the Father (there is only one Father); but he is all that the Father is. The Spirit is not the Son, because he comes from God (there is only one Son); but he is all that the Son is. The three are one in their godhead; the One is three in the personal distinctions. Thus we avoid the Sabellian notion of the unity, and the recent perverse doctrine of the division in the Trinity.

'What? So you mean that the Spirit is God?' Certainly. 'So you really mean that he is consubstantial with the Father?' Yes; if he is God. 'Well then, show me that there are two beings from the same source, one a son, the other not a son; show me that they are consubstantial; and then I will acknowledge each of them to be a god.' If you show me that there is more than one sort of god, and more than one nature of god, then I will show you this same Trinity of yours, names and entities.[1]

---

[1] 'Consubstantiality' follows from the unity of God. Eunomius, by insisting on differences of *nature* between the Persons, implies tritheism.

What was Adam? 'God's handiwork.' What was Eve? 'A portion taken from that handiwork.' What was Seth? 'The offspring of the two.' Does it appear to you that the handiwork, the portion, and the offspring have the same nature? 'Certainly.' Are they consubstantial, or not? 'To be sure they are.' Then this is an admission that beings who come into existence in different modes can be of the same substance. In saying this I am not literally applying to the godhead the notion of handiwork, or portion, or any other physical notion (I would not have any captious critic seize on this point); I am simply using those illustrations as a kind of stage upon which to observe our conceptions of higher realities. It is quite impossible for our speculations to arrive at the whole truth without admixture of error . . .

For us there is but one God, because there is but one kind of godhead. The Beings that issue from a single source are referred back to that source, although we believe in them as being three: for it is not the case that one is more, another less, of a god than the other; nor is one prior, another secondary. There is no severance of will, no division of power; nor are any of the distinctive marks of separate individuals to be seen in the Godhead. To put it shortly; the Persons are divided, but the Godhead is entire and undivided in each: as three suns might be joined to each other, producing one mingled light. Thus when we look at the Godhead, and the first cause, and the monarchy, it is one thing that we imagine: but when we observe the beings in whom the Godhead subsists, which issue from the First Cause, deriving their being from it timelessly and with equality of honour, there are three objects of our worship.

But, they might say, do not the Greeks speak of one Godhead, according to the teaching of their more profound philosophers: and we speak of a single humanity, comprising the whole human race? And yet there are many gods, not one god; in the same way as there are many men? Yes, but in this case the common nature has a merely conceptual unity; while the individuals are widely separated from each other in time, in experience, and in capacity. And we are not only composite beings; we are also opposite, to each other and to ourselves, not remaining completely the same even for a single day, still less for the whole of our life.   *or.* 31. 8-11, 14, 15

VII. The Trinity

(a) Three Persons: One Godhead

We do not postulate three origins, to avoid Greek polytheism. Nor do we believe in a God who is one in the narrow, jealous, impotent sense, like the Jewish god: nor do we preserve the unity by making the Godhead self-consuming, as in the theory which produces the Son from the Father and then resolves him back into the Father: nor by degrading the natures of the second and third Persons and removing them from godhead as the clever ones of our time have decided to do—as if the Godhead feared that these derivative beings might set themselves in opposition; or as if the Divinity would not do what is impossible in the created world. We do not speak of the Son as unbegotten, for there is but one Father; nor do we speak of the Spirit as a son, for there is but one Only-begotten; so that the Persons have their singularity in a divine manner, the one in respect of sonship the other in respect of procession, not sonship. . . . The Father, the Son, and the Holy Spirit have this in common; that they are uncreated, and they are divine. The Son and the Holy Spirit have this in common; that they are derived from the Father. Peculiar to the Father is his ingeneracy; to the Son, his generation; to the Holy Spirit, his being sent . . .

Be content to know this, that the Unity [Monad] is adored in the Trinity [Triad], the Trinity [Triad] in the Unity [Monad]

or. 25. 16, 17

The three most ancient opinions about God are atheism (or anarchy), polytheism (or polyarchy), and monotheism (or monarchy). The children of Greece played with the first two; let us leave them to their games. For anarchy is disorder: and polyarchy implies factious division, and therefore anarchy and disorder. Both these lead in the same direction—to disorder; and disorder leads to disintegration; for disorder is the prelude to disintegration. What we honour is monarchy: but not a monarchy confined to a single person; for a single entity may be divided against itself and become many. For us the monarchy is formed by equality of nature, harmony of will, and identity of activity, and the concurrence with the One of the Beings which derive from the One, a unity impossible among creaturely beings, so that while they are numerically distinct there is no severance in substance [*ousia*]. The original unity comes into action as a duality and reaches its final form as a trinity: and thus we have the Father, the Son, and the Holy Spirit. The Father is the begetter and the emitter; but this does not mean that he undergoes a change, and that there is any temporal succession, or any physical relation. The Son and the Spirit are respectively offspring and emission; for I know no other terms which could be applied, such as to avoid completely any material suggestions . . .

'When did this happen?' Those acts are above and beyond time. But, if one must speak childishly, they are simultaneous with the being of the Father. 'When did the Father come to be?' There was not when he was not.[1] The same applies to the Son and the Holy Spirit. Ask me again, and I shall answer you. 'When was the Son begotten?' When the Father was not begotten. 'When did the Spirit proceed?' When the Son did not proceed, but was begotten timelessly, in a way we cannot understand. When we try to avoid the suggestion of temporality in illustrating timelessness we are frustrated; for 'when', and 'before', and 'originally', cannot be divested of temporal implication, however hard we try. The only thing we can do is to take eternity as denoting a period commensurate with supra-temporal realities, a period not divided and measured by the course of the sun or any kind of motion, as time is measured. If those Beings are co-eternal, must they not be equally without beginning? They derive from the First Being, though they are not *after* him. 'Without beginning' implies 'eternal'. Yes; but 'eternal' does not necessarily imply 'without beginning', seeing that these Beings are referred to the Father as their origin. Thus they are not without beginning in respect of *cause*. But it is clear that a cause is not necessarily prior in time to its effects; for the sun is not prior to the sunlight. Yet they are in a sense without beginning, in respect of *time* (even though you may use this notion as a bogey to scare simple minds), for they are not subject to time, since time originates from them.   *or.* 29. 2

(b) *Technical Terms—Substance, Nature, Person, Hypostasis*

'My sheep follow me'. . . . They will flee from . . . the 'analysis' of Sabellius and his 'fusion' (which I would rather call 'absorption'), when he contracts the three into one, instead of defining the one in

---

[1] The negative of the phrase used by the Arians of the Son, 'there was when he was not', ἦν ὅτε οὐκ ἦν.

three subsistent beings.[1] They will flee from Arius, and his subordinates, with their diversity of the natures, and the form of Judaism which confines the Godhead to the unbegotten, and Photinus[2] with his earthly Christ, who took his origin from Mary. But they will worship the Father, and the Son, and the Holy Ghost, one Godhead; for them the Father is God, the Son is God, the Holy Spirit (if you will not be exasperated at this) is God. They adore one nature in three particular manifestations,[3] which are intelligent and perfect, having their own individual subsistence, numerically distinct, but not distinct in Godhead.

or. 33. 16

The knowledge of the mutual relations and dispositions of the Trinity is a matter we are content to leave to the Trinity itself, and to those men to whose purified minds the Trinity has already revealed it or will reveal it later. For ourselves, we know that there is one and the same nature of godhead which is made known to us by existence without beginning, by generation, by procession; answering to our mind, speech, and spirit (so far as things in the sensible world can represent realities in the intelligible order, as small things hint at transcendent realities, since no analogy can attain to the truth). . . . Each Entity is God, when considered by itself, when the mind separates the inseparable; the three are God, when thought of together, by reason of identity of activity and nature.   *or.* 23. 11

God is three in regard to distinctive properties, or subsistences [*hypostases*], or, if you like, persons [*prosôpa*]: for we shall not quarrel about the names, as long as the terms lead to the same conception. He is one in respect of the category of substance, that is, of godhead. The Godhead is distinguished, so to say, without distinctions, and is joined in one without abolishing the distinctions. The Godhead is one in three, and the three are one. The Godhead has its being in the three; or, to speak more accurately, the Godhead *is* the three. We must avoid any notion of superiority or inferiority between the Persons; nor must we turn the union into a confusion, nor the distinction into a difference of natures. We must keep equally aloof from the Sabellian identification and the Arian differentiation—errors diametrically opposed, but equally irreverent.   *or.* 39. 11

[1] ἐν τρισὶν ὑφεστῶσιν, the verb from which ὑπόστασις (hypostasis) is derived.   [2] Bp. of Sirmium 344–51. No writings extant; but he evidently taught a kind of Sabellianism. The 'Photinians' were condemned at the Council of Constantinople, 381.   [3] ἐν τρισὶν ἰδιότησιν.

(c) Generate and Ingenerate

'For us there is one God the Father, from whom are all things; and one God the Son, through whom are all things';[1] and one Holy Spirit, 'in whom are all things'. The phrases 'from whom', 'through whom', 'in whom', do not make a severance in the natures (if they did, there would never be an interchange of the prepositions, or of the order of the names), but they mark the personal distinctions within the one unconfused nature. This is made clear by the fact that they are combined in another place, if one gives a more than cursory attention to the passage where the Apostle writes: 'From him, and through him, and for him, are all things: to him be the glory for ever, Amen.'[2] The Father is father, and without beginning, for he is underived. The Son is son, and not without beginning, in that he derives from the Father. But if one thinks of a *temporal* beginning, then the Son is without beginning; for the author of time is not subject to time. The Spirit is truly holy spirit, as proceeding from the Father, not in the manner of the Son, since not by generation, but by procession (if one must coin new terms for the sake of clarity). *or*. 39. 12

That which is without beginning, and the beginning, and that which is with the beginning—these are one God. Neither lack of beginning, nor lack of generation, constitutes the nature of that which has no beginning: for an entity's nature is never constituted by what it is *not*, but by what it *is*: it is defined by positing what it is, not by removing what it is not. The beginning is not separated, by virtue of its being a beginning, from that which has no beginning: for beginning is not the nature of the former, nor is lack of beginning the nature of the latter. These are attributes of the nature, not the nature itself. And that which is with the unoriginate, and with the originate, is not something other than what they are. But the unoriginate has the name of Father; the originate has the name of Son; that which is with the originate is called the Holy Spirit. But these three have the same nature, namely, Godhead. The Father is the principle of unity; for from him the other two derive their being, and in him they are drawn together: not so as to be fused together, but so as to cohere. There is no separation in time, or in will, or in power. These factors make us men a plurality, each individual at odds with himself and with others. But

[1] 1 Cor. 8. 6.   [2] Rom. 11. 36.

unity properly belongs to those who have a single nature and whose
essential being is the same.   *or.* 42. 15

VIII. The Sacraments

(*a*) *Baptism*

(i) *Five Kinds of Baptism*

Moses baptized, but only in water: and before that, in the cloud and
in the sea.[1] But this, as Paul judged, was figurative: the sea stood for
the water; the cloud, for the Spirit; the manna, for the bread of life;
the drink, for the divine drink. John also baptized; but he did not
merely continue the Jewish baptism, for he did not merely baptize
with water, but also for repentance. However, it was not yet wholly
spiritual; for he does not add 'with Spirit'. Jesus also baptizes, but
'with Spirit'. This is the perfection of baptism. And (if I may in passing
make a somewhat bold statement) God must be the source of your
deification. I also know a third kind of baptism, the baptism by means
of martyrdom and blood, the baptism which Christ himself received,
which is more to be revered than the other kinds, since it is not defiled
by any subsequent stains. There is also a fifth kind; the baptism of tears
. . [*e.g. Manasses, the Ninevites, the publican in the temple, the Canaanite
woman*[2]].   *or.* 39. 17

(ii) *Infant Baptism*

Have you an infant? Do not let wickedness seize its chance. Let him be
sanctified from babyhood, and consecrated by the Spirit in his tender
years. Are you afraid of the seal because of the weakness of the child's
nature? What a faint-hearted mother you are! How weak your faith
is! Why, Hannah vowed Samuel to God before he was born, and no
sooner was he born than she made him a priest and reared him in a
priestly robe;[3] for she had no human fears but put her trust in God.
You have no need of charms and spells. With these the Devil gains an
entrance, and with these baubles steals for himself the honour due to
God. Give your child the powerful and lovely amulet of the Trinity.

or. 40. 17

[1] Cf. 1 Cor. 10. 2.   [2] 2 Chron. 23. 15; Jonah 3. 5; Luke 18. 13; Matt. 15. 22 ff.
[3] 1 Sam. 1. 11 ff.

What about infants, who cannot feel loss or grace? Shall we baptize them also? Certainly, if there is any pressing danger. It is better to be sanctified without being conscious of it than to depart without being sealed and initiated. And we find our justification for this practice in the fact that circumcision, which was in some degree prefigurative of the baptismal seal, was administered on the eighth day to babies who were still irrational. Similarly, the anointing of the doorposts protected the firstborn though applied to unconscious objects. In other cases my judgement is that they should wait for three years, more or less, by which time they are capable of some spiritual understanding and are able to reply; even if they cannot fully understand, their characters and minds are in process of formation. Then we should sanctify their souls and bodies by the great mystery of full initiation. For the case stands thus. Children begin to be answerable for their actions as soon as their reason is fully developed and they have been instructed in the divine revelation; they are not answerable for the sins of ignorance which are due to their tender years. But because of the dangers which so suddenly assail us, and which are too strong for human aid, it is on every consideration more profitable for children to be fortified by the baptismal washing.   *or.* 40. 28

(b) *The Eucharist*
(i) *Realism*

This is my opinion about the staff [*the 'staff in hand' at the passover*, Ex. 12. 11] and its allegorical significance. There is the staff for support, and the staff of the shepherd (the staff of teaching, which brings back the 'sheep' endowed with reason). It is the staff of support that the Law now prescribes for you, lest you should stumble at all in your mind when you hear of the blood of God, and his passion and death; lest you should wander erratically, deserting God when you should be God's advocate. You must without shamefacedness, without wavering, eat the body, and drink the blood, if you are eager for life. Do not disbelieve the sayings about the flesh, nor be put off by the teaching about the passion.[1]   *or.* 45. 19

(ii) *The Eucharistic Anamnesis and Eschatology*

We shall be partakers of the Passover, yet still by way of a type,

[1] Cf. John 6. 41–66, and e.g. Matt. 16. 21 f.

although more directly than under the ancient Law (for I make bold to say that the Passover of the Law was a type of the most obscure sort): later on we shall partake perfectly and purely, when the Word 'drinks it new with us in the Kingdom of the Father',[1] revealing and teaching what he has now shown us only up to a certain point. For what is now understood is something which is always new. But the full meaning of the drinking, and the full enjoyment of it, is ours to learn and his to teach, and to communicate to his disciples. For the teaching is our sustenance, the teaching of him who gives the food.[2] But come, let us partake of the Law,[3] not in the literal fashion, but in the spirit of the gospel; perfectly and eternally, not incompletely and temporarily. Let us take as our capital not the earthly Jerusalem, but the heavenly mother-city,[4] not that which is now trampled on by armies,[5] but that which is glorified by angels. Let us sacrifice not young calves, and lambs 'with horns and hoofs',[6] which are to a great extent without life or feeling; but let us sacrifice to God the sacrifice of praise[7] on the heavenly altar, with the heavenly dances;[8] let us draw aside the first curtain, approach the second, and look into the Holy of Holies. I will go further than that: Let us sacrifice ourselves to God; or rather, let us continually sacrifice ourselves, every day, ourselves and our every activity. Let us accept everything for the sake of the Word. By our sufferings let us imitate his suffering; by shedding of blood let us do honour to the blood that he shed: let us be ready and eager to mount the cross. The nails are sweet, though bitterly cruel. It is more desirable to suffer with Christ, and for Christ, than to enjoy delights with others.

Celebrate the feast of the Resurrection; act the parts of Peter and John in hastening to the sepulchre.[9] . . . When he descends to Hades, go down with him, and learn the mysteries that the Christ reveals there also; and learn what is the plan and design of his double descent, whether he saves all by his appearing, or whether there also he only saves those who believe.

When he ascends into heaven, go up with him; join the angels who escort him, or those who welcome him; bid the gates to be lifted up,[10] and to become more exalted, that they may receive one who was exalted as a result of his suffering.[11]   *or.* 45. 23, 24

[1] Matt. 26. 29.   [2] Cf. John 6. 63.   [3] sc. of. the Passover.   [4] Cf. Gal. 4. 25 f.   [5] Cf. Luke 21. 20.   [6] Ps. 69. 31.   [7] Ps. 50. 14.   [8] Cf. Ps. 149. 3, 150. 4.   [9] Cf. John 20. 17. [10] Ps. 24. 7.   [11] Cf. Phil. 2. 8 f.

(iii) The Heavenly Realities

I know of another altar, of which the present visible altars are merely types; an altar to which no axe or hand went up, nor was the noise of iron heard, nor any work of craftsman or skilful artist.[1] It is all the work of the mind, and the ascent is by contemplation. It is at this altar that I will stand, and on it I will sacrifice acceptable offerings, sacrifice, oblations and burnt-offerings; as much better than those which are now brought as the reality is better than the shadow. David also seems to me to be speaking philosophically about this altar, when he says: 'I will go to the altar of God, who gladdens my spiritual youth.'[2]   or. 26. 16

(iv) Reservation of the Sacrament

[Gregory's sister, Gorgonia, was desperately ill.] What remedy did she find for her suffering? Here is her secret. She despaired of any other relief, and had recourse to the Physician of all mankind. She waited till dead of night, during a slight alleviation of her condition, and fell on her knees before the altar with faith, calling with a loud cry and with every kind of invocation upon him who is honoured upon the altar, recalling to him all his mighty acts, whenever they were performed (for she was well versed in the stories of the old and the new dispensation). Then at last she ventured on an act of reverent and noble impudence, imitating the woman who staunched the flow of blood by means of the fringe of Christ's shawl.[3] What did she do? She bowed her head over the altar, and with another loud cry, and with a wealth of tears, like the one who in time gone by bathed Christ's feet,[4] and she threatened that she would not leave off until she was restored to health. Then she applied to her whole body this medicine which she had with her, namely so much of the antitypes[5] of the precious body and blood as she treasured in her hand, mingling it with her tears. And, wonder of wonders, she at once perceived that she was healed, and went away, light in body and soul and mind, having received what she hoped for as a reward for that hope, and having gained strength of body because of her strength of soul. An extraordinary story, but quite true.

or. 8 [or. funebris in laudem sororis]. 18

---

[1] Cf. 1 Kings 6. 7.   [2] Ps. 42 (43) 4. But 'spiritual' is not in LXX.   [3] Matt. 9. 20.   [4] Luke 7. 38.   [5] i.e. symbols. The language is obscure, but it appears that Gorgonia took the sacrament reserved on the altar.

(v) *The Eucharistic Sacrifice*

[*Julian*[1] *the Apostate*] unhallows his hands, sterilizing them from the bloodless sacrifice by means of which we have fellowship with Christ, both in his sufferings and in his Godhead. He sets up his palaces with the slaughter and sacrifice of animals, employing evil counsellors to establish an evil reign.   *or.* 4. 52

[*Defending his flight to avoid exercising the priestly functions.*] I know that no one is worthy of the great one who is God and sacrifice and high priest, who has not first offered himself to God as a living sacrifice and holy, and displayed the rational service which is acceptable,[2] and has sacrificed to God a sacrifice of praise,[3] and a contrite spirit[4] (the only sacrifice demanded from us by him who gives all). How then was I to make bold to offer to him the external sacrifice, the antitype of the great mysteries?[5] How was I to put on the fashion and name of a priest, until I had consecrated my hands with holy works?   *or.* 2. 95

I have at last recovered from my troublesome illness, and I hasten to write to you, as one responsible for my restored health.

For the tongue of a priest, speaking wisely of the Lord, arouses the sick to health. Now therefore do something even greater when you exercise the priestly office: release me from the great burden of my sins, as you take hold of the resurrection sacrifice.[6] . . . Do not hesitate to pray for me, to be my ambassador, when by your word you draw down the Word, when with a stroke that draws no blood you sever the body and blood of the Lord, using your voice as your sword.

         ep. 171

IX. Discipline

Forgiveness after Baptism

I accept this 'baptism of tears'[7] eagerly, for I confess myself to be a man, a changeable creature of unstable nature, and I adore him who has bestowed it, and I accord it to others, offering mercy in exchange for

---

[1] 332–63, became Emperor 361. Attempted to re-establish a reformed paganism throughout the empire. He had been G.'s fellow-student at Athens.   [2] Rom. 12. 1.   [3] Ps. 50. 14.   [4] Ps. 51. 17.   [5] i.e. the representation of Christ's sacrifice.   [6] Probably the Easter Eucharist.   [7] i.e. repentance and absolution, cf. p. 120.

mercy. For I know that I am myself 'beset by weakness',[1] and that I shall receive in proportion as I give.[2] But what do you say? What law do you lay down, you Pharisee, you who are pure in name but not in conduct. You bluster to us the teachings of Novatus,[3] teachings full of the same infection of Pharisaism. Do you not admit repentance? Do you not give any scope to lamentations? Do you not shed a tear of mercy? I hope you may not encounter such a judge as yourself! Do you not revere the kindness of Jesus, who 'bore our weaknesses and carried our diseases',[4] who 'did not come to call the righteous, but to call sinners to repentance',[5] who 'wished for mercy rather than sacrifice',[6] who pardons sins 'seventy times seven times'?[7] Your lofty attitude might be a matter for congratulation if it were purity and not swollen pride, when you impose laws from above upon mankind and remove the possibility of amendment by instilling despair. Condemnation without hope of pardon is as bad as condemnation without correction; the latter lets the reins go loose; the former pulls on them so hard as to strangle. Show me your purity and I will allow your self-confidence. As it is, I am afraid that you impose a ban on healing while you are yourself a mass of sores. Do you not admit the penitence of David,[8] whose penitence preserved for him the gift of prophecy? Or that of the great Peter, after he succumbed to human weakness at the time of our Saviour's passion?[9] Well, Jesus accepted him, and healed him by the threefold question and the threefold profession.[10] Do you not even admit one who has been made perfect[11] by shedding his blood? Your arrogant folly does not stop short of this. Nor the transgressor at Corinth? Yet Paul 'decided in favour of showing love to him', when he saw his reformation, giving this reason; 'Lest a man like that should be overwhelmed with excess of sorrow',[12] crushed by excessive reprobation.

But, you say, these were not sins after baptism. What is your proof? Either establish your argument or refrain from condemnation. Or if there is a doubt, let kindness have the benefit of it. But Novatus, you say, did not receive those who lapsed in persecution. Why? If he refused those who were not truly penitent, then he was right. I myself

---

[1] Heb. 5. 2.   [2] Cf. Matt. 7. 2.   [3] A widespread schism in the third century, of those who advocated rigorism in the treatment of baptized offenders, especially those who lapsed in persecution, was led by Novatian (called by Greek writers Novatus) of Rome, abetted by Novatus of Carthage.   [4] Isa. 53. 4.   [5] Luke 5. 32.   [6] Hos. 6. 6; Matt. 9. 13, 12. 7.   [7] Matt. 18. 22.   [8] Cf. 2 Sam. 12. 13.   [9] Cf. Matt. 26. 69–75.   [10] Cf. John 21. 15–17.   [11] i.e. 'has received full initiation', cf. Heb. 2. 10.   [12] Cf. 1 Cor. 5. 6; 2 Cor. 2. 7, 8.

do not receive those who show no contrition, or inadequate contrition, and who do not counterbalance their offence with amendment: and when I receive penitents I assign to them a suitable position. But if Novatus repulsed those who were wasted with tears, then I do not imitate his conduct. Why should his ruthlessness be a precedent for me? He did not punish avarice, which is a second kind of idolatry.[1] But he harshly condemned sexual immorality, as though he himself was not made of flesh and blood. What do you say to this? Do my arguments persuade you? Come on, stand here on our side, on the side of human beings: let us magnify the Lord together.[2] Let none of you dare to say, however great his self-confidence: 'Do not touch me, for I am pure;[3] and who is as good as I am?' Please let us share your moral grandeur! You are not convinced? Then we will weep for you. Very well then. Let those men, if they will, follow our way, which is also Christ's way. If not, let them go on their own road. Perhaps in another life they will receive their baptism of fire.   *or.* 39. 18, 19

X. The Last Things

(a) Judgement

Then Christ will come again in the glory of the Father, to show his body to those who put God to death. Then comes the resurrection, the re-uniting of soul and body in a composite being. Then the final consummation, the dissolution of all that is; and there is a kind of change into a better state. There follows the fearful judgement. And what is the judgement? The weight which each man feels within his conscience, or the lightness, and the weighing of his life against the law. Blessedness, I think, is living well. And what is the Kingdom? To behold God, and to sing his praise with the angels. But the darkness for the wicked is to fall away from God: and the 'worm' and the 'fire' stand for the dissolution of carnal passions.   *poem. mor.* 34. 249 ff

You hear of a book of the living, and a book of those who are not being saved. There we shall all be inscribed or rather have been inscribed already, according to the deserts of each man's life on this

[1] Cf. Eph. 5. 5.   [2] Cf. Ps. 34. 3.   [3] Cf. Isa. 65. 5, and John 20. 17.

earth. Wealth has no advantage there, poverty no disadvantage: nor is justice corrupted, as here, by favour or hatred or any other such influence. We have all been entered in the book by God's finger, and that book will be opened in the day of revelation.   *or.* 19. 15

(b) Heaven

'What is man, that thou rememberest him?'[1] What is this newly revealed truth about me? I am small, yet great; lowly, yet exalted; mortal, yet immortal; on earth, yet in heaven. One set of attributes belongs to me because of my connexion with this lower world; the other, because of my fellowship with God. The one, in respect of my flesh; the other, in respect of my spirit. I must be buried with Christ, raised from the dead with Christ: I must be a co-heir with Christ, and become a son of God, even myself be deified.   *or.* 7. 23

[From the funeral oration on Basil of Caesarea.]

Do you, Basil, there also welcome me in your dwelling,[2] when I have departed this life; that we may live together and gaze more directly and perfectly at the holy and blessed Trinity, of which here on earth we have been granted but fleeting glimpses. Thus we shall attain the fruition of our desire, and receive the reward of the battles we have fought and the attacks we have resisted.   *or.* 43. 82

(c) Punishment
[*Sundry Scriptural passages referring to light, and fire.*]
I know the purifying fire, which Christ 'came to throw upon the earth';[3] and Christ himself is allegorically spoken of as fire. This fire is able to consume base matter and the evil dispositions; and Christ wishes it to be kindled with all speed, for he longs to hasten his beneficent work, since he gives us coals of fire for our assistance. I also know the fire which is not purifying, but punitive: whether the fire of Sodom, which rains down on all sinners, mixed with 'sulphur and tempest';[4] or that which is 'prepared for the devil and his angels';[5] or that which 'goes before the face of the Lord and will burn up his enemies round about';[6] and there is a yet more fearful fire, which is

[1] Ps. 8. 4.   [2] Cf. Luke 26. 9.   [3] Luke 12. 49.   [4] Cf. Gen. 19. 24.   [5] Matt. 25. 41.
[6] Ps. 97. 3.

found combined with the unsleeping worm, a fire which is not quenched, an everlasting fire for the punishment of sinners.[1] All those fires have the power of annihilation; unless one prefers even here to suppose a more kindly fire, an interpretation more in keeping with him who imposes the chastisement.   *or.* 40. 36

[1] Cf. Isa. 64. 24; Mark 9. 44 etc.

Gregory of Nyssa

I. Man

(a) Creation and Fall

If the subsistence of the whole world depends on the power of the Word, we are inescapably compelled to conceive that the only cause of the various parts of the world is the Word himself, through whom the whole scheme of things issued into being. If anyone desires to call him Word, or Wisdom, or Power, or God, or any other exalted and honoured name, we shall not quarrel with him. For whatever term or name is discovered to describe the subject, one thing is indicated by the expressions, namely the eternal power of God, maker of all that exists, discoverer of what is not, which maintains all that has come into being, and foresees all that is to be. Then this Word of God (or Wisdom, or Power) has been shown by logical argument to be the maker of human nature, not compelled by any necessity to man's creation, but effecting the origin of such a being through superabundance of love. For it could not be that his light should be unseen, his glory without witness, his goodness unenjoyed, or that all the other things which are observed as belonging to the divine nature should be idle, with none to share and enjoy them. If therefore man came into being for this purpose, to share in the good things of God, he must inevitably be created with the capacity of enjoying those goods. The eye comes to partake of the light in virtue of the beam which is naturally implanted in it, attracting what is akin to it through its innate capacity. In the same way it was necessary that a certain affinity with the divine should be mingled with the nature of man, so that by means of this correspondence it might have an impulse towards what is congenial to it. Irrational creatures, to whom the water or the air has been allotted as their environment, must be given a constitution adapted to their manner of life, so that because of the particular organization of their bodies each finds its own congenial and kindred element, the one kind in the air, the other in the water. Similarly, it was necessary that man, who came into being in order to enjoy the good things of God, should have something in his nature akin to that in which he is to share. Therefore he has been equipped with life and reason and wisdom and all the

qualities appropriate to God, so that through each of those he might
have a desire for what is congenial to him. Now since one of the good
things pertaining to the divine nature is eternity, it was absolutely
necessary that the organization of our nature should not be deprived
of this attribute, but should contain an immortal element, so that by
reason of his innate capacity man might recognize the transcendent
and be seized with a desire for the divine eternity. The narrative of the
creation in fact demonstrated this, in a comprehensive expression, by
one phrase: the statement that man came into being 'after the image of
God'.[1] For in the 'likeness' which is 'after the image' we have a
summary of the characteristics of the divinity; and all that Moses
explains about these characteristics, by means of an historical record,
belongs to the same kind of teaching; for he presents to us doctrines
in the form of narrative. There is that paradise and its unique fruits, the
eating of which did not satisfy the appetite of those who tasted, but
offered them knowledge and eternal life. This is in complete harmony
with our previous observations about man, namely that our human
nature was in the beginning good and surrounded by good. But anyone
who observes the present state of things and thinks he can show the
falsity of our argument, may object that man is not now seen in that
condition but in a state almost completely opposite. 'Where is this
godlike element in the soul, the body's freedom from passions, that
eternity of life? Man's life is fleeting, he is subject to passions, doomed
to death, liable to every kind of suffering in body and soul'. . . . But
the fact that man's life is now in an abnormal state is no valid proof
that he did not at one time come into being surrounded by good: for
since man is a work of God, who brought this creature into being
because of his goodness, no one could plausibly suspect that he was
brought into being by his creator surrounded by evil, since goodness
was the cause of his constitution. . . . He who made man for participation in his own unique good and equipped his nature with the capacity
for all kinds of excellence, in order that his impulse might be directed
by a corresponding movement of like to like through every endowment of his nature, would never have deprived him of that noblest
and most precious of goods; I mean the gift of freedom and self-
determination. For if necessity in any way ruled the life of man, the
'image' would have been falsified in that particular, since it would
have become remote from its original by this lack of resemblance.

[1] Cf. Gen. 1. 26. f.

How could a nature which was subjugated and enslaved to any kind of necessity be called an 'image' of the nature of the King? Surely that which resembles the divine in every respect must inevitably possess in its nature the principle of self-determination and freedom, so that participation in good becomes the reward of virtue. How is it then, you will ask, that he who had been honoured with the whole range of excellent endowments has exchanged those good things for worse? The reason is plain. No evil which came into being had its origin in the divine will. To be sure, evil would not be blamed if it could claim God as its creator and father. No; evil is engendered in some way from within, arising in the will, when there is a retreat of the soul from the good. Sight is a natural activity, while blindness is a deprivation of the natural activity: there is a like opposition between virtue and evil. For it is impossible to conceive the origin of evil except as the absence of virtue. Darkness supervenes on the removal of light: while light is present, darkness does not exist. Similarly, as long as the good is present in the nature, evil has no existence in its own right. . . . It is not God who is responsible for the present evils, since he has constituted your nature so as to be uncontrolled and free. The responsibility is with the perverse will which has chosen the worse rather than the better.

or. cat. 5

(b) Physical and Moral Evil

The utmost grievance is felt by one who considers the dissolution of the body and regards it as cruel that this life of ours should be dissolved by death, and asserts that extinction of our being by mortality is the supreme evil. Let him then observe, through this gloomy state of affairs, the excess of the divine benevolence. Those who partake of life find life worth having because they enjoy life's agreeable features: a man who passes his life in agony judges non-existence to be far preferable to existence in pain. Then let us examine whether he who equips us for living has any other end in view than that we should live in felicity. Now by the exercise of our free will we have contracted a fellowship with evil, mixing evil with our nature by some indulgence in pleasure, like a harmful substance sweetened with honey, and therefore we have fallen away from the happiness which our thought associates with freedom from suffering. For this reason man is dissolved back into earth, like some earthenware pot, so that the filth which he has acquired may be separated out and he may be re-fashioned to his original form by the resurrection. This is the sort of teaching which Moses sets before us in a cryptic form, in the guise of historical narrative; but the veiled language conveys an obvious teaching. He tells us that when the first human beings were involved in what had been forbidden, and were stripped of that original happiness of theirs, the Lord clothed his first-created beings in coats of skins. Moses did not, in my opinion, intend those skins to be taken in the literal sense.[1] What sort of animals were killed and skinned to devise clothing for them? Rather, since hide is always dead when separated from an animal, I feel certain that the meaning is that the healer of our wickedness, in his foresight, endued man after his fall with the capacity of dying, which was the special characteristic of the brute creation; but this capacity was not intended to remain for ever. For a coat is one of the external things put upon us: it lends itself for the body's use for a time; it is not part of our natural endowment. Therefore this mortality, taken from the brute creation, was put upon the nature created for immortality, by way of accommodation. It covers the outward, not the inward, part; it attaches itself to the sentient element in man: it does not cling to the actual image of God. But the sentient element suffers dissolution only, it does not disappear; for disappearance is passing over into non-existence, whereas dissolution is the diffusion again into the basic ingredients of the earth, from which it had its composition . . . [*The sentient part of our nature is dissolved, to be refashioned in its original beauty when the alien substance has been removed.*]

Now since both soul and body are bound together by participation in the sinful affections, there is also an analogy between the death of the body and the death of the soul. In the case of the flesh we call the separation of the sentient life, death: in regard to the soul we give the name of death to the separation of the real life. . . . The death of dissolution cannot affect the soul; for how could the uncompounded suffer dissolution? But the stains that sin has engendered in the soul must be removed by some remedial treatment: therefore the medicine of virtue has been applied in this present life for the healing of those blemishes. If the soul should remain untreated the remedial treatment has been kept in store in the life hereafter . . . [*Remedial treatment, like surgery, involves suffering*]. . . . Thus if anyone keeps in view the final aim of the wisdom of him who administers the universe, he would be

[1] This allegorical interpretation, derived from rabbinic exegesis, was suggested also by Clement of Alexandria and Origen.

unreasonable and little-minded to call the creator of man the author of evil, either asserting that he was ignorant of what was going to happen, or else that by creating man in full knowledge of the future he is involved in the impulse towards wickedness: he knew what would happen, and he did not prevent that impulse towards what actually happened. . . . What would have been the better course? Not to have brought human nature into existence, since he foresaw that this future being would stray from the good? Or to bring him back and restore him by repentance to his original state of grace even when he had become diseased?

But to call God the maker of evil because of physical pain, which is the necessary consequence of the instability of human nature, or to refuse to regard him as the creator of man, lest he should be supposed responsible for what gives us pain; that is the extremity of little-mindedness shown by those who judge of good and evil on the basis of mere feeling. They do not understand that the only intrinsic good has no connexion with physical feeling, and that the only real evil is estrangement from the true good . . .

Whose task was it to recall man to his original state of grace? Who was concerned to restore the fallen, to recall the lost, to lead the wanderer by the hand? Who but the supreme Lord of his being? Only he who originally gave life had the power and the right to recover it when it had been lost.

The human birth, the growth from infancy to maturity, the eating, drinking, weariness, sleep, sorrow, tears, the false accusation, the judgement-hall, the cross, the death, the entombment—all those things, which are included in the revelation, blunt the faith of the more little-minded, so that they reject the sequel because of the prologue; for they will not admit the resurrection as congruous with the deity, because of the incongruous circumstances of the death. I think it necessary to begin by removing our reasoning a little from the grossness of the physical, and to consider the good-in-itself and its opposite, and to ask what are the distinctive marks by which each of those is recognized. For I suppose that no one who has carefully thought about it will dispute the assertion that one thing, and one thing only, is intrinsically disgraceful, and that is moral evil; while what is free from moral evil is a stranger to any kind of disgrace. Now what has no admixture of disgrace is certainly to be classified as good: and what is truly good has no admixture of the opposite. Whatever is found in the category

of good is congruous with the character of God. . . . If it is allowed
that the circumstances of his life and death are free from moral evil . . .
one can only pity the folly of those who flatly assert that what is
morally good is incongruous with the character of God.   *or. cat.* 8. 9

II. The Person of Christ

(a) Immanence and Incarnation

The birth of godhead in our nature should not reasonably present
itself as a strange novelty to those whose notions are not too limited.
For who, surveying the whole scheme of things, is so childish as not
to believe that there is divinity in everything, clothed in it, embracing
it, residing in it? For everything that is depends on Him–Who–Is,[1]
nor can there be anything which has not its being in Him–Who–Is.
Then if all things are in the divinity, and the divinity is in all things,
why are men embarrassed at the divine plan[2] displayed in the revelation
which tells us of the birth of God in humanity, since we believe that
God is not outside mankind even now? For even though the miracle
of God's presence in us is not the same as that of his Incarnation, still
we equally acknowledge his existence in us now as then. Now he is
mingled with us as sustaining nature in existence; then he was mingled
with our nature in order that our nature, by this admixture with the
divine, should itself become divine, being rescued from death and put
out of reach of the tyranny of the Enemy; for Christ's return from
death becomes for the mortal race the beginning of the return to
immortal life.   *or. cat.* 25

It was not in respect of his divinity, as he is in himself, that he was
born of a woman. Existing before creation, he receives a birth in flesh,
but not his existence. The Holy Spirit prepared the way for the entrance
of the Son's own power. The Son did not need any physical material
to make ready a special 'habitation', but, as is said of Wisdom, he
'built himself a house'[3] and made into a man the 'dust' from the Virgin,
by means of which he was mingled with human nature.   *antirr.* 9

---

[1] Cf. Exod. 3. 14.   [2] 'the economy', God's 'management of his household' (the biblical
term is 'dispensation') by which he fulfils his purpose in the world. The term is used
especially with reference to Christ's incarnation.   [3] Prov. 9. 1.

(b) God–Flesh: God–Man

How will Apollinarius ascribe the feeding at the breast, the swaddling clothes . . . growth, weariness . . . [*the details of the Passion*] burial, the tomb, the stone? How are these congruous with God? For if his 'God-in-flesh' was always that which became visible as a result of his birth from Mary, and that which appeared was godhead, then the godhead experiences all those things; the godhead is suckled . . . is weary, sleeps, grieves. . . . The godhead runs to the fig-tree, and does not know when the tree bears fruit; the godhead does not know the day and the hour; the godhead is beaten, bound, buffeted, receives the nails, bleeds, becomes a corpse, is buried and placed in a new tomb. . . . Who cried out that he was forsaken by God? If it was the one godhead of the Father and the Son, who did the forsaking? . . . [*To say that the godhead was not the same would be Arianism.*] But he cannot avoid ascribing those utterances and experiences which display suffering and humility to the humanity; he cannot help admitting that the divine nature is unchangeable and impassible even when associated with human sufferings. *antirr.* 24

Apollinarius says, 'The Greeks and the Jews plainly refuse to believe because they will not hear of a God who was born of a woman'. Why does he now, when talking of his birth, pass over the flesh in silence, although what was born of the flesh was undoubtedly flesh, as the Lord says in one place? No; he wants the flesh itself, which was born, to be divinity, and to make out that God has not been displayed in flesh. And therefore he says, 'But God was endued with flesh before the ages, and subsequently was born by means of a woman and underwent the experience of death, as the necessary consequence of assuming human nature'. By this assertion he does not allow him true humanity, he makes him submit to suffering *as* a man, but he does not grant him participation in human nature. For how can that be a man which is said to be not of the earth? For Scripture says that humanity takes its origin from Adam, and that he came into being at the beginning from the earth. That is why Luke, in drawing up the genealogy of him 'who was regarded as the son of Joseph', ends by saying, 'the son of Adam',[1] tracing the origin of his descent step by step through his ancestors. Therefore one who was not born of the human race is assuredly not a man but some other kind of being. What then may this 'God endued

[1] Luke 3. 23 and 38.

with flesh' be, which our writer speaks of, if he is neither man, as having no real connexion with the human race; nor God, as not being incorporeal? . . . [*Elijah in the fiery chariot as a type of Christ.*] Fire has by nature an upward tendency, but by divine power it is brought down to earth; and Elijah is himself raised on high[1] when he has been enveloped in the heavenly flame which then hastens to resume its natural upward motion. In the same way the power of the Highest which is something without matter or form, receives the form of a servant in the subsistence (*hypostasis*) it receives through the Virgin, and brought it to its own sublimity, transmuting it to its divine and imperishable nature.   *antirr.* 25

[Greg. Naz. also accuses Ap. of teaching a pre-existent, heavenly flesh (e.g. in *ep.* 101. 6). Ap. indignantly repudiates such a fantasy: 'We do not assert that the Saviour's flesh descended from heaven; nor that his flesh is consubstantial with God. But it is God in that it is united with the godhead to constitute one person' (*fr.* 164. Lietzmann).]

(c) The Two Natures: 'Communicatio idiomatum'

Apollinarius must not falsely represent our argument, saying that we assert that the Only-begotten God was not always Christ. Christ existed always, not only in the time of the dispensation,[2] but also afterwards. But the human nature did not exist before or after but only during the season of the dispensation. For the humanity did not exist before the birth from the Virgin, nor did the flesh remain, with its own properties, after the ascent to heaven. 'If once we knew Christ in the flesh, we do not still know him in this way.'[3] For the flesh did not continue in being because God had been displayed in flesh. Human nature is subject to change, whereas the divine nature is unchangeable; therefore the godhead remains unmoved in face of every change, not being altered for the worse (for it does not admit of deterioration, nor is it susceptible of improvement), while the human nature in Christ undergoes a change for the better, from perishable to imperishable . . . from short-lived to eternal, from corporeal to incorporeal, freed from the limits of a physical shape.

They allege that we say that it was the man, not the God, who suffered. Let them listen to what we say. We affirm that the godhead was in him who suffered; we deny that the impassible nature became

[1] 2 Kings 2. 11.   [2] The economy; cf. p. 134.   [3] 2 Cor. 5. 16.

capable of suffering. Human nature takes its subsistence from the conjunction of an intellectual soul with a body. . . . In the case of man in general we think of some life-giving power coming upon matter, as a result of which man is formed, consisting of soul and body. In the case of the Virgin Birth the power of the Highest was implanted immaterially in the undefiled body and took the Virgin's purity as the material for the flesh, employing it as the contribution of the virgin body towards the formation of one who was in truth a New Man . . . created after the likeness of God, not in the fashion of man. The divine power spread through all this compound nature equally, so that neither part was without its share in the Godhead; in both parts (that is, in body and soul) the two elements (the divinity and the humanity) duly coalesced and corresponded. . . . The divine nature was implanted in both body and soul in corresponding measure and became united to both.

antirr. 53, 54

We assert that the body in which he accepted his suffering, being mingled with the divine nature, became through that intermixture identical with the nature which assumed it . . . we believe that whatever in our lowly nature was assumed in the fulfilment of his divine plan of love for man was also transformed to what is divine and immortal. [Acts 2. 36, '*God made this Jesus, whom you crucified, Lord and Christ*'.] This passage of Scripture asserts that two things happened to one person; suffering at the hands of the Jews, honour from God. It is not meant that one person suffered and another was honoured by exaltation. The Apostle makes his meaning clearer by his following statement, 'being exalted by the right hand of God'. Who was exalted? . . . God surely needs no exaltation, since he is the highest. Then he must mean that the humanity was exalted: and it was exalted by becoming Lord and Christ. And this happened after the passion. . . . The lowly nature of him who was crucified . . . in virtue of its commixture with the infinite and unlimited nature of the good, remained no longer confined to the limits of its own properties, but was raised up with the divine element by the right hand of God, and became Lord instead of servant, King Christ[1] instead of subject, Highest instead of lowly, God instead of man . . . *c. Eunom.* 5. 5

In our thought we distinguish the working out of the divine plan[2] by means of the flesh from the divine power considered by itself. . . .

[1] 'Anointed King.' [2] Cf. p. 134.

The flesh was not identical with the godhead, until this too was transformed into the nature of divinity. So that it necessarily follows that one set of attributes is fitting for God the Word, another set to 'the form of the servant'[1]. . . . He who was 'highly exalted'[1] as a result of his suffering became Lord and Christ through his union with him who is in reality Lord and Christ. We say this, knowing, through what we have been taught, that the divine nature is always identical and consistent, while the flesh, in itself, is what reason and sense-perception apprehend it to be. But when mingled with the divine it no longer keeps within the limits of its own natural properties, but is taken up to the level of the prevalent and transcendent. But our idea of the different properties of the flesh and the godhead remains unconfused so long as we contemplate each of these by itself. For example, 'The Word existed before the ages: but the flesh came into being in these last times'. One could not reverse this statement, and say that the flesh was pre-temporal, or that the Word came into being in recent times. The flesh is passible in nature; the Word is active. The flesh is not capable of creating the universe; the Godhead's power is not capable of suffering. . . . It is not the human nature which raises Lazarus; it is not the impassible power that weeps for him. . . . It is clear that the blows of the passion belong to the servant in whom the Master was; but the honours belong to the Master who was enveloped by the servant; so that because of the conjunction and connexion the attributes of each nature become common to both, and the Master takes upon himself the servant's stripes while the servant is glorified by the Master's honour. Hence the cross is said to be the cross of 'the Lord of Glory',[2] and 'every tongue confesses that Jesus Christ is Lord'[3] . . .

The godhead 'empties itself'[4] in order that it may come within the capacity of the human nature; the humanity is renewed by becoming divine through commixture with the divine. . . . As fire that often lies hidden below the surface of wood is not observed by the senses of those who see or even touch the wood, but is manifest when it is kindled into flame; so . . . he who, because he is 'the Lord of Glory', thought nothing of that which men think shame, and concealed, as it were, the embers of his life beneath his bodily nature in fulfilling the divine plan by means of his death, kindled it to flame again by the power of his own Godhead, warming into life that which had been brought to death, pouring that limited first-fruit of our nature into the

[1] Phil. 2. 7 and 9.   [2] 1 Cor. 2. 8.   [3] Phil. 2. 11.   [4] Phil. 2. 7.

infinity of his divine power. Thus he made it to be what he himself was, making the form of the servant to be Lord, the human son of Mary to be Christ, him who was crucified through weakness to be life and power, and making all that is reverently conceived as belonging to God the Word to be also in that which the Word assumed; so that those properties no longer seem to be in either nature by way of distinction and division. Rather it seems that the perishable nature is re-created by commixture into the divine, since the divine prevails over it; and thus it partakes of the power of the Godhead; as if one should say that a drop of vinegar[1] mixed in the ocean is turned into sea by that mixture, since the natural qualities of the liquid do not remain in the infinity of the prevailing element. . . . That which was crucified because of weakness has itself become, through the prevailing power of him who dwelt within it, what the indweller is in fact and title, namely, Christ and Lord.   c. Eunom. 5. 5

We do not ascribe our salvation to a mere man; nor do we admit that the incorruptible divine nature is liable to suffering and death. But we must certainly believe the inspired utterances which proclaim that the Word 'which was in the beginning was God', and that afterwards the 'Word made flesh' was 'seen on the earth and lived in intercourse with men.'[2] And therefore we admit into our faith those ideas which accord with the inspired utterance. When we are told that he is light, power, righteousness, life, and truth, that 'through him the whole universe was made',[3] we count all such statements as worthy of belief, and we refer them to the Word who is God. But when we hear of pain, sleep, need, distress, bonds, nails, the spear, the blood and the wounds and the burial and the tomb and other things of this kind, then, even though these are somewhat contrary to the epithets mentioned above, we nevertheless accept them as things to be believed and as true, in respect of the flesh, which we accept as part of our faith, together with the Word. It is impossible to consider the attributes proper to the flesh as existing in the Word which 'was in the beginning'; it is equally inadmissible to conceive the properties of the godhead as existing in the flesh. Therefore, since the teaching of the gospel about the Lord displays a mixture of sublime elements congruous with the

[1] This simile is used in antirr. 42, where 2 Cor. 5. 4 is quoted as 'what is mortal has been swallowed up by life'.   [2] John 1. 1, 14; Baruch 3. 37 (speaking of Wisdom).   [3] John 1. 4; 1 Cor. 1. 24, 30; Col. 3. 4; John 14. 6; John 1. 3.

godhead and lowly attributes, we fit each particular conception to one or the other of the natures which have been revealed to our understanding; ascribing the human element to the humanity, the sublime to the godhead. We assert that the Son, as God, is utterly impassible and incorruptible; and when his suffering is mentioned in the gospel, he achieved that by means of his human nature which was capable of suffering. For the godhead assuredly achieves man's salvation by means of the body which enveloped it; so that the suffering belonged to the body, but the achievement was the work of God . . .

The human nature is glorified by his assumption of it, the divine nature humbles itself by this act of condescension, but consigns the human element to suffering, while achieving, through its divine power, the resurrection of the element which suffered. Thus the experience of death is ascribed to him who has partaken of our passible nature because of the union of the humanity [the man] with him; while the sublime appellations, congruous with divinity, descend upon the human nature [the man]: so that he who was displayed upon the cross is called 'the Lord of glory', because of the mingling of his divine nature with the lowly element, and the transference of the grace of those names from the divine to the human . . .

God the Word highly exalted that which was lowly, and on him who had a human name he bestowed the name above all names. Thus came about that ineffable mixture and conjunction of human littleness and divine immensity, in virtue of which even those majestic divine names are rightly applied to the humanity, and the godhead conversely is addressed by human names. For it is the same person who has the name above all names who is also worshipped by all creation under his human name of Jesus. 'At the name of Jesus every knee shall bow . . . and every tongue confess that Jesus is Lord.'[1]   c. Eunom. 6. 1, 2, 4

(d) The Two Wills

['Not my will, but thine, be done.' Luke 22. 42.] To feel dread when faced with suffering belongs to human weakness . . . to endure the suffering in fulfilment of the divine plan belongs to the divine decision and the divine power. There is a distinction between the divine and the human will, and he who made our sufferings his own utters, as from his human nature, the words which suit the weakness of humanity;

[1] Phil. 2. 11.

but he adds the second utterance because he wishes the exalted will, the will that is worthy of God, to prevail over the human, for man's salvation. In saying, 'Not my will', he indicated his manhood: in adding, 'but thine', he displayed the conjunction of his godhead with that of the Father; and in that godhead, because of the communion of nature, there is no difference of will. *antirr.* 32

III. The Work of Christ

(a) *The Ransom from the Devil*

The heathen fable tells of a dog who caught sight of the reflection in the water of the food he was carrying in his mouth. He opened his mouth wide to swallow the reflection, and dropped the real food; and so he went hungry. It is thus that man's mind has been cheated of its desire for what is really good and has been diverted to that which is not, persuaded by the advocate and inventor of wickedness to confuse good with its opposite. For his guile would have been ineffective, if the false semblance of good had not been spread upon the hook of wickedness like a bait. Such was man's predicament: he had brought himself of his own accord into subjection to the enemy of his life. On the other hand, examine those attributes which accord with our conception of God; goodness, wisdom, justice, power. . . . As good, he feels pity for fallen man; as wise, he knows well the means for his restoration: and the decision of his justice must be a decision of wisdom; for one could not connect the true justice with folly.

In these circumstances, how was God's justice shown? In not using tyrannical power against him who held us in his sway. . . . Those who have sold their freedom for money are the slaves of their purchasers . . . and it is illegal to use force against a purchaser, though perfectly legal to buy a person out of slavery, if anyone so wishes. On the same principle . . . it was necessary that a just method of restoration should be devised by him who in his goodness rescued us from bondage. The method is something like this: to make over to the master whatever ransom he should be prepared to take in exchange for the slave in his possession. . . . Now the origin of the tendency to evil [*in Satan*], and the foundation and as it were the mother of all other wickedness was the love of power, which was a disease in him. Then what would he accept in exchange for his possession except, of course, something higher and better, so that by gaining through the transaction he might give greater satisfaction to his inflated pride? . . . Seeing the power [*displayed in the miraculous birth of Christ and in his miracles*] the Enemy recognized in him a proposed bargain which would give him a profit in the exchange for what he held. Therefore he chose him as a ransom in exchange for those who were shut up in death's prison. But it was beyond his power to look upon the unveiled appearance of God; he would only see in Christ a part of the fleshly nature which he had of old subdued through wickedness. That was the reason why the Godhead was veiled in flesh, that Satan should observe what was familiar and congenial and thus have no fear in approaching the transcendent power. He only noticed the power which shone quietly more and more in his miracles; and what he saw seemed to him an object of desire rather than fear. Thus you see how goodness was combined with justice, and wisdom was included. For you have a demonstration of goodness, wisdom, and justice in the device by which the divine power became accessible through investment in a human body so that the divine plan for us should not be thwarted by the fear inspired by a manifestation of divinity. His choosing to save man is evidence of his goodness; his making the ransoming of the captive a matter of exchange displays his justice; while his pre-eminent wisdom is demonstrated by the device by which something was made accessible to the Enemy which had been beyond his grasp.

In order that the exchange for us might be easily accepted by him who sought for it, the divine nature was concealed under the veil of our human nature so that, as with a greedy fish, the hook of divinity might be swallowed along with the bait of flesh.   *or. cat.* 21–24

[The notion of the 'deceit of the Devil' appears in Irenaeus, Origen, Ambrose' Augustine (see pp. 180 f; 222), Leo the Great, and Gregory the Great. Gregory Naz. repudiates it (see p. 112). The simile of the fish-hook and the bait was made familiar in the West in the free rendering of Rufinus of Aquileia (*c.* 400), and reproduced by Gregory the Great (*moral.* 33.7.)]

(b) Reconciliation

[*On the words to Mary Magdalene, 'Touch me not. . . .'* John 20. 17.]
Our life had been alienated from God; and its return to the high and heavenly place[1] was beyond its own unaided contrivance. For this reason, as the Apostle says, 'he who had no acquaintance with sin is

[1] Cf. Eph. 1. 20; 2. 6.

made to be sin', and frees us from the curse by making our curse his own; and taking up the enmity that had come between us and God, 'he slew' (in the words of the Apostle) 'the enmity in his own person'.[1] Sin, indeed, *was* the enmity. Thus, by becoming what we were, through his own person he again united humanity to God. For through purity he brought into the closest kinship with the Father of our nature that 'new man which is created after the likeness of God', in whom 'the whole fulness of the Godhead dwelt in bodily form'.[2] And along with himself he drew to the same state of grace all the nature which shares in his human body and is akin to him. And through the agency of this woman he proclaims this good news, not only to those disciples but also to all those who up to this present time have become disciples of the word. The good news is that man is no longer an outcast, nor expelled from God's kingdom; but is again a son, again God's subject, in that the whole mass of humanity is hallowed along with its first-fruits.[3] 'For behold', he says, 'I and the children whom God has given me.'[4] He who for our sake shared in flesh and blood has taken you up and brought you back again to the place from which you strayed, and became through your sin mere flesh and blood. And so he from whom we had been estranged through our rebellion has become our Father and our God. Therefore in those words ['*my Father, and yours; my God, and yours*'] the Lord proclaims the good news of this benefit. The words are not a proof of the humiliation of the Son; they are the good news of our reconciliation to God. For what happened in the human nature of Christ is a boon shared by all men who believe. . . . The fact that this boon was revealed by the agency of a woman is itself also consonant with the interpretation we have given. 'The woman', says the Apostle, 'was deceived and fell into transgression.'[5] By her disobedience she led the rebellion from God; and this is why woman is the first witness of the resurrection, so that she may retrieve, by faith in the resurrection, the catastrophe which resulted from her transgression: that, as she brought into human life the beginning of evil and its consequences by making herself at the beginning the assistant and supporter of the serpent's suggestions, so, by conveying to the disciples the words of him who put to death the apostate serpent, she may become for men their leader in the faith through which the first pronouncement of death is rightly annulled. *c. Eunom.* 12. 1

[1] 2 Cor. 5. 21; Gal. 3. 13; Eph. 2. 16.   [2] Eph. 4. 24; Col. 2. 9.   [3] Cf. Rom. 11. 16.
[4] Heb. 2. 13 [Isa. 8. 18].   [5] 1 Tim. 2. 14.

(c) Restoration

[*The deception of Satan may be thought inconsistent with divine justice and wisdom.*] But the essential feature of justice is to give to each according to his deserts; of wisdom, not to pervert justice, and at the same time not to separate the good aim of love for mankind from the decision of justice, but to combine the two skilfully: in respect of justice, rendering due recompense; in respect of goodness, not departing from the aim of love for mankind. Let us observe, then, whether these two qualities are not to be discerned in what happened. The due recompense, by which the deceiver was himself deceived, displays justice; the aim of the transaction testifies to the goodness of him who effected it. It is the property of justice to allot to everyone whatever belongs to him as responsible for its cause and beginning, just as the earth gives back its produce according to the kind of seeds that have been sown. It is the property of wisdom not to fail in the better purpose of love in the method of giving the equivalent recompense. An intending murderer may mix a drug in food; so may a physician, to cure the intended victim: in the one case it is a poison; in the other, an antidote. And the method of the cure does not spoil the beneficent purpose. In both cases the drug is mixed with food; but we observe the different intention and praise one man and are indignant with the other. In this instance the deceiver, in accordance with the requirements of justice, receives the return of the seeds which he had sown of his own free choice; for he deceived man by the bait of pleasure and is himself deceived by the presenting to him of a human being. But the purpose of the action changes its character and makes it good. The one effected his deceit with a view to the destruction of human nature: the other, who is at once just and good and wise, employed the device of his deception for the salvation of him who was destroyed.

This benefited not only the ruined but also the worker of our ruin. For the result of this approach of death to life, of darkness to light, of corruption to incorruption, is the disappearance of the worse element, which passes away into nothingness, and the bringing of succour to him who is cleansed from these evils. As when inferior material is mixed with gold the refiners burn away the foreign and worthless matter and restore the valuable metal to its natural lustre . . . so the approach of the divine power acts like fire and effects the disappearance of the unnatural contamination, and by purification confers upon that nature a boon, even though the separation is painful. Thus even the Enemy himself would not dispute that the action was just and salutary, if he should attain to a perception of the blessing conferred. Those who submit to surgery or cautery are angry with their doctors as they smart under the agony of the operation; but if restoration to health follows, and the pain passes, then they are grateful to those who effected the cure. In the same way, when after tedious processes the evil is expelled which had been mixed with human nature and had grown up with it, and when there has taken place the restoration to the original state of those who are now lying in wickedness, then will arise a unison of thanksgiving from all creatures, as well as from those who have suffered chastisement in the process of purification as from those who needed no purification at all. Such are the benefits conferred by the great mystery of the divine incarnation. By mingling with humanity, sharing all the distinctive features of our nature—birth, nurture, growth —and going right on to the experience of death, he effected all those aforementioned results, freeing man from wickedness and healing even the inventor of wickedness himself. For the purification of the disease, however painful, is the healing of infirmity.   *or. cat.* 26

(d) Man's Response

If anyone thinks to refute our argument on the ground that even after the application of the remedy man's life is still discordant through his errors, let us guide him to the truth by an illustration from familiar experience. Take the case of a snake: it may receive a fatal blow on the head, but the coil behind is not immediately deprived of life along with the head; the head has died, but the tail part is kept alive by its own spirit, and is not deprived of its vital motion. Similarly, we can see wickedness fatally smitten, but still troubling the life of man in its remnants. Abandoning this complaint against the teaching of the revelation, our opponents make it a ground of accusation that the faith has not spread through all mankind. 'Why', they ask, 'has grace not come upon all mankind? Some have adhered to the word, but the portion remaining unconverted is no small one. Is it that God lacks the will to bestow his benefits on all without stint? Or is it that he altogether lacks the power?' . . . Now, if in our argument we had adopted the position that it was God's will that faith should be dealt out by lot to man, some being called, the rest having no share in the call, there would be an occasion for bringing this charge against our revelation. But the call came to all on an equal footing, without distinction of rank, age, or race; for that was the reason why, at the first beginning of the preaching of the gospel, those who ministered the word were by divine inspiration enabled to speak the languages of all nations, so that no one might be robbed of a share in the blessings of the teaching. How then can anyone reasonably blame God because the word has not attained dominion over all men? For he who has control over the whole universe, because of the exceeding honour in which he held man, has allowed something to be under our control, over which each individual alone is sovereign. This is our free will, which cannot be enslaved, with the power of self-determination, which resides in the freedom of our thought. Therefore the charge ought with more justice to be transferred to those who did not adhere to the faith . . .

But they are not at a loss for a captious rejoinder. They say that God, if he wished, had the power to have dragged the obstinate to acceptance of the gospel by main force. But then where would have been their free will? What room would there be for merit? What room for praise for moral success?   *or. cat.* 30. 31

(e) *The Significance of the Cross*

[*Another objection: the death of Christ was unseemly and unnecessary; and especially crucifixion. But without death the human nature would be incomplete.*] Yet it may be that one who had a thorough and exact understanding of the revelation would say with more justification that the birth was accepted for the sake of the death rather than that the death followed as a necessary consequence of the birth. For he who exists eternally did not submit to a bodily birth because he wanted to live, but in order to recall us from death to life. Then since what was needed was the ascent of the whole of our nature from death to renewal of life, he stretched out a hand as it were to the prostrate body, and in bending down to our dead corpse he came so near to death as to come in contact with our state of mortality and by his own body to bestow on human nature a beginning of the resurrection, by raising up through his power the whole of man along with himself. For that humanity which received the godhead[1] and through the resurrection was raised up with the godhead came from no other source than from the mass

[1] θεοδόχος ἄνθρωπος.

of human nature.[1] Therefore, just as in our human body the activity of one of the sense-organs communicates a sensation which is felt in common by the whole system which is united with that particular member; so the resurrection of a member passes to the whole race, as though the whole of humanity were one living being; and it is distributed from the part to the whole, by reason of the continuity and solidarity of the human race. Then is there anything beyond the bounds of probability in what we are taught in the revelation: that he who stands upright stoops to the fallen to raise him up?

The cross may have another meaning known to those versed in mystical interpretation. But the following is the traditional teaching which has come down to us. All the words and events in the gospel have a higher and divine meaning, and there is nothing therein which is not of this kind, nothing which fails to display a complete mingling of the divine and the human, where the utterance or the action takes place on the human level, while the secret meaning manifests the divine element. It would follow that in this particular case we should not observe the one aspect and ignore the other; we should notice the human element in the fact of death, while in the manner of the death we should be concerned to see the divine. Now it is characteristic of the divinity to penetrate all things and to extend throughout the whole of natural existence in every part; for a thing would not continue in existence if it did not remain in the existent, and the divine nature is that which is properly and primarily existent; and the continuance of things in being forces us to believe that this divine nature is in all that exists. This is what we learn from the cross. It is divided into four parts, so that there are four projections from the centre, where the whole figure converges. This teaches us that he who was stretched out at the destined hour, when by his death he fulfilled the redemptive plan,[2] is he who binds together all things to himself, bringing together in harmonious and concordant unity the diverse natures of existing things. For in all that exists there is the conception of something above, or below, or else thought passes to the boundaries on either side. Thus if you consider the system of things above the heavens, or beneath the earth, or the boundaries of the universe on either side, everywhere your thought is preceded and met by deity, which alone is observed in all that exists in every part and holds all things together in existence. . . . The great Paul starts from the spectacle of the cross when he initiates the

[1] ἡμετέρου φυράματος. [2] 'economy' cf. p. 134.

people of Ephesus, and instils in them the power, through his teaching, to know what is 'the depth and height and breadth and length'.[1] For he names each projection of the cross by its proper appellation: the upper part he calls 'the height', the lower 'the depth', the extensions on each side 'the breadth and length'. And in another passage he makes this idea still plainer, in my opinion, when he says to the Philippians 'At the name of Jesus every knee shall bow, of things in heaven, things on earth and things under the earth'.[2] In this passage he includes the central cross-beam in one appellation using the phrase 'on the earth' to describe all that is between things in heaven and things under the earth. This is the lesson revealed to us by the shape of the cross.

or. cat. 32

[There are similar interpretations in Athanasius (*de inc.* 25), Irenaeus (5. 17. 4), and Augustine (*de doctr. christ.* 2. 41).]

IV. The Holy Spirit

Equal in Divinity with Father and Son

[*Those who deny the divinity of the Spirit*[3]] assert that this appellation [*sc. of God*] indicates *nature*; that the nature of the Spirit is not shared with the Father and the Son; and that it follows that the Spirit should not share the common name. Then they must show by what means they have recognized the diversity of nature. Now if it were possible for the divine nature to be observed as it is in itself, and if we could discover what is proper to it and what is foreign by means of direct observation; then we should not stand in need of arguments or other evidence to bring us to the apprehension of the subject of our inquiry. But the divine nature is too exalted for such comprehension of the subject, and about things which are beyond our knowledge we reason on evidence of probability: we are therefore constrained to conduct a search into the divine nature guided by the evidence of its activities. Thus, if we see that the activities of the Father, the Son, and the Holy Spirit are different from one other, we shall conjecture, from the diver-

---

[1] Eph. 3. 18.   [2] Phil. 2. 10.   [3] The *Pneumatomachi*, under the leadership of Eustathius of Sebaste. They are often called Macedonians, after Macedonius, the semi-Arian bishop of Constantinople, who was deposed by the Arian Synod of Constantinople in 360.

sity of activities, that the natures behind those activities are different. It is also impossible that things which are distinct in respect of nature should combine in respect of the form of their activities. Fire does not freeze; ice does not warm: differences of natures lead to differences of the activities arising from them. If then we see that the activity of the Father, the Son, and the Holy Spirit is one and the same, showing no difference or variation in any respect, then from this identity of activity we necessarily infer the unity of nature.

The Father, the Son, and the Holy Spirit alike sanctify, enliven, illuminate, comfort, and the rest. No one can attribute to the activity of the Holy Spirit a special and exclusive power of sanctification, when he has heard in the gospel the Saviour saying to the Father about his disciples, 'sanctify them in thy name'.[1] In the same way all other activities are performed, in all who are worthy, equally by the Father and the Son and the Holy Ghost. [Basil] *ep.* 189. 6, 7

[Generally attributed to Greg. Nyss.]

Luke makes it plain that the intention of the clause 'Thy kingdom come' is to implore the aid of the Holy Spirit. For in his gospel, in place of 'Thy kingdom come', he says 'Let the Holy Spirit come upon us and purify us'.[2] In view of this, what will these talkers say against the Holy Spirit? How can they contrive to transform the dignity of kingship to the lowliness of slavery. For Matthew uses 'kingdom' where Luke speaks of 'Holy Spirit': how then can the enemies of God reduce that which is thus described to the level of subordinate creation? This would be to bring it down from the condition of ruler to the condition of subject. Creatureliness implies slave status, and slavery is not kingship. But the Holy Spirit is a kingship . . . 'Let the Holy Spirit come, and purify us'. The word of the gospel testifies that it is the proper and particular power and activity of the Holy Spirit to purify and forgive sins. This testimony carries with it the definite assertion of the deity of the Holy Spirit. The Apostle says precisely the same thing about the Only-begotten, that, 'he achieved the purification of our sins, and then took his seat at the right hand of the Father's majesty'.[3] Thus the activity of the Spirit is identical with the activity of Christ; and identity of activity inescapably implies identity of nature. . . . The Son

[1] John 17. 17. [2] Luke 11. 2. A reading found in no major MS. but occurring in two late cursives, and quoted by Maximus of Turin (*fl. c.* 420). [3] Heb. 1. 3.

is identical in nature with the Father, and the activities of the Spirit
are proof of his identity in nature with the Son. The proof of the unity
in nature of the Holy Trinity follows inevitably.   *de or. dom.* 3

We acknowledge the Holy Spirit to be of equal status with the Father
and the Son, so that there is no difference between them in any attribute
which piety can ascribe to the divine nature, in thought or name. We
acknowledge the Holy Spirit to be indeed *from* God, and *of* Christ,
according to the Scriptures; save that in respect of his personal subsistence [*hypostasis*] he is observed to have his particular attributes.
Since he is not ingenerate, he is not to be confused with the Father;
nor with the Son, since he is not the Only-begotten. Thus he is
distinguished by certain properties, but in all other respects he is
inseparable from them.   *c. Maced.* 2

Our opponents cannot make use of the plea in self-defence that the
Holy Spirit is bestowed by the Lord on his disciples and is therefore
third in order, and thus remote from our notion of complete deity.
There is no diminution or alteration of beneficent activity; how absurd
to suppose that the numerical order indicates any diminution or alteration in nature! It is as if a man were to see three torches burning with
separate flames (assuming that the flame has been conveyed by the
first torch to the second, and by the second to the third), and were to
maintain that the first had more heat than the others; . . . that the third
could not be said to be a fire at all, even though it burned and shone
like fire, and behaved like fire in every respect.   *c. Maced.* 6

V. The Holy Trinity

(a) *Logos and Spirit*

Even those who are outside our doctrine do not conceive of the Deity
as without *Logos*. . . . Now human speech [*logos*] is designated by the
same term. Thus anyone who says that he understands what is meant
by the Word of God on the analogy of human activities, will be led
on to a higher conception, since he is compelled to believe that an
utterance [*logos*] corresponds to the nature of the speaker. For there is
power, of a sort, and life, and wisdom, observable in a human context;
but no one would imagine, from the use of the same terms, that the

life, power, wisdom ascribed to God are of the same kind as the human: the meanings of such words are scaled down to the lowly level of our human nature. Our nature is perishable and weak; therefore our life is fleeting, our power unsubstantial, our utterance [*logos*] unstable. But when we refer to the transcendent nature, everything that is said about it is elevated to that level, because of the greatness of the contemplated object. Thus, although we speak of the Word of God, it will not be considered as having its subsistence [*hypostasis*] in the mere act of speech, and then passing into non-existence, as our utterance does. Our nature is doomed to destruction; so is our speech [*logos*]: that imperishable and ever-existing nature has speech [*logos*] which is eternal and subsistent. . . . The world is good and all that it contains is observed to be wisely and skilfully ordered. All things, indeed, are the works of the Word, who is living and subsistent, because he is the Word of God, and who wills, because he is living: who also has the power to effect his will, and who wills what is completely good and wise, and everything else that signifies excellence. . . . This Word is therefore distinct from him whose Word he is. For we have here, in a sense, a relative term, since the Father of the Word is inescapably implied along with the Word; for a word could not exist without being the word of someone. . . . In a human context we say that a word comes from the mind, being neither completely identical with the mind nor utterly different from it: for it is distinct, as being from it; yet it cannot be conceived as different, since it reveals the mind itself; it is in nature identical with the mind but distinct, as being a separate subject. Similarly the Word of God is distinct from God by reason of its self-subsistence; while by displaying in itself the qualities which are regarded as belonging to God it is identical in nature with him who is recognized by the possession of the same qualities . . .

Thus we have recognized the Word in the transcendent nature by an ascent from the facts of human nature. By the same method we shall be led on to the conception of the Spirit by observing in our human nature certain shadows and resemblances of his indescribable power. In us the spirit [*breath*] is the drawing in of air, which is something of a different nature . . . which, on the occasion of uttering the word, becomes a sound which expresses the meaning of the word. In the case of the divine nature the existence of a Spirit [*breath*] of God has been considered a religious belief. . . . But it is irreverent to suppose that, as in the case of our breath, something foreign from outside comes as an influx into God and becomes the Spirit [*breath*] in him. When we hear of the Word of God we think of it ... as essentially self-subsistent, with a will, ever active, and all-powerful. In the same way, when we have learnt that there is a Spirit of God, accompanying the Word and displaying its activity, we do not conceive of it as a mere emission of breath ... but as a power with a real existence,[1] regarded as self-subsistent in its own right, and yet not capable of separation from God in whom it is, nor from God's Word, which it accompanies: nor yet dissolving into nothingness, but existing as an individual subsistence, like God's Word, possessed of will, self-moving, active, always choosing the good; and being the power corresponding to the will for the effecting of every purpose.   *or. cat.* 1. 2

(b) Unity and Distinction

Thus a man who carefully inspects the depths of the mystery receives in his soul in secret a certain limited apprehension of the doctrine of the knowledge of God; and yet he is unable to make clear in words the inexpressible profundity of the mystery. He cannot explain how the same thing admits of number and yet evades numerical explanation; is perceived as admitting distinctions and is apprehended in a unity; is distinguished in individual subsistence [*hypostasis*] and is not divided in substrate [*hypokeimenon*[2]]. For in subsistence the Spirit is one thing and the Word is another, and again that to which Word and Spirit belong is another. But when you have conceived these distinctions, the unity of the nature still does not admit division; so that the might of the monarchy is not split up by division into different godheads.

Now this statement does not agree with the Jewish dogma, but the truth proceeds in the mean between two conceptions, overthrowing both heresies while receiving what is useful from each of them. The Jewish dogma is overthrown by the acceptance of the Word and by belief in the Spirit: the polytheistic error of the hellenists is annihilated because the unity of nature cancels the supposed plurality. On the other hand, of the Jewish conception, the unity of nature must be retained; of the hellenistic doctrine, only the distinction of the subsistences. A corrective is supplied for the irreverent notion on either side. For the number of the Trinity is as it were a remedy for those who are in error

---

[1] οὐσιώδης, 'substantial'.   [2] As the term is used by Stoic philosophers to describe the reality 'underlying' the sensible appearance. Hence it comes to be a synonym for οὐσία.

in respect of the unity; while the assertion of the unity is a remedy for those whose belief is dispersed among a plurality of divinities.

or. cat. 3

[*The nature of God incomprehensible; we can only know some of his qualities and his operations.*] The word 'godhead' signifies activity rather than nature. Now when a number of men participate together in the same pursuits they are enumerated and spoken of in the plural; but the deity is spoken of in the singular, as one God and one godhead, even though the three persons [*hypostases*] are inseparable from the meaning expressed by 'godhead'.

It would be reasonable to explain this fact by saying that even when a number of men are engaged on the same activity each of them works separately at his appointed task without participating, in respect of his individual activity, with the others who are engaged in the same occupation. For instance, there are many orators, but since they follow the same pursuit, the same name is given to their activity in the different instances: but each member of this profession is engaged on his own particular activity, functioning individually. Therefore because of the separate activity of men when engaged in the same pursuits, they are properly spoken of in the plural, since each of them is marked off from his fellows in his separate sphere of activity, fulfilling his particular purpose. But in the case of the divine nature it is not so. We are not told that the Father does anything by himself in which the Son does not co-operate; or that the Son has any isolated activity, apart from the Holy Spirit. All activities which extend from God to creation are described by different names, in accordance with the different ways in which they are presented to our thought: but every such activity originates from the Father, proceeds through the Son, and is brought to fulfilment in the Holy Spirit. For this reason the name of the activity is not split up among the plurality of the agents, since the energy of each in any matter is not separate and individual. Whatever happens, whether it concerns his providence for us, or the government and ordering of the whole universe, takes place through the action of the three; but what happens is not three things.

There is no absolute necessity, in my opinion, to contend against those who make the counter-assertion that it is wrong to conceive of 'godhead' as the name of an activity. Because we believe the divine nature to be unlimited and incomprehensible, we can have no comprehension of it, but we postulate that that nature is to be thought of as infinite in all respects: and what is absolutely infinite is not limited in one respect and unlimited in another; infinity escapes any kind of limitation. That which is without limit is certainly not limited by name. Therefore, to ensure consistency in our notion of the infinity of the divine nature, we assert that the divine is above every name. But 'godhead' is a name: thus it is impossible that the same thing should at the same time be a name and be regarded as above every name.

Still, if it pleases our opponents to assert that the meaning of 'godhead' is a nature, not an activity, we shall fall back on our original argument, that usage wrongly applies the name of a nature to denote plurality. For, in strict logic, a nature receives neither increase nor diminution when it is observed in a greater or a lesser number of instances. . . . We affirm that gold, even if cut up into various shapes, is one, and is spoken of as one. But we speak of many coins, without finding that the nature of gold is increased by the number of coins. Thus we speak of 'much' gold, when we observe it in greater bulk, in plate or coin; but not of 'many golds'. . . . Therefore, as gold is one, though there are many gold coins, so we are supplied with many individual instances of human nature, as Peter, James, and John; but the man [the humanity] in them is one. . . . But Scripture, while using the plural 'men' . . . is careful to use the word 'God' in the singular only, to guard against introducing the notion of different natures in the divine essence.

But if anyone cavils at our argument, on the ground that by not admitting a difference in nature it produces a confusion of the persons [hypostases], we shall reply thus to the charge: that, while acknowledging the unchanging character of the nature, we do not deny the difference in respect of cause and what is caused; and it is in this respect only that we conceive one to be distinguished from another; that is, by our belief that one is the cause, another derived from the cause. And again we conceive of a further difference in what is derived from the cause: for one is derived immediately from the first cause, another through that which is thus immediately derived. So that the status of Only-begotten attaches incontrovertibly to the Son, while the Spirit is unambiguously derived from the Father: the mediation of the Son safeguards his character as Only-begotten, without precluding the Spirit's relationship to the Father by way of nature. But in speaking about 'cause' and 'caused' we do not mean to indicate a difference of nature, but only a difference in manner of existence.

quod non sunt tres dei

(c) *Equality of Persons*

[*Eunomius argues that the subordination of the Holy Spirit is shown by his being mentioned always in the third place.*] We have never yet heard of this kind of philosophy, which relegates to the rank of the inferior and dependent that which is mentioned in the second or third place because of some kind of sequence. Yet this is what he wants to do, in contending that the traditional order in the enumeration of the persons is a proof of superiority and inferiority in rank and nature. In fact he lays it down that the sequence of order indicates difference in nature. The source of this fantasy is not clear, nor the cogency of the reasoning which landed him in this supposition. Numerical order does not produce a diversity of nature: things which are counted remain the same in nature whether they are counted or not. Number is indicative of the quantity of things; it does not invariably assign to the second place things which are by nature inferior in value, but it creates a sequence of the objects numerically indicated in reference to the intention of the enumerators. 'Paul and Silvanus and Timothy'; here is a mention of three persons as the reference to a particular intention on the part of the speaker. Does the placing of Silvanus, second after Paul, indicate that he was something other than a man? Timothy is placed third. Is he therefore considered to belong to a different natural species, because he is mentioned in this sequence? Not at all. Each of them is a human being, before and after this enumeration. But because it is impossible to refer to all three at once in one utterance, our usage is to mention each separately in an order which commends itself, but to unite the names by the intervening copula; to indicate, as I think, by this connexion of the names, the harmony of purpose subsisting between the three. *c. Eunom.* 1. 16

[*The fundamental division in the universe is between the intelligible (or intellectual) level of existence and the world of sense. The 'sensible' world consists of things differentiated by quantity and other sensible properties.*] But in the sphere of intellectual (or intelligible) existence (I am speaking here of the *created* 'intelligible' world) the principle of differentiation which is found in the sensible world has no place, and another method is found for detecting superiority and inferiority. For the fount and origin and source of supply of every good is regarded as being in the uncreated sphere; and the whole intellectual creation has a tendency towards that archetypal good because the higher level of existence has fellowship with it; and this intellectual creation comes into contact with it, and participates in it of necessity, in proportion as it partakes of existence on the higher level. But there are different degrees of this participation, varying according to the exercise of responsible freedom of choice: and thus in the sphere of the intellectual creation the superiority or inferiority of each member is adjudged in proportion to this tendency towards the first good. For that part of creation which is in the sphere of intellect is situated on a kind of borderline between good and its opposite, so that it is capable of either, in virtue of its power to incline towards objects of its own choosing. This is the teaching of Scripture. Thus we are able to speak of degrees of excellence in virtue in proportion as it departs from evil and approaches the good. The uncreated nature, on the other hand, is far removed from such distinctions, since it does not possess the good as something acquired, nor does it receive goodness into itself through participation in some superior good. It is in itself good by nature and is so conceived of; it is the source of good, simple, uniform, incomposite, as is admitted by our opponents. But it has its own internal differentiation, consonant with the majesty of its own nature. But this differentiation is not, as Eunomius imagines, a matter of more and less. To admit the notion of any deficiency of good into our belief in the Holy Trinity is inevitably to introduce the idea of some admixture of the opposite quality in that which is deficient; and such a supposition, in the case either of the Only-begotten or of the Holy Spirit, is impious. We contemplate this uncreated nature as being supremely perfect and incomprehensibly excellent, yet it contains within itself clear-cut distinctions owing to the special properties which belong to each of the Persons. It has the character of immutability in virtue of the property of uncreatedness which is shared by all the Persons; but it is differentiated by reason of the separate and distinct character of each person. The individual character observed in each of the Persons clearly and sharply divides them from one another. For instance, the Father is acknowledged to be uncreated and also ingenerate; he is neither generated nor created. This uncreatedness is a property he holds in common with the Son and the Holy Spirit: but ingeneracy, like fatherhood, is his special and incommunicable property, not found in the other Persons. The Son is linked to the Father and the Holy Spirit in his uncreatedness: in his status and name of Only-begotten he has a unique character which does not belong either to the Supreme Deity or to the Holy Spirit. The Holy Spirit is joined to the Father and the Son by the common property of uncreatedness, but he is distinguished from them by his own particular characteristics. His most individual mark and characteristic consists in his not showing either the property of ingeneracy or of being only-begotten, which we have observed as characterizing the Father and the Son respectively. He simply *is*, without being ingenerate or only-begotten, and this is what constitutes his special character and distinction for the other persons. Linked to the Father by being uncreated, he is disjoined by not being Father. United with the Son by the bond of uncreatedness, and by deriving his being from the Supreme God, he is separated by the distinction of not being the Father's Only-begotten, and of having been manifested through the Son himself. On the other hand, since the created world came into existence through the Son, we must guard against the idea that the Spirit has anything in common with the created world because it was through the Son that he was revealed; and therefore he is distinguished from creation by being unalterable and unchangeable and by his independence of any goodness outside himself.   *c. Eunom.* 1. 22

[*Space and time begin with the creation.*] Our busy and over-active intellect, when employed in this lower world, makes distinction of early and later between things separated by intervals of time. But how can we suppose this to apply to the uncreated existence, 'before all ages'? It is in this uncreated sphere that those wonderful realities, with their wonderful names of Father, Son, and Holy Spirit, are thought of as existing. For there we think of the Father, without beginning, without generation and always Father; and with him comes the conception of the Son, without any interval of separation; and through the Son and with him, in inseparable conjunction, the Holy Spirit is thought of as existing without the interposition of any idea of an empty and insubstantial gap. He is not subsequent in existence to the Son, as if the Only-begotten could even be conceived as being without the Spirit. The Spirit derives his being from the Supreme God, whence comes the being of the Only-begotten Light; and through that true Light the Spirit has shone forth, not being divided from the Father and the Son either by temporal interval or by diversity of nature. There are no intervals in the sphere of existence 'before the ages': nor are there any differences of being. . . . The generation of the Son is not within time, any more than the creation was before time. It is utterly wrong to introduce division into an order of existence which admits no separation and to interpolate an interval of time into the creative cause of the universe by asserting that there was a time when the author of all existence did not exist.[1]　　　　　　　*c. Eunom.* 1. 26

There is one and the same Person [*prosôpon*] of the Father, from whom the Son is begotten, and the Holy Spirit proceeds. He is the cause of those Persons who are caused by him; and therefore we rightly assert One God, since he co-exists with them. For the Persons of the Godhead are not divided from each other in time, place, will, occupation, activity or any qualifications of this sort, the distinguishing marks observed in human beings. The only distinction here is that the Father is father, not son: the Son is son, not father; similarly, the Holy Spirit is neither father nor son.　　　　　　　*de comm. not.*

VI. The Sacraments

(a) Baptism

(i) Symbol of Resurrection

The descent into the water, and the threefold immersion, involves another mystery.[2] The method of our salvation became effectual not so much as a result of instruction by way of teaching as by the act of him who established a fellowship with man, bringing life to man by effective action; so that by means of the flesh which he assumed and deified everything kindred and related to it may be saved. Therefore it was necessary that a means should be devised by which there should be in what is done by the follower some kinship and likeness to the leader. . . . What do we see in the case of the captain of our salvation? A state of death for three days and then life again. Something resembling this must therefore be devised for us. . . . Since the death of him who leads us to life involved burial under the earth . . . the imitation of death on our part is represented in water, the neighbouring element. That man from above,[3] after he had assumed a state of death after his

---

[1] ἦν ὅτε οὐκ ἦν, 'there was when he was not', was an Arian slogan, referring to the Son.
[2] i.e. inner teaching conveyed by external rite.　　[3] Cf. John 3. 13; 1 Cor. 15, 47.

deposition in the earth, came back to life on the third day. So every one who is linked to him in virtue of his bodily nature and fixes his eyes on the same victory (and by this I mean the consummation, which is life) has water poured upon him, instead of earth, and thus, by submitting to this element three times, represents the grace of resurrection attained after three days. . . . In the case of the leader of our salvation the divine purpose of death was fully attained [i.e. *the restoration of nature to its primal purity*]. . . . But in the case of his followers their nature is not capable of exact and complete imitation, but it receives now as much as it is able, while the remainder is reserved for the time to come. In what, then, does this imitation consist? In the effecting of the annihilation of the wickedness mingled in our nature. This is the meaning conveyed by the image of mortification presented by the water. It is not, however, a complete annihilation; but a kind of breach in the continuity of evil, two things concurring to effect the removal of wickedness—the repentance of the offender and the imitation of the death of Christ. . . . It is necessary for us to undergo, by means of water, this preparatory rehearsal of the grace of the resurrection, so that we may realize that it is as easy for us to rise again from death as to be baptized with water. Now in matters which concern our ordinary life there are some things which take priority as being essential to the achievement of a certain result, although the beginning would seem of no account when compared with the end. . . . Similarly, the great resurrection has its beginnings and its causes here, in baptism. . . .

Without the regeneration by means of the laver it is impossible, I say, for man to be in the resurrection. I am not here referring to the refashioning and renewal of our composite being; for to this our nature must in any event attain, under compulsion of its own natural laws in accordance with the divine plan of him who so ordained, whether it has received the grace of the laver or remains without that initiation. I am referring rather to that restoration to a blessed and divine state, removed from all shame. For all who receive through the resurrection a return to existence do not return to the same kind of life. There is a wide separation between those who have been purified and those who need purification. Those who have previously been purified in this life by the laver are restored to a state which suits them: and the appropriate state for the pure is a condition of freedom from passion, and it is beyond dispute that blessedness consists in this freedom from passion. But for those who have become encrusted with passions, to whom no purification from defilement has been applied, no sacramental water, no invocation of the divine power, no reformation by means of penitence, it is utterly necessary that they should be in their appropriate place. The appropriate place for adulterated gold is the smelting furnace, so that the wickedness which has been mingled in them may be melted away in the course of long ages and their nature may be restored pure to God. There is a cleansing power in fire, as in water. Those who have washed away the filth of wickedness by means of the sacramental water do not need the other kind of purification; those who have not been initiated into this kind of purification must be purified by fire.　　　　　　　　　　　　　　　　　　　　　　　　　　*or. cat.* 35

(ii) *Regeneration and Response*

The transmutation of our life which comes through the regeneration will not be a transmutation, if we continue in the same condition as before. . . . Humanity in itself does not admit of any change as a result of baptism; neither the reason, nor the intellect, nor the faculty of knowledge, nor any other of the special characteristics of human nature undergoes change. Indeed the transmutation would be for the worse, if any of these properties of our nature were exchanged. If the 'birth from above'[1] is a refashioning of man's nature, we must ask what change is made to bring the grace of regeneration to perfection. Clearly the change for the better follows when the wicked thoughts of our nature have been eradicated. . . . We have become better men and have been transmuted to a better condition. . . . If the life after initiation is of the same quality as the uninitiated life, then, though it may be a bold thing to say, I will say it without flinching; in the case of such people the water is merely water, for the gift of the Holy Spirit in no way shows itself in what takes place. . . . A child born to any one is entirely akin to his parent. If then you have received God, and have become the child of God,[2] display in the purpose of your life the God that is in you, display in yourself the Father who gave you birth.　　　　　　　　　　　　　　　　　　　　　　　　　*or. cat.* 40

(iii) *Water and Spirit*

Baptism is a purification of sins, a remission of transgressions, a cause of renovation and regeneration. By regeneration you must understand a regeneration perceived by thought, not observed by the eyes. . . .

[1] Cf. John 3. 3.　　[2] Cf. John 1. 12.

We shall not change the old man into a child . . . but we do bring back, by kingly grace, one scarred with sins and grown old in evil habits, to the innocence of a babe. For just as the new-born infant is free from accusations and penalties, so too the child of regeneration has no charges to answer, being released from accountability by kingly bounty. It is not the water that bestows this bounty (for then it would be exalted above all creation), but the commandment of God and the intervention of the Spirit, which comes sacramentally to give us liberty. But water has a part to play, by giving an outward sign of the purification. For when our body has been soiled by dirt and mud it is our practice to make it clean by washing in water. We therefore use water in the sacramental action also, signifying, by something perceived by the senses, a shining cleanliness which is not a bodily cleanliness.

Now pray let us persevere, in a more searching inquiry into the laver of baptism. Let us begin with Scripture, as the fountain-head. 'Unless a man is born from water and spirit, he cannot enter the Kingdom of God.'[1] Why are those two things mentioned? Why is not the Spirit alone considered necessary for the fulfilment of baptism? Man, as we very well know, is composite, not simple: and therefore, for the healing of this twofold and conjunct being, medicines are assigned which suit and resemble his double nature. For his visible body, the sensible water; for his invisible soul, the unseen Spirit, invoked by faith, which comes in a fashion we cannot describe. 'The Spirit breathes where he wills, and you hear his voice. But you do not know from whence he comes, and whither he departs.'[2] He blesses the body which is being baptized, and the water that baptizes. Therefore do not despise the divine laver, nor make it of no account, as something common, because of the use of water. For the power at work is mighty, and the effects accomplished thereby are wonderful.

This holy altar, where we now stand, is in itself an ordinary stone slab, in no way different from other slabs with which our walls are built and our pavements are adorned. But since it has been consecrated for the service of God, and has received the blessing, it is a holy table, an undefiled altar, no longer touched by the hands of all, but only by the priests, and by them with reverence. Again, the bread is, to begin with, common bread, but when the sacramental act has consecrated it, it is called, and becomes, the body of Christ. So with the sacramental oil, and the wine; though things of small value before the blessing,

[1] John 3. 3.   [2] John 3. 8.

after the sanctification by the Spirit each of them has its special effectiveness. Again, the same power of the word also makes the priest revered and honourable, separated from community with the general public by the new quality given by the blessing. Yesterday he was one of the crowd, one of the people; he is suddenly made into a leader, a president, a teacher of religion, a guide into hidden mysteries: and he performs these functions without being changed in any way in body or in form. He continues to be the same as before to all appearance; but he is transformed to a higher state in respect of his invisible soul by an invisible power and grace.

What are the words of the Lord's command? 'Baptizing them in the name of the Father, and of the Son, and of the Holy Spirit.'[1] Why in the name of the Father? Because he is the First Cause of all things. Why in the name of the Son? Because he is the agent of creation. Why in the name of the Holy Spirit? Because it is his power which brings all to perfection. We therefore bow down to the Father, that we may be sanctified. We bow down to the Son, for this same end. We bow down to the Holy Spirit, that we may become what he is in fact and in name. There is no distinction in the sanctification, as if the Father sanctified in a higher degree, the Son less, the Holy Spirit less again. Why then do you chop up the three Persons into different natures, and produce three Gods, unlike to one another, when from all three you receive one and the same grace?   *in bapt. Chr.*

(b) The Eucharist

[*The soul is united to God in baptism: the body by the Eucharist receives the antidote to the poison of sin, the immortal Body of Christ, which assimilates and transforms our body.*] How can that Body of Christ give life to the whole of mankind that is, all those in whom there is faith, and, though divided among all, itself be not diminished? . . . The subsistence of every body depends on nourishment . . . and the Word of God coalesced with human nature and did not invent some different constitution for man's nature when he came in a body like ours. It was by the usual and appropriate means that he ensured his body's continuance, maintaining its subsistence by food and drink, the food being bread. Now in our case one may say that when any one looks at bread he is looking at a human body, for when the bread gets into the body it *becomes* the

[1] Matt. 28. 19.

body. Similarly in the case of the Word of God, the body which received the godhead, when it partook of nourishment in the form of bread, was in a manner of speaking identical with that bread, since the nourishment was transformed into the natural qualities of the body ... the body which by the indwelling of God the Word was transmuted to the dignity of godhead. If this is so, we are right in believing that now also the bread which is consecrated by the Word of God is transmuted into the body of God the Word. For that body was virtually bread, but was consecrated by the indwelling of the word which 'tabernacled'[1] in the flesh. A similar result now takes place from the same cause as that by which the bread that was transmuted into that body was changed to divine potency. In that case the grace of the Word made that body holy, whose subsistence was derived from bread: in this case the bread, as the Apostle says, is 'sanctified by the Word of God and prayer'.[2] It is not a matter of the bread's becoming the body of the Word through the natural process of eating: rather it is transmuted straightway into the body through the Word, just as the Word himself said, 'This is my body'[3] ... The God who was manifested mingled himself with the nature that was doomed to death, in order that by communion with the divinity human nature may be deified together with him. It is for this purpose that by the divine plan[4] of his grace he plants himself in the believers by means of that flesh, composed of bread and wine, blending himself with the bodies of believers, so that man also may share in immortality by union with the immortal. He bestows those gifts by the virtue of the blessing, 'transelementing'[5] the nature of the visible things into the immortal body. *or. cat.* 37

VII. The Last Things

Resurrection. Soul and Body re-united

The soul has a natural inclination of affection towards the body that has dwelt with it; and it has therefore a disposition, in virtue of this commixture, to recognize the body that belongs to it, as if certain marks had been imprinted by nature, by means of which the community between them remains unconfused, being marked by these distinctive signs. Now since the soul attracts again to itself that which is connected

[1] John 1. 14. [2] 1 Tim. 4. 5. [3] Matt. 26. 26 etc. [4] 'economy'. [5] μεταστοιχειώσας.

with it and belongs to it, what difficulty, I ask you, would be presented to the divine power to hinder the coming together of related things which are drawn towards each other by a kind of mysterious natural attraction? The fact that there still remain in the soul some tokens of our composite nature, even after its dissolution, is attested by the dialogue in Hades.[1] For although the bodies had been committed to the tomb, some physical means of identification still attached to the souls, by which Lazarus was recognized, and the rich man was known.

And so there is nothing improbable in the belief that when our bodies rise again there will be a return from the common stock to the individual. This will be especially clear to one who takes the trouble to make a careful examination of human nature. For our being is not entirely a subject to flux and change; if it had by nature no stability at all it would be utterly incomprehensible. A more accurate account would be that part of our constituents is stable, while the remainder undergoes a process of change. The body alters by increase and diminution . . . it is the stable and unalterable elements in our composition, not that part which is subject to change, flux and alteration, that is attached to the soul, which is in the likeness of God. The differences of forms are the products of particular kinds of combination, this combination being simply the commixture of the elements (and by elements we mean those which provide the basic ingredients for the composition of the universe, and make possible the constitution of man). The form remains in the soul as if by the impression of a seal; and thus it is inevitable that those things which have been impressed by the seal with this stamp should not fail to be recognized by the soul. In fact, at the time of the general restoration the soul inevitably receives back to itself whatever corresponds to the stamp of the form: and clearly all those things which in the beginning were thus stamped by the form would so correspond. Thus there is nothing improbable in the supposition that what properly belongs to the individual returns to it from the common stock.   *hom. opif.* 27

It seems to me that the argument of the Apostle [*in* 1 Cor. 15. 35–49] agrees in all respects with our conception of the resurrection, and displays the same notion as is contained in our definition of it, which asserted that the resurrection is nothing other than the reconstitution of our nature to its pristine state. For we learn from Scripture, in the

[1] Cf. Luke 16. 23–31.

first cosmogony, that the earth first brought forth the green plant, then seed was produced from this plant, and from this, when it had been shed on the ground, the same form of the original growth sprang up. Now the inspired Apostle says that this is what happens also at the resurrection. Thus we learn from him not only that human nature is changed into a far nobler state, but also that what we are to hope for is just this; the return of human nature to its primal condition. The original process was not that of an ear from the seed, but of the seed from the ear, the ear thereafter growing from the seed.

The order of events in this simile clearly shows that all the happiness which will burgeon for us through the resurrection will be a return to our original state of grace. Originally we also were, in a sense, a full ear, but we were withered by the torrid heat of sin; and then on our dissolution by death the earth received us. But in the spring of the resurrection the earth will again display this naked grain of our body as an ear, tall, luxuriant, and upright, reaching up as high as heaven, and, for stalk and beard, decked with incorruption and all the other godlike characteristics. For 'this corruptible thing must put on incorruption';[1] and this 'incorruption', and 'glory', and 'honour', and 'power'[2] are confessedly the distinguishing marks of the divine nature, once the property of him who was created in God's image, now hoped for hereafter. The first ear was the first man, Adam. But with the entrance of evil human nature was divided into multitude; and, as happens with the ripe grain in the ear, each individual person was stripped of the beauty of the ear and mingled with the earth. But in the resurrection we are reborn in that pristine beauty, becoming the infinite myriads of the harvest-fields instead of that original ear.   *de anim. et res.*

[1] 1 Cor. 15. 53.   [2] Cf. 1 Cor. 15. 41–3.

Theodore of Mopsuestia

The Doctrine of Christ

(a) The Soul of Christ

The disciples of Arius and Eunomius say that he took a body, but not a soul; the divine nature, they say, supplied the place of a soul.[1] They abased the divine nature of the Only-begotten to such an extent that, declining from its natural grandeur, it performed the actions of the soul, imprisoning itself in that body and performing the functions necessary for the body's existence. Consequently, if the divinity took the place of a soul, he would not have felt hunger or thirst; he would not have been tired, or had need of food: for all these experiences come to the body because of its weakness, and because the soul is incapable of satisfying its needs.

It was necessary that the Son should assume not only a body but also an immortal and rational soul. It was not only the death of the body that he had to abolish, but also the death of the soul, which is sin.... It was necessary that sin, the cause of death, should be removed, and consequently death would be abolished with the removal of sin.

It is evident that the tendency to sin has its origin in the will of the soul. *cat. hom.* 5. 9, 10, 11

It was necessary, therefore, that Our Lord should take a soul, so that the soul should first be saved from sin and, by God's grace, should achieve immortality ... *cat. hom.* 5. 14

Our blessed Fathers said: 'He was incarnate, and became man', in order that we should believe that he was a complete man who was assumed and in whom God the Word dwelt: that he was complete in all that belongs to human nature, composed of a mortal body and a rational soul, since it is 'for man and for his salvation that he came down from heaven'.... He put on himself a man like Adam, who after sinning received the sentence of death, so that by a like being sin should be abolished from us, and death annihilated. *cat. hom.* 5. 17

[1] Cf. p. 11 f.

(b) The Two Natures

He is not merely God, nor is he merely man: but in truth he is both by nature, God and man. He is God the Word, he who assumed; and he is the man who was assumed. He who is 'in the form of God' assumed 'the form of a servant';[1] and the form of a servant is not the form of God. In the form of God he is one who is God by nature, who assumed the form of a servant: while the form of a servant is one who is man by nature and who was assumed for our salvation. He who assumed is not the same as he who was assumed; the one who assumed is God, while the one who was assumed is man. The one who assumed is by nature the same as God the Father, for he is 'God with God'.[2] . . . But he who was assumed is by nature the same as David and Abraham, whose son he is, and from whom he is descended. Hence he is both the Lord of David and his son.[3] *cat. hom.* 8. 1

(c) The Unity of Person

We learn from the Sacred Books the distinction between the natures. . . . That which assumed was the divine nature, which does everything for us; while the other is the human nature, which was assumed on behalf of us all by him who is the cause of everything, and is united to it in an ineffable union, forever indissoluble. *cat. hom.* 8. 10

We must hold fast to the knowledge of that indissoluble conjunction. Never for a single moment can that form of a servant be separated from the divine nature which has put it on. The distinction of natures does not annul the exact conjunction; nor does that exact conjunction destroy the distinction: the natures remain distinct in their existence, and their conjunction remains of necessity, because that which was assumed is associated with the assumer in honour and glory.

cat. hom. 8. 13

The fact that we speak of two natures does not mean that we are forced to speak of two Lords, or two Sons. This would be utter foolishness. When things are two in one respect, and one in another respect, their conjunction, which makes them one, does not annul the distinction of natures, nor does that distinction prevent their unity.

cat. hom. 8. 14

[From the version of the Syriac text (see p. 17) in *Les Homélies Catéchétiques de Théodore de Mopsuestia*, tr. Raymond Tonneau and Robert Devreesse, Biblioteca Apostolica Vaticana, 1949.]

[1] Phil. 2. 6. [2] John 1. 1. [3] Cf. Matt. 22. 45.

When God is said to dwell in the apostles, or, more generally, in righteous men, he makes his dwelling there as taking pleasure in righteous men, as rejoicing in 'those who excel in virtue'.[1] But we do not say that he dwelt in Christ himself in this way (we would never have been so mad), but as in a Son. For he dwelt in him because it was in this way that he 'was well pleased'[2]. What is meant by dwelling 'as in a Son'? We mean that when he took his dwelling there he wholly united to himself him whom he had assumed, and contrived that the assumed should share with himself all the honour which the indwelling Son himself shares, being by nature Son; so that the result is one person [*prosôpon*], in virtue of the union, and the sharing of authority. He operates through the assumed in all things, so that he effects the judgement and trial of the whole world through him and through his coming; while we recognize the difference between assumer and assumed in the distinctions imposed by difference of nature.   *de inc.* 7

When we distinguish the natures we speak of the nature and person of God the Word as perfect. We cannot talk of an impersonal existence [*hypostasis*]. Similarly, we speak of the nature and person of the man as perfect. But when we consider the conjunction [*synapheia*], then we speak of 'one person'.   *de inc.* 8

To the question: 'Is Mary the bearer of man, or the bearer of God?', we must answer: 'Of both'. She is the first in the physical sense, the second by implication. Bearer of man on the natural level, seeing that he who was in her womb and issued from it was human: bearer of God, seeing that God was in the man who was born; not in him as confined there naturally, but in him by an act of will.   *de inc.* 15

The manner of union according to divine favour[3] ensures that the natures are not confused, and demonstrates the unity of the two persons without division, and the unity of will, of activity, together with the authority and lordship which accompanies them.   *ep. ad Domnum*

---

[1] Ps. 16. 3.   [2] Matt. 3. 17.   [3] εὐδοκία, the noun from the verb translated 'I am well pleased'.

John Chrysostom

I. Man's Condition

(a) Original Sin

'Through the wrong-doing of one man many became sinners.' That, when Adam sinned and became mortal, those who were descended from him should become mortal also has nothing improbable about it. But how should it follow that from his disobedience anyone else should become a sinner? For unless a man becomes a sinner on his own responsibility he will not be found to deserve punishment. Then what does 'sinners' mean here? I think it means those liable to punishment, that is, condemned to death . . .   *hom.* 10 *in Rom.* [on Rom. 5. 19]

That one man should be punished on another's account seems to most people unreasonable. That all should be justified because one man had done right would be more reasonable, and more suited to God.

hom. 16 *in Rom.* [on Rom. 11. 10]

We do baptize infants, although they are not guilty of any sins.

ad neoph.

[From this passage Julian of Eclanum concluded that C. disbelieved in original sin. Augustine argued that *sins* (plural) meant personal sins and quoted passages in which he found, to his satisfaction, the doctrine of original *sin*. (*C. Julianum* 1. 21 f.)]

(b) Grace

God waits for the chances we give him to show his great generosity. Let us not then through idleness deprive ourselves of his gifts; but let us hasten with eagerness to get started on the road to virtue, that we may avail ourselves of help from above and be able to reach our destination. For it is not possible to do anything really good, unless we enjoy the benefit of the decisive influence from above.   *hom.* 25 *in Gen.* 1

(c) Free Will

Our choice shows great variability, choosing now the one, now the other. It has a bent towards evil. . . . Grace does not anticipate our wills, so as not to injure our freedom of decision. But when we choose, it brings us much assistance. . . . God calls us, but he waits for us to come to him of our own will and choice. Then, when we come to him, he affords us every help.　　　　　*hom.* 12 *in Heb.* [on Heb. 7. 2, 3]

II. The Person of Christ

(a) *Co-eternal with the Father*

Someone may ask, 'How can Christ be a Son, without being younger than the Father: for anything which derives its being must be later than its source?' We answer that such arguments suppose a human context . . . while we are discussing the nature of God. . . . Come now, does the sun's radiance proceed from the sun's own substance, or from elsewhere? Any sensible person is bound to acknowledge that it proceeds from the sun's own substance. But although the radiance proceeds from the sun, we cannot assert that it is later in time than the substance of that body, for the sun has never appeared without its rays. . . . Why then do you not believe this to be so in the case of the invisible and ineffable nature? . . . That is why Paul calls him the *Brightness*;[1] thus showing his derived existence, and his co-eternity. Moreover, were not all the ages, and every measure of time, created by him? . . . Therefore there is no interval of time between Son and Father. If so, then the Son cannot be 'after', but co-eternal; since 'before' and 'after' are ideas which imply time . . .　　　*hom.* 4 *in Jo.* 1

(b) *The Union of Word and Flesh.*

By a union and conjunction God the Word and the flesh are a unity: there is no confusion or annihilation of substances, but an ineffable and incomprehensible union.　　　　　*hom.* 11 *in Jo.* 2

From the words 'He reduced himself to nothing'[2] you must not suppose a change or transfiguration, or any kind of annihilation. While he remained what he was, he assumed what he was not: though he became flesh he remained God, in that he was the Word. In his flesh he was like a man: hence 'in shape like a man'. His nature did not alter: there was no confusion. . . . The phrases, 'he became', 'he assumed', are never used to govern 'godhead'; . . . but they are used to govern

[1] Heb. 1. 3.　　[2] Phil. 2. 7.

'manhood'. The latter he 'became', and he 'assumed': the former was always his. We must make no confusion, nor admit separation. One God; one Christ, the Son of God. But when I say 'one', I refer to a union, not a confusion: one nature is not transformed into the other, but is united with it. *hom. 7 in Phil.* [on Phil. 2. 7]

(c) The Human Experience of Christ

'I [*sc. Christ*] assumed manhood, but never left it unmingled with the divine activity. I have acted now as man, now as God, thus showing my [*human*] nature and at the same time supporting faith in the incarnation:[1] teaching that the humbler things are to be attributed to the manhood, the nobler to the Godhead, and by this unequal mixture of actions explaining the unequal union of the natures. By control over human experiences I showed that my sufferings were voluntary. As God, I restrained nature, and endured a forty-day fast: as man, I was hungry and weary. As God, I calmed the fury of the sea: as man, I was tested by the devil. As God, I cast out devils; as man, I am going to suffer on man's behalf.' *in quatrid. Laz. 1*

Thus, in saying, 'If possible, let this cup pass away from me' and, 'Not as I will, but as thou wilt',[2] he is merely demonstrating that he is really clothed with flesh which is afraid of death: for it is characteristic of the flesh to be afraid of death, and to shrink from it in horror. And so sometimes he leaves the flesh deprived and stripped of his own activity, so that, by showing its weakness, he may help men to believe in the reality of his physical nature: while sometimes he hides this very weakness so that you may learn that he is not a mere man. . . . As God, he foreknows the future: as man, he trembles.

in eos qui ad syn. 6

III. The Work of Christ

(a) The Devil Defeated

'Now is the judgement of this world: now the prince of this world will be cast out.'

It is as if he said, 'There will be a trial, and justice will be done. How will it be done? The devil put to death the first man; for that man

---

[1] 'the economy'; cf. p. 134.　[2] Matt. 26. 39

was guilty of sin, and it was "through sin that death came on the scene".[1] But in me he did not find sin. Why then did he assail me, and hand me over to death? Why did he put into the soul of Judas the resolve to bring about my death?' Do not tell me now that God had so ordained it; for the fulfilment of God's plan does not belong to the devil, but to God's own wisdom: let us observe the treatment of the Evil One. How then is 'the world to be judged in me?' It is as if the devil was being examined before a court in session. 'Very well. You put them all to death because you found them guilty of sin: but why did you put the Christ to death? Is it not obvious that you acted unjustly? Therefore all the world shall be acquitted through him.'

Let me illustrate this by an example. Imagine a violent tyrant who afflicts with untold sufferings all who fall into his power: If he were to encounter a king, or a king's son, and killed him unjustly, his death would be able to extend acquittal to the others also. Or let us suppose that a man is collecting his debts: he beats his debtors and flings them into prison. Then suppose that with the same madness he imprisons one who owes him nothing. Such a man will pay the penalty for what he did to the debtors: for the innocent man will bring him to destruction. That is the situation in the case of the Son. The devil will be punished for what he has done to you, as a result of what he had the effrontery to do to Christ.   *hom. 67 in Jo.* 2 [on John 12. 31]

(b) Redemption

We have been freed from punishment, have put away all wickedness; we have been re-born from above; our old human nature has been buried and we have risen again; we have been renamed, sanctified, adopted as sons; we have been justified and have become brothers of the Only-begotten, made co-heirs with him and of the same body; we are counted as his flesh, and are united with him as a body to its head. That is what Paul calls the 'abundance of grace',[2] showing that we have received not only a medicine adequate to deal with our hurt, but also health and beauty, honour, glory, and rank far surpassing our nature. Each of those by itself would have been able to destroy death: but when all those join together, as we see, then death is utterly annihilated, and no trace or shadow of him is left. . . . For Christ paid far more than the death we owed, as much more as the boundless ocean exceeds a tiny drop of water.   *hom.* 10 *in Rom.*

[1] Rom. 5. 12.   [2] Rom. 5. 17.

(c) *Sacrifice*

'Thus Christ also was once offered.'[1] By whom? By himself, to be sure. Here the author shows that he is not only a priest, but also victim and sacrifice. Then he gives the reason for his being offered: 'Offered once to bear the sins of many'. Why 'many' and not 'all'? Because all did not believe. He, for his part, did indeed die for all, to save all; for his death was equivalent to the death of all. *hom.* 17 *in Heb.*

IV. The Eucharist

(a) *The Consecration*

Christ is now also present. He who adorned that table [*of the Last Supper*] is he who now also adorns this. It is not man who makes the gift of the oblation to become the body and blood of Christ, but Christ himself, who was crucified for us. The priest stands, fulfilling the original pattern, and speaks those words; but the power and grace come from God. 'This is my body', he says. This statement transforms[2] the oblations: and as the command, 'increase and multiply', spoken once, extends through all time, and gives to one human nature the power of reproduction; so the statement, 'This is my body', uttered once, makes complete the sacrifice at every table in the churches from that time until now, and even till Christ's coming. *de prod. Jud.* 1. 6

He who did this at the Supper is the same who now performs the act. We rank as ministers: it is he who consecrates and transmutes[3] [*the oblations*]. *hom.* 82 *in Matt.*

(b) *The Epiclesis*

When the priest stands before the Table, holding up his hands to heaven, and invokes the Holy Spirit to come and touch the elements, there is a great silence, a great stillness. When the Spirit gives his grace, when he descends, when he touches the elements, when you see the sacrifice of the lamb completed; do you then indulge in uproar, riot, quarrelling or abuse? *de coemet.* 3

[1] Heb. 9. 28. [2] μεταρρυθμίζει. [3] μετασκευάζει.

(c) The one Sacrifice

We offer every day, making a memorial of his death. This is one sacrifice, not many. And why? Because it was offered once. It resembles in this the sacrifice which was taken into the Holy of Holies. This [Jewish] sacrifice is a type of that sacrifice [of Christ]: We always offer the same person . . . the same oblation: therefore it is one sacrifice. . . . By the same token, the offering of the sacrifice in many places does not, of course, mean that there are many Christs. Christ is everywhere one, entire in this place and in that, one body . . . and so, one sacrifice. Our High Priest is he who offered the sacrifice for our purification. We offer now what was offered then, an inexhaustible offering. . . . We offer the same sacrifice: or rather we make a memorial of that sacrifice.   *hom.* 17 *in Heb.* 3

We have our victim, our priest, our sacrifice, in heaven. Then let us offer such sacrifices as can be offered on that altar . . . 'our reasonable service',[1] the oblation made through the soul, 'through the spirit'; gentleness, moderation, patience, endurance, humility, and the like; things which are independent of material vehicles and particular places.   *hom.* 11 *in Heb.* 2

(d) The Sacramental Presence

The Magi worshipped this body even when it lay in a manger. Those heathen foreigners left home and country and went on a long journey, and came and worshipped him with fear and great trembling. We are citizens of heaven; let us imitate those foreigners. . . . For you behold him not in a manger, but on an altar; not with a woman holding him, but with a priest standing before him: with the Spirit descending with great bounty upon the oblations.   *hom.* 24 *in* 1 *Cor.*

I would give up my own life rather than grant the reception of the blood of the Lord unworthily: I would shed my own blood rather than wrongfully grant reception of blood so awesome.

hom. 82 *in Matt.*

(e) Realism

What the Lord did not endure on the cross [*the breaking of his legs*] he submits to now in his sacrifice for his love of you: he permits himself

[1] Rom. 12. 1.

to be broken in pieces that all may be filled. . . . What is in the chalice is the same as that which flowed from Christ's side. What is the bread? Christ's body. *hom. 24 in 1 Cor.*

Not only ought we to see the Lord: we ought to take him in our hands, eat him, put our teeth into his flesh, and unite ourselves with him in the closest union. *hom. 46 in Jo.*

V. The Priesthood

The office of the priesthood is performed on earth, but it ranks among the heavenly things. And with good reason; for this ministry was set up not by an angel, or an archangel, or by any created power, but by the Paraclete himself. . . . He commanded that men who are still in the flesh should imitate the actions of angels. Therefore the priest ought to be as pure as if he stood among those Powers in heaven itself. . . . When you see the Lord offered there in sacrifice, and the priest standing and praying, and all being reddened by the precious blood, do you feel that you are still standing among men, on earth? Do you not rather feel transported straightway into heaven? . . . Imagine the scene when Elias stands with the immense throng surrounding him, the victim laid on the altar, and everywhere is stillness and profound silence. The prophet stands alone and prays: and immediately the fire comes down from heaven upon the altar. Then change the scene to the sacrifice which is now offered, and you will see a wonder; rather, something beyond admiration. For the priest as he stands there brings down not fire, but the Holy Spirit. His long prayer is not that fire may come down from heaven to consume the oblation, but that grace may descend upon the sacrifice, and through that sacrifice kindle the souls of all, to make them brighter than silver which has been tried in the fire. . . .

You will easily realize to what dignity the grace of the Holy Spirit has raised priests, if you consider how great a matter it is for a man yet clothed in flesh and blood to approach that pure and blessed nature. For it is by priests that these things are accomplished, and others of no less importance, that concern our redemption and salvation. For men who inhabit the earth and spend their lives there have been entrusted with responsibility for heavenly things. They have received a power which God did not give to angels or archangels. For it was not said to them: 'Whatever you bind on earth will be bound in heaven . . .' [Matt. 18. 18]. Earthly rulers have the power to bind; but they only bind the body. This bond extends to the soul itself, and passes on through the heavens: for what priests do on earth God confirms on high: the Lord ratifies the decision of his servants. What is given to them is nothing less than a heavenly authority. 'If you forgive man's sins, they are forgiven . . .' [John 20. 23]. 'What greater authority could there be? 'The Father has entrusted all judgement to the Son':[1] and here I see the Son giving it all into the hands of his priests.   *de sacerd.* 3, 4

[1] John 5. 22.

Ambrose

I. Man and Sin

(a) Original Righteousness

When Adam was in paradise, he was a heavenly being.

in Ps. 118. 15, 36

He was supremely happy, breathing ethereal air, and knowing nothing of the cares and tedium of this life. in Ps. 118. 4, 5

He was in the sight of God; he flourished in paradise; he was resplendent with celestial grace; he talked with God. in Ps. 43. 75

(b) Original Sin—'Seminal identity'

We all sinned in the first man, and by natural inheritance an inheritance of guilt has been transferred from one man into all. . . . Adam was in each one of us: for in him human nature [*condicio humana*] sinned, because through one man sin passed over into all. apol. Dav. 2. 12, 71

Adam existed; and in him we all existed: Adam perished, and in him all perished. in ev. Luc. 7. 234

I fell in Adam; I was expelled from paradise in Adam: I died in Adam. How can God recall me unless it is in Adam that he finds me? So that I am justified in Christ, as I became subject to guilt, in debt to death, in Adam. de excess. frat. Sat. 2. 6

(c) Inherited Guilt

Before we are born, we are defiled by a contagion; before we enjoy the light, we receive the injury of our very birth. We are 'conceived in wickedness'[1] (it is not clearly stated whether they are our sins, or the sins of our parents), and each one's mother gives birth to him 'in sins'. And here it is not expressly stated whether it is in her own sins that the mother gives birth or whether there are already some sins of the child who is being born. It may be that both are meant. Conception

[1] Ps. 51. 5 (50. 7.)

is not untainted by wickedness, since the parents do not escape the fall:
and not even a day-old child is without sin.   *apol. Dav.* 1. 76

If that first man, who was placed in paradise, who talked with God,
could fall so easily, though he was created from virgin earth . . . not
yet polluted by crime and shame, when our flesh was not yet condemned by the curse of a guilty posterity; how much more easily
thereafter has the slippery path to sin brought a headlong descent to
humanity, when mankind has deteriorated through successive generations.   *ep.* 45. 13

Peter was clean, but he needed foot-washing: for he had inherited,
from the first man, the sin which began when the serpent tripped him
by his feet and persuaded him to transgress. Therefore his foot is
washed, that hereditary sins may be removed: for our personal sins
are removed by baptism.   *de myst.* 32

'He who washes does not need to wash again, only wash his feet.'[1]
Why? Because in baptism all guilt is washed away. Therefore guilt
departs. But because Adam was tripped by the devil, and his feet
were drenched with poison, you wash your feet so that an additional
defence of sanctification should be given in that part where the devil
made his attack; so that afterwards the devil may not be able to trip you.
You wash your feet, to wash away the serpent's poison.   *de sacr.* 3. 7

II. The Person of Christ

(a) *The Two Natures*

Let there be an end of useless disputes about words, for the Kingdom of
God, as Scripture says, does not consist in persuasive arguments but in
clear demonstration of power.[2] Let us observe the distinction between
the divinity and the flesh. It is the one and the same Son of God who
speaks in both, for both natures are present in one and the same subject.
But though it is the same person who speaks, he does not always speak
in the same way. In him you may see at one time the glory of God,
at another the feelings of man.   *de fid.* 2. 77

When the Scripture has set out, as I said above, the twin substance in
Christ, so that you may understand both the substance of divinity
[1] John 13. 9.   [2] Cf. 1 Cor. 2. 4.

and the substance of flesh, it begins in this place [sc. John 1. 30, 'A man
is coming after me, who came into being before me'] with the flesh. For in
Holy Scripture there is no consistent rule: sometimes we begin with
Christ's divinity and descend to the mystery [sacramenta] of his incarnation; sometimes the starting-point is the humility of the incarnation,
and we rise up to the glory of the godhead. . . . Here the writer
begins with the Lord's incarnation, and he is to proceed to speak of his
divinity; not in such a way as to confuse the human and divine elements,
but to distinguish them.   de fid. 3. 65

(b) 'Communicatio Idiomatum'

When we read that 'the Lord of majesty was crucified',[1] we must not
imagine him crucified in respect of his majesty. It is because he is both
God and man (God in virtue of his divinity, man in virtue of his taking
flesh upon him) that Jesus Christ, the Lord of majesty, is said to be
crucified: for, since he partook of both natures, the human and the
divine, he underwent his suffering in the nature of man, so that without
distinction he who suffered may be called, 'the Lord of glory', and he
who descended from heaven may be called, in the scriptural phrase,
'the Son of man'.   de fid. 2. 58

(c) The Human Soul in Christ

I therefore ask on what principle some men assume that a soul was not
taken by the Lord Jesus. Is it because of a fear that Christ might slip
through having human sensuality? It is certainly said that the lust of the
flesh is in conflict with the law of the mind.[2] But the author of this
saying is far from supposing that Christ could have been brought
into the bonds of sin by the law of the flesh. In fact, he himself believed
that he could be helped by Christ, when he was in the turmoil of
human frailty. He says: 'Unhappy man that I am! Who will free me
from the body of this death? Thanks be to God through Jesus Christ our
Lord.'[3] . . . When he took upon him man's flesh, it follows that he took
the perfection and fullness of incarnation: for there was no imperfection
in Christ. And so he took flesh, to bring flesh to life: he assumed a soul;
but it was a perfect, rational, and human soul which he assumed and
took. For who can deny that he took a soul, when he himself says:
'I lay down my soul for my sheep'.   de inc. dom. sacr. 64–6

[1] 1 Cor. 2. 8.   [2] Cf. Rom. 7. 23.   [3] Rom. 7. 24 f.

God the Word did not take the place of the rational soul, capable of understanding, in the flesh that was his own. God the Word took on him a rational soul, capable of understanding; a human soul, of the same substance as ours. He took flesh like ours, of the same substance as our flesh. He was indeed a perfect man, but without any stain of sin.

de inc. dom. sacr. 76

III. The Work of Christ

(a) *The Sinless Victim*

Jesus approached the snares, to set Adam free: he came to liberate what had perished. We were all held in the toils; no one could rescue another, for no one could deliver himself. What was needed was one who was not held by the bonds incurred by the sins of human generation; one who had not been caught by avarice, or enslaved by deceit. Jesus alone was that one; for when he encompassed himself with the bonds of this flesh, he was not caught, nor was he ensnared. Rather he broke the bonds and loosed them, and, looking out through the snares, and rising up above the toils, he called to himself the Church, so that the Church also might learn how to escape being held by the bonds. In fact, so far was he from avoiding the bonds that he even submitted to death for our sake. Yet he was not made death's slave; he was 'free among the dead'[1] free, because he had the power to abolish death . . .

in Ps. 118. 6 22

The Devil Deceived

[1 *Cor.* 2. 7 f.] 'If they had known, they would not have crucified the Lord of glory'; that is, they would never have accomplished my redemption through the death of the Lord. Thus he deceived the powers for us: he deceived so that he might conquer. He deceived the Devil when he was tested, when he was questioned, when he was called the Son of God, so that he should on no occasion admit his own divinity. Above all, he deceived the 'princes of the world': for the Devil, though for a time he doubted, when he said: 'If you are the Son of God, throw yourself down';[2] still, in the end, he failed to recognize him, and 'departed from him'. The demons recognized him; for they said: 'What have we to do with you, Son of God?'[3] . . . For the wickedness of

[1] Ps. 88. 5.   [2] Matt. 4. 6.   [3] Matt. 8. 29.

demons easily apprehends even hidden things: but those who are absorbed in this world's trivialities are unable to know divine matters.

exp. ev. Luc. 2. 3

[*Ps.* 56. 7: '*They have fallen into the pit they dug for me*'.] This trick had to be practised on the Devil, by the taking of a body by the Lord Jesus; and the taking of a body that was corruptible and weak: so that it might be crucified, because of its weakness. *exp. ev. Luc.* 4. 12

The Lord's hunger was a holy deception, so that where the Devil was being cautious, fearing a greater power, he might be elated by this show of hunger, and test him as if he were mere man; so that Christ's triumph should not be hindered. *exp. ev. Luc.* 4. 16

(b) Payment of Debt

Let no one be alarmed by the title 'creditor'.[1] We were before under a harsh creditor, who could not be fully paid and satisfied except by the death of the debtor. The Lord Jesus came; he saw us bound by a load of debt. No one could pay his debt with the patrimony of innocence; I could have nothing of my own with which to free myself. He brought to me a new kind of clearance, by which I changed my creditor, since I had no means to pay my debt. It was not nature which made us debtors, but guilt. We contracted heavy debts by our sins, so that we lost our freedom, and became liable: for he is a debtor who has received any of his creditor's money. Sin comes from the devil: the Wicked One has, as it were, these riches in his patrimony. Just as the riches of Christ are virtues, so crimes are the devil's wealth. He had reduced the human race to perpetual captivity by the heavy debt of inherited liability, which our debt-laden originator had transmitted to his posterity by inheritance of debt. The Lord Jesus came; he offered his own death for the death of all; he shed his blood for the blood of all. So we have changed our creditor; we have not escaped. Or rather we have escaped, for the debt remains, but the interest is cancelled. ... Scripture says that he has freely forgiven 'all sins, wiping out the writing of the writ against us'.[2] *ep.* 41. 7, 8

---

[1] Cf. Luke 7. 41. [2] Col. 2. 13 f.

IV. The Trinity

Unity of Father and Son

There is fullness of divinity in the Father, fullness of divinity in the Son:
this is not a diverse divinity, but one and the same. There is no confusion, for it is one thing: no multiplicity, for there is no difference. For,
as Scripture says, there was 'one soul and one heart in all believers';[1]
everyone 'who cleaves to the Lord is one Spirit':[2] the Apostle said, a
man and wife are 'in one flesh';[3] all we men are of one substance, as far
as regards our nature: Scripture says this of human beings, that they,
though many, form a unity.[4] Now there can be no comparison between
human and divine persons; so if there can be such unity in human
beings, how much more are the Father and Son a unity in divinity,
where there is no difference either of substance or will.   *de fid.* 1. 17-19

V. The Baptismal Rite

(i) *The Effeta*

What then did we do on the Saturday [*i.e. Easter Eve*]? The 'opening', to
be sure. Those mysteries [*sacramental acts*] of opening were performed
when the priest touched your ears and nostrils. What does it signify?
When in the gospel a deaf-mute was presented to our Lord Jesus Christ,
he touched his ears and mouth . . . and said 'Effetha' a Hebrew word
meaning 'be opened'.[5] The reason why the priest touched your ears was
so that they might be opened to the discourse and address of the priest.

(ii) *The Unction at the Font*

We came to the font: you entered; you were anointed . . . A levite
[*i.e. a deacon*] met you, and a presbyter [*i.e. a priest*]. You were anointed
as an athlete of Christ, about to wrestle in this world's contest.

(iii) *The Renunciations*

He[6] asked you, 'Do you renounce the devil and his works?' What did
you reply? 'I renounce.' 'Do you renounce the world and its pleasures?'

---

[1] Acts 4. 32.   [2] 1 Cor. 6. 17.   [3] 1 Cor. 6. 16; Eph. 5. 31; Gen. 2. 24.   [4] Acts 17. 26.
[5] Mark 7.   [6] According to *de myst* 3. 8, the questions were put by the bishop, who also
performed the consecration.

What did you reply? 'I renounce.' Remember what you said, and never let the terms of your bond slip from your mind.   *de sacr.* I. 2, 4, 5

(iv) *The Blessing of the Water*

. . . The customary form of baptism prescribes that the font should first be consecrated, and then the person to be baptized should descend. As soon as the priest enters, he performs an exorcism over the created element of water; after that, he offers an invocation and a prayer, that the font may be hallowed and the presence of the eternal Trinity[1] may be there.   *de sacr.* I. 18

The priest comes, and he says a prayer at the font. He invokes the name of the Father, the presence of the Son and of the Holy Spirit. He uses heavenly words: heavenly, because they are Christ's words, who said that we should 'baptize in the name of the Father and Son and Holy Spirit.'[2]   *de sacr.* 2. 14

(v) *The Baptism*

You came to the font; you went down into it; you watched the high priest; you saw the levites and the presbyter in the font.   *de sacr.* 2. 16

You were asked: 'Do you believe in God the Father Almighty?' You said; 'I believe', and you dipped; that is, you were buried. Again you were asked: 'Do you believe in our Lord Jesus Christ, and in his cross?' You said: 'I believe', and you dipped, therefore you were 'buried with Christ'.[3] . . . A third time you were asked: 'Do you believe also in the Holy Spirit?' You said: 'I believe', and you dipped for the third time, so that the threefold confession might cancel the fall of your earlier life.
                                                            de sacr. 2. 20

(vi) *The Unction*

You came to the priest. What did he say to you? 'God the Father Almighty, who has given you new birth by water and the Holy Spirit, and has forgiven you and your sins, himself anoint you to eternal life.' See to what you have been anointed—'to eternal life'.

You received ointment on the head. . . . For wisdom is lifeless without grace: but when it has received grace, then it begins to have its full effect.   *de sacr.* 2. 24

---

[1] *de myst.*, 3. 14 adds the signing of the water with the cross.   [2] Matt. 28. 19.   [3] Rom. 6. 4.

(vii) *Washing of the Feet*

You came up from the font. What followed? The priest was girded up
(for, though presbyters also performed the service, it is begun by the
priest) and washed your feet. We are well aware that the Roman church
has not this custom . . . perhaps on account of large numbers. . . . But
there are some who say . . . that this should not be done in a sacrament,
at baptism, in the regeneration. . . . Learn, then, that it is a sacrament,
and an act of sanctification: 'Unless I wash your feet, you will have no
share with me'.[1] I say this, not to criticize others, but to commend my
own usage. In general, I desire to follow the Roman church; and yet we
also have some discrimination: and therefore we have the advantage
of retaining a usage which has also been retained elsewhere.

de sacr. 3. 4, 5

(viii) *The Spiritual Seal*

Then follows the spiritual seal. . . . After the font, it remains for the
'perfecting' to take place, when, at the invocation of the priest, the
Holy Spirit is poured upon you 'the spirit of wisdom and understanding
the spirit of counsel and strength, the spirit of knowledge and godliness,
the spirit of holy fear'.[2]   *de sacr.* 3. 8

VI. The Eucharist

(a) *'Transfiguration' of the Elements*

He added: 'For my flesh is truly food, and my blood is truly drink'.[3]
You hear of 'flesh' and 'blood': you recognize the sacraments of the
Lord's death. . . . Now we, whenever we take the sacraments, which
through the mystery of the sacred prayer are transfigured into his flesh
and blood, 'proclaim the Lord's death'.[4]   *de fid.* 4. 125

(b) *The Symbol*

Do you wish to know how it is consecrated by heavenly words? Hear
what those words are—the priest says: 'Make for us this oblation rati-
fied, reasonable, acceptable, because it is the figure of the body and
blood of our Lord Jesus Christ.'   *de sacr.* 4. 21

First of all, I told you about the saying of Christ, whose effect is to
change and convert the established kinds of nature. Then came the

[1] John 13. 8.   [2] Cf. Isa. 11. 2 f.   [3] John 6. 56.   [4] 1 Cor. 11. 26.

saying of Christ, that he gave his flesh to be eaten, and his blood to be drunk. His disciples could not stand this, and they turned away from him. Only Peter said: 'You have the words of eternal life; how can I take myself away from you?'¹ And so, to prevent others from saying that they are going away, because of a horror of actual blood, and so that the grace of redemption should continue, for that reason you receive the sacrament in a similitude, to be sure, but you obtain the grace and virtue of the reality. 'I am', he says, 'the living bread who came down from heaven.'² But the flesh did not come down from heaven; that is to say, he took flesh on earth from a virgin. How, then, did bread come down from heaven—and bread that is 'living bread'? Because our Lord Jesus Christ shares both in divinity and in body: and you, who receive the flesh, partake of his divine substance in that food.

de sacr. 6. 3, 4

(c) The Miracle

[*A. has spoken of the nature-miracles of Moses and Elisha.*] Thus we observe that grace is more powerful in its operation than nature: and yet it is only the grace of a prophet's blessing that we have instanced. But if a human blessing had the power to effect a change in nature, what are we to say of the divine consecration, where the very words of the Lord and Saviour are in operation? For the sacrament which you receive is effected by the words of Christ. Now if the words of Elijah had the power to call down fire from heaven,³ will not the words of Christ have power to change the character [*species*] of the elements? You have read, in the account of the creation of the universe: 'He himself spoke, and they were made: he commanded, and they were created'.⁴ The words of Christ, then, could make out of nothing that which did not exist; can it not change things which do exist into what they are not? For to give things their original natures is more marvellous than to change their natures. But why do we use arguments? Let us make use of appropriate examples, and by the mysteries [*sacramenta*] of the incarnation let us establish the truth of the mystery [*sacramenti*]. When the Lord Jesus was born of Mary did that birth have the normal, natural antecedent? In the usual order of things, birth results from the union of man and woman. It is clear, then, that the Virgin gave birth outside the order of nature. And this body which we bring about by consecration is from the Virgin. Why do you look for the order of nature

¹ John 6. 68. ² John 6. 41. ³ 1 Kings 18. 38. ⁴ Ps. 33. 9.

here, in the case of the body of Christ, when the Lord Jesus himself was born of a virgin outside the natural order? It was certainly the genuine flesh of Christ that was crucified, that was buried: then surely the sacrament is the sacrament of that flesh. The Lord Jesus himself proclaims, 'This is my body'. Before the blessing of the heavenly words something of another character [*alia species*] is spoken of; after consecration it is designated [*significatur*] 'body'. He himself speaks of his blood. Before consecration it is spoken of as something else; after consecration it is named 'blood'. And you say 'Amen', that is, 'It is true'. What the mouth speaks, let the mind within confess; what the tongue utters, let the heart feel.   *de myst.* 52–4

(d) The Eucharistic Sacrifice

We have seen the High Priest coming to us; we have seen and heard him offering his blood for us. We priests follow, as well as we can, so that we may offer sacrifice for the people. Though we can claim no merit, we are to be honoured in the sacrifice; for, although Christ is not now visibly offered, yet he is himself offered on earth when the body of Christ is offered. Moreover, it is made clear that he himself offers in us, since it is his words which sanctify the sacrifice which is offered.

in Ps. 38. 25

Here is the shadow and the symbol; there is the reality: the shadow in the Law; the symbol in the Gospel; the reality in Heaven. Formerly a lamb was offered, and a calf; now Christ is offered. But he is offered as man, accepting suffering; and he offers himself as priest, so that he may forgive our sins: here in symbol; in reality there, where he intercedes for us as an advocate before the Father.   *de off.* 1. 238

Jerome

I. Scripture

Apocrypha

[The Canon of Scripture: Five books of Moses (Gen., Ex., Lev., Num., Deut.); the Prophets: Joshua, Judges, Ruth, Kingdoms (2), Kings (2), Isa., Jer., Ezek., the Twelve Prophets; Hagiographa: Job, Ps., Solomon (Prov., Eccl., Song of Songs), Dan., Chron. (2), Ezr. (2), Esther.]

This prologue can be attached, as a kind of helmeted[1] introduction, to all the books which we have translated from Hebrew into Latin, so that we can be sure that anything outside this list is to be classed among the apocrypha. Thus Wisdom, generally entitled 'of Solomon', the book of Jesus son of Sirach, Judith, Tobias [sic], and the Shepherd,[2] are not in the Canon. I found the first book of Maccabees in Hebrew. The second is in Greek, a fact which can also be deduced from the style.

prolog. in Sam. et Mal.

We have the authentic book of Jesus son of Sirach, and another pseud-epigraphic work, entitled the Wisdom of Solomon. I found the first in Hebrew, with the title, 'Parables', not Ecclesiasticus, as in Latin versions. . . . The second finds no place in Hebrew texts, and its style is redolent of Greek eloquence: a number of ancient writers assert that it is a work of Philo Judaeus.[3] Therefore, just as the Church reads Judith, Tobit, and the books of Maccabees, but does not admit them to the canon of Scripture; so let the Church read these two volumes for the edification of the people, but not to support the authority of ecclesiastical doctrines.

praef. in lib. Sal.

II. Man

Freedom and Grace

It is for us to make a beginning: it is for God to bring it to fulfilment.

c. Pel. 3. 1

[1] Presumably so called as prepared to defend the authenticity of the contents. [2] 'The Shepherd' of Hermas, a second-century work widely accepted as Scripture in the second and third centuries, especially in the E. In Codex Sinaiticus it is included, with the Epistle of Barnabas, after the N.T. It was rejected by the Muratorian Canon, and little regarded in the E. after the fourth century. [3] Of Alexandria, c. 20 B.C.–c. A.D. 50, philosopher and biblical exegete.

It is for God to call: it is for us to believe.   *in Isa.* 49. 4

It is for us to will, or to refuse: but this ability is only ours by God's mercy.   *ep.* 130. 12

The Saviour in his passion was strengthened by an angel, and yet my friend Critobulus does not need God's help, since he has the power of free will. . . . 'Why', he said, 'are you asleep? Get up and pray, that you may not come into temptation.'¹ According to you, he should have said: 'Why are you asleep? Get up and resist, for you have free will, and when once this power has been given you by God, you need no help from anyone. If you do this, you will not come into temptation.'
        c. Pel. 2. 16

As I said at the start, it has been placed in our power to sin, or not to sin, and to hold out our hand either to the good or the bad, so that the will may be kept free. But this freedom is proportional to the context and the situation, and to the frail condition of man. Perpetual sinlessness is reserved for God alone, and for him who was the Word made flesh, who did not suffer the disabilities and sins of the flesh. Because I have the ability for a short time you cannot force me to have that ability continually. I have the ability to fast, to keep vigil, to walk, to read, to sing psalms, to sit, to sleep. But can I do so for ever?   *c. Pel.* 3. 12

God has, to be sure, commanded only what is possible. I concede that: but not every one of us can achieve all these possibilities.   *c. Pel.* 1. 23

III. The Church

(a) *The Roman Primacy*

I follow no one as supreme leader except Christ only; hence I attach myself in communion with your Beatitude, that is, with the see of Peter. I know that the Church is built upon this rock. Whoever eats a [passover] lamb outside this house,² is profane. Anyone who is not in Noah's ark will perish when the flood prevails.   *ep.* 15 [*ad Damasum*³]

¹ Matt. 26. 41. ² Cf. Ex. 12. 46. ³ Pope, 366–84; commissioned Jerome to undertake the Vulgate version of the Bible.

(b) The Episcopate

Hence a presbyter is the same as a bishop, and before ambition came into religion, by the prompting of the devil, and people began to say: 'I belong to Paul: I to Apollo; I to Cephas',[1] the churches were governed by the direction of presbyters, acting as a body. But when each presbyter began to suppose that those whom he had baptized belonged to him, rather than to Christ, it was decreed in the whole Church that one of the presbyters should be chosen to preside over the others, and that the whole responsibility for the Church should devolve on him, so that the seeds of schism should be removed. [*J.* cites *Phil.* I. 1, 2; *Acts* 20. 17, 28; 1 *Pet.* 5. 1, 2.].   *in ep. ad Tit.* 1. 1, 5

IV. The Eucharist

After the completion of the passover which was a 'type', and after he, with his apostles, had eaten the meat of the lamb, he took bread, which 'strengthens man's heart',[2] and proceeded to the true sacrament of the passover; so that, as Melchisedech, priest of God the Highest, offered bread and wine,[3] and thus prefigured him, Christ himself should represent his offering in the reality of his body and blood.   *in Matt.* 26. 26

The blood and flesh of Christ are to be understood in two ways. There is that spiritual and divine flesh and blood, of which he himself said: 'My flesh is really food, and my blood is really drink'; and: 'Unless you eat my flesh and drink my blood, you will not have eternal life'.[4] There is also the flesh which was crucified, and the blood which was poured out under the soldier's spear. A corresponding distinction is to be understood, in the case of his saints, between the flesh which is to 'see the salvation of God',[5] and the flesh and blood which 'cannot possess the Kingdom of God'.[6]   *in Eph.* 1. 7

V. The Last Things

Those who wish the punishments to come to an end eventually, and the torments to have a limit, even if after long ages, call upon this evidence:

---

[1] 1 Cor. 1. 12.   [2] Ps. 104. 15.   [3] Gen. 14. 18.   [4] John 6. 56.   [5] Isa. 52. 10.
[6] 1 Cor. 6. 19.

'When the full number of the nations have entered, then all Israel will be saved'.[1] ... We believe that there will be eternal torments for the devil, for all deniers of God and the impious, who have 'said in their heart: God does not exist';[2] while in the case of sinners, and the impious who are yet Christians, whose deeds are to be tested and purified in the fire,[3] we think that the sentence of the judge will be moderate, and mingled with clemency.   *in Isa.* 66. 24

There are many who say that there will not be physical punishments for sins, and that torments will not be applied externally, but that the sin itself, and the consciousness of wrong-doing act as punishment, while 'the worm' in the heart 'does not die',[4] and the 'fire' is kindled in the mind, like a fever, which does not torment the sick man externally, but merely seizes on the body and administers punishment, without applying any tortures from outside. Paul called such persuasive but deceptive arguments 'empty and idle words'.[5] They seem to have an attraction, and they are soothing notions for sinners; but in fact, by giving them false confidence, they convey them more surely to eternal punishment.   *in Eph.* 3. 56

[1] Rom. 11. 29 f.   [2] Ps. 13. 1.   [3] Cf. 1 Cor. 3. 13.   [4] Mark 9. 48.   [5] Eph. 5. 6.

Augustine of Hippo

I. God

(a) The Divine Government

[*In the heavenly realm.*] The will of God, 'who makes spirits [winds] his messengers and flaming fire his servants'[1] ... presiding, as it were, in the lofty and holy and secret dwelling-place, as in its own house and temple, diffuses itself from thence through all things by certain ordered motions of created things, motions first spiritual, then corporeal; and employs all things to the fulfilment of the unalterable decision of its intention, things incorporeal or corporeal, spirits rational or irrational, those who, through the grace of God, are good, or those who, through their own choice, are evil. But as the grosser and inferior bodies are ruled in a certain order by the subtler and more powerful; so all bodies are governed by the spirit of life, and the spirit of irrational life by the rational spirit of life, and the rational spirit of life which is a renegade and a sinner by the rational spirit of life which is devout and righteous, and that spirit by God himself. So the whole creation is governed by its Creator, from whom and by whom and in whom it was founded and established. And thus the will of God is the first and supreme cause of all corporal appearances and motions. For nothing happens in the visible and sensible sphere which is not ordered, or permitted, from the inner, invisible and intelligible, court of the most high Emperor, in this vast and illimitable commonwealth of the whole creation, according to the inexpressible justice of his rewards and punishments, graces and retributions.   *de trin.* 3. 9

(b) Substance—Essence

God is without doubt a substance, or better, an essence, which the Greeks call *ousia* ... 'Essence' is derived from *esse*, 'to be'; and who *is* more fully than he who said to his servant Moses 'I am HE WHO is'?[2] Other essences, or substances, are capable of 'accidents', which produce in them change in some degree; but no 'accident' of this kind can happen to God: therefore there is one unchangeable substance, or essence, namely God, to whom 'being' (from which 'essence' is derived) is most fully and truly

[1] Ps. 104. 4.   [2] Ex. 3. 14.

applicable. Anything that changes does not preserve its being: anything capable of change, even if it remains unchanged, can cease to be what it was; and thus only that which not only does not change but is utterly incapable of change deserves the title of 'being' in the truest sense, without qualification.   *de trin.* 5. 3

Is it right to speak of God as 'subsisting'? Subsistence is correctly ascribed to things which are the subjects of accidents, as colour or shape are attributes of a body. The body subsists, and is therefore a substance; but attributes are attached to a subsistent body, as their substratum; they are not substances, but exist *in* a substance. Thus, if that particular colour, or that particular shape, disappears, their disappearance does not mean that the body ceases to exist, since its existence does not involve the retention of a particular shape or colour: therefore things which are changeable and which are not simple are rightly described as substances. Now, if God subsists, and can rightly be described as a substance, then some attribute or attributes have him as their subject, and he is not simple, since his existence entails that certain external attributes can be applied to him, as 'great', 'almighty', 'good', and other such attributes as may fittingly be applied to God. But it is unthinkable that God should be the substratum of his goodness; that his goodness is not a substance, or rather essence; that God *is* not his goodness, but that goodness is related to him as accident to subject. Thus it is clear that the title of 'substance' is improperly applied to God: and so this more familiar term should be interpreted as 'essence'. 'Essence' is the true and proper term: so much so that perhaps it ought only to be applied to God; for God alone *is* in the true and full sense, because he is unchangeable.
                                                            de trin. 7. 10

II. Man—Sin—Grace

(a) Pelagius on Grace and Free Will

'I anathematize anyone who denies, either in thought or speech, the necessity of the grace of God, by which "Christ came into this world to save sinners", not only every hour, every moment but also in every act of ours. Let those who try to abolish this grace have eternal punishment for their portion.'   *de grat. Chr.* 1. 2

'We assert free will without denying our perpetual need of the help of God.'   *de grat. Chr.* 1. 36 ·

'We distinguish three elements [in human action], and dispose them, as it were, in a fixed order. In the first place we put the power [*posse*], in the second place the will [*velle*], in the third place the actuality [*esse*]. The power resides in nature, the will in human choice [*arbitrium*], the actuality in realization. The first of these belongs exclusively to God, who has conferred this power on his creatures; the other two are to be attributed to man, because they derive from human choice. Therefore man's praise is in his good will and his good work; or rather it is the praise of man *and* God, who has given the possibility of that good will and good work and always assists that possibility with the help of his grace. Man's power to will the good and to effect it is of God alone. That could exist without the existence of the other two elements; but they could not exist without it. It is open to me not to have a good will or perform a good action; but I cannot avoid having the possibility of good. . . . Our ability to say and think what is good comes comes from him who granted us this power, who also assists it; but right action, speech, and thought depend on us, for it is in our power to misuse those faculties.'   *de grat. Chr.* 1. 5

'God helps us by his teaching and his revelations, when he opens the eyes of our heart; when he shows us the future, lest we should be wholly taken up with the present moment; when he uncovers the snares of the devil; when he enlightens us with the manifold and ineffable gift of heavenly grace.'   *de grat. Chr.* 1. 8

'Let us deserve divine grace, and more easily resist the evil spirit, with the help of the Holy Spirit.'

'While we have within us a free will which is so strong and steadfast to resist sin, a free will which the Creator implanted in human nature universally, we are further strengthened, through his inestimable kindness, by daily help.'

'So that men may more easily fulfil through grace that which they are bidden to do by means of their free will.'   *de grat. Chr.* 1. 28, 29

'There is no congenital evil in us, and we are begotten without fault; and before the exercise of a man's own will there is nothing in him except what God has created.'   *de grat. Chr.* 2. 14

'Man can be without sin, and can keep the commandment of God, if he so wishes. . . . Now we do not say that anyone is to be found who has never in fact sinned throughout his whole life. But when he has turned from his sins, then he can be sinless, through his own effort and the grace of God. He does not become incapable of conversion because of his sin.'   *de gest. Pel.* 20

'I mean by grace that state in which we were created by God with free will.'   *de gest. Pel.* 22

'God wished to bestow on his rational creation the privilege of doing good voluntarily, and the power of free choice, by implanting in man the possibility of choosing either side; and so he gave him, as his own characteristic, the power of being what he wished to be; so that he should be naturally capable of good and evil, that both should be within his power, and that he should incline his will towards one or the other. . . . We have heard and read of many philosophers who have been chaste, patient, self-controlled . . .; we have indeed known them in our own experience. They have spurned worldly honours and delights: they have loved righteousness as much as knowledge. Whence do men who are remote from God acquire those qualities which are pleasing to God? How do they acquire those virtues, except from natural goodness? . . . If men without God show the qualities which God has given them, think what Christians can achieve, since their nature and their life has been trained, through Christ, to a better condition, and they are also helped by the aid of divine grace!

For there is, I say, in our souls a kind of natural sanctity, which presides, as it were, in the citadel of our heart, and exercises judgement between good and bad.'   [*ep. ad. Demetr.*[1]]

(b) Man's First State

(i) The Possibility of Immortality

God created certain beings immortal in the sense of being unable to die: man was created immortal in a different sense, being able not to die, an ability given to him from the Tree of Life, and not from a natural endowment. He was separated from this tree when he had sinned, so that he could die: had he not sinned he would have been able not to die. He was mortal because of the natural state of his animal body; he was immortal through the generosity of his Creator.   *de Gen. ad. litt.* 6. 36

[1] Written by Pelagius in 412/13.

(ii) *Primal Freedom*

The first man had the ability not to sin, not to die, not to desert the good. . . . This was the first freedom of the will, the ability not to sin. The final freedom will be a much greater freedom, the inability to sin. There was at first the *power* of perseverance, the ability not to desert the good; in the end there will be the *happiness* of perseverance, the inability to desert the good. . . . The first man was given the gift of perseverance, not to ensure that he should persevere, but to make it possible that he might persevere by the exercise of his free will.   *de corr. et grat.* 33, 34

God made man upright and therefore, necessarily, of good will; otherwise he would not have been upright, if he had not a good will. Therefore this good will was the work of God, since man was created with it by him. The first evil will, which preceded all his evil acts, was rather a falling away from the work of God to his own works than any particular act.   *de civ. Dei.* 14. 11

(iii) *The Image of God*

The image of the Creator is to be found in the rational or intellectual soul of man, being implanted in the soul's immortality, . . . Although reason or intellect may at times be dormant, may at times show itself small, or at times great, the soul of man cannot but be rational and intellectual. Therefore if it has been created according to God's image in respect that it is able to employ reason and intellect to apprehend God and to behold him, then without doubt . . ., though this image may be so dimmed as almost to cease to be, though it may be obscure and distorted . . ., it never utterly disappears.   *de trin.* 14. 6

(c) *Original Sin*
(i) *Man's Responsibility*

When there is evil will in a man, then acts are done which would not be done if he did not so wish. These acts are voluntary and not necessary failures, and the consequent penalty is just. For the evil is not in the things which occasion our fall, but in the fall itself. The things which cause our fall are not in their own nature evil; but our fall is evil because it is a reversal of the natural order, since it proceeds from the highest level to the lower. Greed is not a fault belonging to money; it belongs to the man with a perverse love of money who abandons justice, which ought to be regarded as incomparably better than riches. . . . Pride is not a fault belonging to the source of power, or the power itself: it belongs to the soul which perversely loves its own power, despising the juster claims of a higher power. Thus if a man perversely sets his heart on any natural good, then, even if he attains it, he himself becomes evil in the attainment of a good, and wretched because deprived of the better.　　　　　　　　　　*de civ. Dei* 12. 8

(ii) *Pride*

The first human beings began to be evil secretly: and so they slipped into open disobedience. For they would not have come to any evil act, had not an evil will preceded: and what could have been the beginning of evil will but pride, since 'pride is the beginning of all sin'?[1] And what is pride but a craving for a perverse elevation, perverse in that it deserts him to whom the soul ought to cleave as its source of life, so as to make itself as it were its own source? This happens when the soul loves itself too much; when it abandons that immutable good, which it ought to love more than itself. This falling-away was voluntary, since if the will had remained steadfast in its love of that higher, immutable good, which gave it light to see it and warmth to love it, it would not have turned away to self-satisfaction, and thus have become so darkened and cold; Eve would not have believed the serpent, nor would Adam have preferred his wife's wish to God's command. . . . The transgression happened because they were already evil; that evil fruit could come only from an evil tree, a tree which had become unnaturally evil through unnatural viciousness of the will. This depravity could only occur in a nature made from nothing. Its existence as nature was due to God's creation: the possibility of failure arose from its creation from nothing. Yet man's failure did not result in his becoming utterly nothing; but his inclination towards himself led to a declension from that state of being which he enjoyed when he adhered to him who supremely is. By deserting God to exist in himself, that is in self-satisfaction, he does not immediately become nothing, but he advances towards nothingness.　　　　　　　　　*de civ. Dei* 14. 13

The grievousness of Adam's fall was in proportion to the loftiness of his position. His nature was such as to be capable of immortality if it had

[1] Ecclus. 10. 13.

refused to sin; his nature was such as to display no strife of flesh against spirit; his nature was such as to show no struggle against vice, not because it surrendered to vice, but because there was no vice in him. ... The sin with which God charged Adam was a sin from which he could have refrained ... and a sin which was far worse than the sins of all other men just because he was so much better than all others. Hence the punishment which straightaway followed his sin was so severe as to make it inevitable that he should die, though it had been in his power to be free from death. ... Now when his happened the whole human race was 'in his loins'.[1] Hence in accordance with the mysterious and powerful natural laws of heredity it followed that those who were in his loins and were to come into this world through the concupiscence of the flesh were condemned with him. ... And so the sons of Adam were infected by the contagion of sin and subjected to the law of death. Though they are infants, incapable of voluntary action, good or bad, yet because of their involvement in him who sinned of his own volition, they derive from him the guilt of sin, and the punishment of death: just as those who are involved in Christ, although they have done nothing of their own volition, receive from him a share in righteousness and the reward of everlasting life. *op. imp. c. Jul.* 6. 22

Julian[2] says, 'If the act of birth derives from the will of God in creation before the commission of sin, whereas the desire of the parents derives from the devil, then holiness will certainly be attributed to birth, while blame attaches to the act of generation. This quite clearly condemns marriage; and therefore such a notion should be removed from the Church's teaching, and we should truly believe that "all things were created through Jesus Christ, and without him nothing was created".[3] This argument assumes that we allege that the devil was responsible for the creation of something substantial in man. The devil encouraged evil, as a sin: he did not create evil, as a part of nature. Man is a part of nature; thus the devil persuaded nature, and perverted it. To inflict a wound is not to create a limb, but to harm it. Now wounds inflicted on our bodies maim our limbs, but they do not harm the virtue by which a man is righteous: but that wound which we call sin affects the very life, the possibility of right living. And the wound inflicted by the devil was far graver and deeper than the familiar sins of man. Hence by that great

[1] Heb. 7. 10.   [2] Pelagian bishop of Eclanum, 416–54, the most powerful critic of Augustine's doctrine of grace.   [3] John 1. 3.

sin of the first man our nature was perverted, becoming not only sinful itself but also productive of sinners. And yet the disease which destroys the power to live a good life is not really a part of nature, but a perversion of nature; just as a bodily infirmity is a perversion, and bodily infirmities of parents are often, though not always, in some way transmitted by inheritance, and appear in the children.

de nupt. et concup. 2. 57

(ii) *The Transmission of Guilt*

This argument is advanced: 'If a sinner begets a sinner, so that the guilt of original sin has to be removed in infancy by the reception of baptism; then it follows that the righteous should beget a righteous offspring.' But it is ineffective; for it assumes that a man begets physically in virtue of his righteousness and not because of the lustful promptings of his body, the 'law of sin' being turned by the 'law of the mind'[1] to serve the purpose of propagation. A man begets because he is still leading the old life among the sons of this world, not because he is advancing towards the new life among the sons of God. For it is the 'sons of this world' who 'beget and are begotten'.[2] And the offspring is of the same kind, since 'what is born of flesh is flesh'.[3] But the righteous are righteous just because they are sons of God; and as sons of God they do not beget by physical means, since they themselves were thus born spiritually, not physically.[4]   *de pecc. mer.* 2. 11

(iii) *'Seminal Identity'*

The Apostle cries, 'Sin entered into the world through one man, and through sin came death, and thus it passed on to all men, for in him all sinned'.[5] Hence it cannot reasonably be asserted that Adam's sin harmed those who did not sin; for the Scripture says, 'All sinned in him'. And those sins are not spoken of as belonging to someone else, as if they did not affect little children: seeing that in Adam all sinned at that time, since all were already united with him by that power to beget them with which his nature was endowed. But those sins are said to be another's in that Adam's descendants were not at that time leading their own lives; however, the life of one man embraces all that was to be in his posterity.   *de pecc. mer.* 3. 14

---

[1] Cf. Rom. 7. 23.   [2] Cf. Luke 20. 34.   [3] John 3. 6.   [4] Cf. John 1. 13.   [5] Rom. 5. 12; ἐφ' ᾧ being rendered 'in quo', as in Vulgate. The Greek almost certainly means 'in as much as' (as EVV).

Although infants do not possess free will, there is no illogicality in calling their original sin voluntary, since it derives from the misused will of the first man, and is theirs as it were by heredity. *retract* 1. 13, 5

(iv) *Guilt and Corruption*

When the Apostle says, 'You have been washed and sanctified',[1] he speaks of a change for the better; bringing, not exemption from concupiscence, which is impossible in this life, but freedom from obedience to it, a thing which can happen in a good life. . . . You are greatly in error in thinking that 'if concupiscence is an evil the baptized person would be exempt from it'. The baptized is exempt from *sin*, not from every evil; or rather, to put it more clearly; he is exempt from the *guilt* of all evils, not from all evils. *c. Jul.* 6. 49

(d) *The Origin of the Soul*

[*A. is writing to Optatus, bishop of Milevis in North Africa.*]
It may be that you fail to discover why or how the souls of infants become sinful, and what it is that compels them, through no wickedness in themselves, to derive from Adam the cause of their condemnation; since you do not believe their souls to have been propagated from that first sinful soul, but to be fresh and innocent when they are confined in that sinful flesh. Nevertheless you should not let yourself be won over too readily to the other opinion, to the belief that their souls are handed on by propagation from the one first soul: it may well be that someone else may be able to discover what you have failed to find, or that you will later succeed in your search. For those who assert that souls are propagated from the one soul which God gave to the first man, and say that they are derived from the parents, may adhere to the view of Tertullian; if so, they contend that souls are not spiritual but corporeal and come into existence from corporeal seeds. And could you have a more perverse statement than that? But it is not surprising that Tertullian should have dreamed such a notion, seeing that he holds that God the creator is himself none other than corporeal.[2]

If this insanity is expelled from the mind and lips of a Christian, then a man who acknowledges the truth that the soul is not body but spirit, and yet is passed on from parents to children, is not entangled in difficulties because the true faith proclaims that all souls contract the original sin which was committed by the first man through the use of his

[1] 1 Cor. 6. 11.   [2] Cf. Tert. *adv. Prax.* 7.

own will; a sin transmitted to all his posterity by generation, and only to be purged by regeneration. This is true of the souls even of infants: the Church does not baptize them for a fictitious remission of sins, but for a genuine remission. The difficulty arises if we begin to examine and discuss the meaning of this statement. It is surprising if any human intelligence can understand how the soul comes into being in the child from the soul of the parent, or is transferred to the child, as a lamp is lit from a lamp, and one light is produced from another, without loss to the source; whether, when a woman conceives, an incorporeal seed of the soul runs from the father into the mother by a separate, secret, and invisible route; or (which is less credible) it is concealed in the corporeal seed. And when seed is emitted without conception, the question arises whether the seed of the soul does not issue; or does it rush back to its source in an instant? Or does it perish? If it perishes, then how can the soul itself be immortal, if its seed is mortal? Does it receive immortality at the moment when it attains the living stage of development, as it receives righteousness when it develops intelligence?[1]   *ep.* 190. 14, 15

[*A. is writing to Jerome.*] Some years ago I wrote some books *On Free Choice*. These had a wide circulation and are in the possession of many at this time. There I put forward four opinions about the incarnation of the soul: (1) That all souls are generated from the soul given to the first man; (2) That a new soul is created for each individual; (3) That souls already existing some where are sent by God into bodies, or (4) glide into bodies of their own will. I thought I ought to deal with these views in such a way as to give free course to my intention of opposing, with all my powers, those who try to blame God for creating a nature endued with its own principle of evil—I mean the Manicheans. . . , I am at a loss to know which of the four opinions to adopt. But whichever is to be adopted it must not clash with the belief, of the truth of which we are convinced, that every soul, even that of a tiny infant, stands in need of liberation from the bond of sin, and that the only liberation comes through 'Jesus Christ, a Christ on the cross[2]. . . [*Jerome is apparently a 'Creationist'.*] Tell me, if souls are individually created at birth, and this creation still goes on, how can infants have in them any sin which makes them need remission of sin by means of the sacrament of Christ? How can

---

[1] 'Traducianism' is the term for the theory that the soul is transmitted by the parents; the less crudely physical belief is often called 'Generationism'. 'Creationism' is the doctrine that each soul is created *de nihilo* at conception or birth.   [2] 1 Cor. 2. 2.

they sin 'in Adam', from whom the sinful flesh has been derived? While if they do not sin, where is the Creator's justice in binding them to another's sin, seeing that they are involved in a mortal organism derived from him, so that condemnation follows unless they receive the help of the Church; for it is not in their power to obtain the aid of baptismal grace. Thousands of souls leave the bodies of children dying without the benefit of the Christian sacrament. Is it equitable that they should be condemned, if they are newly created, with no previous sin? If it was by the will of the Creator that they were separately attached to individuals at birth, since he created them, and bestowed them on those individuals to give them life? If the Creator certainly knew that each of them was destined to leave the body without the baptism of Christ, through no fault of their own? We cannot say that God compels souls to be sinful, or that he punishes the innocent. We cannot deny that souls, even the souls of little children, which leave the body without Christ's sacrament, are bound for condemnation. Tell me, I beg you, how can the view be defended, which holds that all souls do not come into existence from the one soul of the first man, but are separately created for each person, as was his? ... [A. meets certain objections to 'Creationism'.]

But when we come to the punishment of little children, I am bewildered by great perplexities, and I am quite at a loss for an answer. I refer not only to the punishment which results from the condemnation which inevitably falls on them if they depart from the body without the sacrament of Christian grace, but the suffering which takes place before our eyes in this life and brings us sorrow. . . . We are forbidden to say that these things happen without God's knowledge, or that he is powerless to resist what causes these things, or that he causes or permits them unjustly. We rightly say that irrational animals are made to serve the purposes of natures more excellent, even if perverse, as in the gospel we find pigs handed over to the demons for the purpose they desired.[1] Can we rightly say this of human beings? There is a rational soul in that physical organism which is punished with such bitter suffering. God is good; God is just; God is omnipotent: only an utter madman could doubt this. Therefore some just cause must be assigned for terrible suffering of small children . . .

[A. quotes from de lib. arb. 3. 23.] 'God effects some good in correcting adults when they are chastised by the sufferings and the deaths of the

[1] Matt. 8. 31 f.

children who are dear to them.' Why should this not happen, since, when the pain is past, it is as nothing to those to whom it happened? While those on whose account it happened will either be better men if they are corrected by their temporal disasters and decide to live better lives; or else they will have no excuse when they are punished at the future judgement, if they refuse to direct their longing towards eternal life under the stress of this life's pain. And if the hard hearts of adults are softened by the torments of children, if their faith is aroused, and their compassion tested; who knows what ample compensation God has in store for those little children in the secret of his judgements? They have not performed any right actions; but they have endured those sufferings although they have committed no sin . . .

But the question cannot be dismissed as answered unless a reply is given about the children who after the severest torment pass from life without the sacrament of the Christian community. What compensation can be imagined for them, seeing that condemnation is in store for them, over and above their suffering? . . .

If souls are created for each individual at birth, why are they condemned, if they die in infancy without Christ's sacrament? For their condemnation, if they leave the body thus, is testified by Holy Scripture, and by Holy Church. Hence I am ready to accept your view about the creation of new souls if it does not conflict with this fundamental tenet of the faith: if it does conflict, you should abandon it.

ep. 166. 7, 10, 16, 18, 20, 25

[*A. never reached a final position on this question. Shortly before his death he wrote*:] As to the origin of the soul, by which it came into being in the body, whether it derives from the one first-created man, when 'man was made a living soul',[1] or whether a separate act of similar creation gives a soul to each individual, this I did not know then, nor do I know now.   *retr.* I. 1, 3

(e) Concupiscence

If anyone asks, 'How is it that this carnal concupiscence remains in the regenerate man, who has received remission of all sins? Seeing that it is through this same concupiscence that he is conceived, and by reason of it the offspring of even a baptized parent is born carnal.' Or 'Why is concupiscence a sin in the child, if it can exist in the baptized parent

[1] Gen. 2. 7.

without being a sin?' The answer is that carnal concupiscence is not set aside in baptism so that it ceases to exist. but so that it is not reckoned as a sin. But although the guilt of it is removed, the passion itself remains until every infirmity of ours is healed as our 'inward man'[1] is progressively renewed day by day, when the outward man has 'put on immortality'.[2] For it does not remain in the manner of a substance, like a bodily organism, or a spirit: it is a kind of disordered condition, like a bodily sickness . . .

Some sins are over as soon as they are committed: but their guilt remains, and remains for ever, unless forgiven. The guilt of concupiscence is removed when forgiveness is given; for to be free from sin means not be guilty of sin. . . . If freedom from sin merely means to cease from sin, it would be enough for Scripture to admonish us thus: 'My son, have you sinned? Do not go on to sin again.' But it is not enough; and it goes on: 'And pray about your former sins, that they may be forgiven.'[3] Thus they remain, unless forgiven. But how can they remain, if they are past, unless they remain in respect of their guilt, though they are past in respect of action? So it can happen, conversely, that a sin may remain in respect of action, though past in respect of guilt.   de nupt. et conc. 1. 28, 29

(f) Freedom and Grace

Would anyone say that free will disappeared from the human race in consequence of the sin of the first man? It is true that liberty was lost through sin, that liberty which existed in paradise, the liberty of perfect righteousness together with immortality. And therefore human nature stands in need of divine grace: and the Lord says, 'If the Son sets you free, then you will really be free';[4] free, that is, for a good and righteous life. So far is free will from having been lost in the sinner that it is through free will that men sin, especially all who delight in sinning and who love their sin: they decide to do what pleases them. The Apostle says, 'When you were the slaves of sin, you were free from righteousness'.[5] Observe that it is made clear that men can only become slaves to sin because they are free. What frees men from righteousness is just the use of their free choice: what makes them free from sin is nothing but the Saviour's grace. The admirable teacher makes a verbal distinction '. . . free from righteousness . . . freed from sin . . .'. 'Free from righteousness', not 'freed': but not 'free from sin', to prevent them

[1] 2 Cor. 4. 16.   [2] 1 Cor. 15. 53.   [3] Ecclus. 21. 1.   [4] John 8. 36.   [5] Rom. 6. 20.

ascribing the credit to themselves. He is careful to say 'freed', with reference to the Lord's statement, 'If the Son sets you free[1] ...' The sons of men cannot live a good life unless they are made sons of God. How then can this fellow (Julian of Eclanum)[2] try to ascribe to man's free will the power to live a good life? This power is only given by God's grace, 'through Jesus Christ our Lord'.[3] As the Gospel says, 'To all those who received him he gave the power to become sons of God'.[4]

c. duas. epp. Pel. 1, 5

(g) The 'Mass of Perdition'

[*Against the Pelagian contention that there were righteous men in the O.T.*] If anyone contends that in any age human nature did not stand in need of the second Adam as its physician, on the ground that it was not corrupted in the first Adam, he is shown up as an enemy of the grace of Christ, being in error not in respect of some question where uncertainty or error is possible without detriment to the faith, but in respect of the rule of faith itself, which is the basis of our Christianity. How strange of our opponents to praise that human nature of ancient times, as if it were as yet less corrupted by evil behaviour. They do not observe that humanity was then sunk in such grievous and intolerable sins that by a just judgement of God the whole world was wiped out by a flood, save for one man of God, and his wife, and their three sons and their wives; just as later the small territory of Sodom was destroyed by fire. Thus from the moment when 'through one man sin came into the world, and death through sin, and thus passed to all mankind, since all sinned in him',[5] the whole mass of perdition became the possession of the destroyer. So that no one, no one at all, has been set free from that situation, or is being set free, or will be set free, except by the grace of the Redeemer.

de grat. Chr. 2. 34

[cf. also below, p. 210 f.]

(h) Prevenient Grace

'Reveal your way to the Lord, and hope in him: and he himself will do it'.[6] This corrects the notion of some, that they themselves do it: for the Scripture in saying, 'He himself will do it', clearly has in mind those who say, 'we ourselves do it'; that is, 'we justify ourselves'. Certainly we also are active in this: but it is in co-operation with his action, for

---

[1] John 8. 36.   [2] See p. 197.   [3] Rom. 7. 25.   [4] John 1. 12.   [5] Rom. 5. 12 (see note on p. 198).   [6] Ps. 36 (37). 5.

'his mercy goes before me'.[1] It goes before us so that we may be cured: it will follow so that we may be glorified; it goes before so that we may live faithfully: it will follow so that we may live forever with him, for 'without him we can do nothing.'[2] . . . In saying this we are not doing away with free will. For who could benefit except one who willed; but who willed in humility, not pluming himself on the strength of his will, as if that alone sufficed for perfect righteousness?

de nat. et grat. 35, 36

(i) *Grace Available and Grace Effective*

The first man did not have the grace to prevent him from willing evil; what he had was the grace to enable him to be good, if he continued in it, the grace without which he had no power to be good even with free will, though he could abandon it through the use of free will. Thus God did not wish him to be without his grace, and he made this grace depend on his free will. Now free will is capable of evil, but incapable of good, unless it is assisted by the all-powerful good: but if that man had not abandoned this assistance by the use of his free will he would have been always good; but he did abandon it, and was himself abandoned. The assistance was of such a kind that he could abandon it when he wished, and continue in it, if he so wished. It was not such as to ensure that he should so wish. Such was the first grace, given to the first Adam: the grace that comes through the second Adam is more powerful. The first grace ensures that a man should have righteousness, if he wills: the second has more power; for it ensures that he should will, and will so strongly, and love so ardently as to give the spirit the victory over the 'will of the flesh' which 'lusts against the spirit'.[3] The first was no small grace, for it showed the power of free will; since the assistance was so offered that without it the will could not continue in goodness, while it could abandon this aid if it so willed. The second grace was so much greater that it was not enough for it to effect the recovery of man's freedom, not enough that it alone should enable man, if he so willed, to attain goodness and to continue in goodness. It had also to ensure he should so will.

The larger gift is given through Jesus Christ our Lord. God decided to grant to us not only the aid without which we cannot persevere in goodness, even if we will; but such powerful aid as makes us will. Through this grace of God it comes about that in receiving goodness,

[1] Cf. Ps. 59. 10. [2] John 15. 5. [3] Gal. 5. 17.

and in holding to it steadfastly, we are not merely able to attain our
wish but to will what we can attain.

Two kinds of assistance are to be distinguished: that without which
something cannot happen, and that by which something happens. We
cannot live without food, but a supply of food does not ensure life, if a
man wants to die. . . . The first man was created in a state of good; and
in that right condition he received the possibility of avoiding sin, of
escaping death, of continuing in that state of good. He was given the
aid to perseverance not so as to ensure that he would persevere, but
because without it he would not, by the use of his free will, be able to
persevere. But it is not this aid to perseverance which is now given to
the saints who are predestined for the kingdom of God through the
grace of God; the aid bestowed on them is perseverance itself. It is not
merely that without that gift they could not continue to persevere, but
that because of this gift they cannot but persevere. For the Lord did not
only say, 'Without me you can do nothing'.[1] He added, 'You did not
choose me; I chose you.'[2]   de corr. et grat. 31, 32, 34

(j) Grace Co-operating

He provides the will, and by co-operation brings to fulfilment what he
begins by his operation: . . . the Apostle says, 'I am convinced that he
who effects a good work in us will fulfil it up to the day of Christ'.[3] He
operates without us to effect our will; when we have the will, and the
will to act, he co-operates with us. But we have no power to perform
the good works of godliness without his operation to make us will, and
his co-operation when we will. . . . About his operation in producing
our will the Scripture says, 'It is God's operation that effects our will';[4]
and concerning his co-operation when we have the will, and act in
consequence. 'We know that for those who love God his co-operation
brings all things to good'.[5] And what is meant by 'all things' but
horrible and cruel sufferings? Indeed, that burden of Christ, which is
heavy for our weakness, is made light[6] for our love. For the Lord called
his burden light for those who resemble Peter when he suffered for
Christ, not Peter when he denied his Lord.   de grat. et lib. arb. 33

(k) Free will and Predestination

We always have free will, but it is not always a good will. For it is
either 'free from righteousness', and then it is bad: or else 'free from

[1] John 15. 5.   [2] John 15. 16.   [3] Phil. 1. 6.   [4] Phil. 2 .13.   [5] Rom. 8 .28.   [6] Cf. Matt. 11. 30.

sin, because it is the slave of righteousness',[1] and then it is good. But the grace of God is always good; and through this grace it comes about that a man is 'a man of good will',[2] whereas he was formerly a man of bad will. Through this grace it also comes about that the good will, which has just come into being, is increased and becomes strong enough to be able to fulfil the divine commands which it has willed, when it has willed them strongly and entirely.   *de grat. et lib. arb.* 31

Are we robbing free choice of all power through grace? Not in the least. We are in fact putting free choice on a firm basis, just as the law is not made powerless, but is put on a firm basis, by faith. For the law is only fulfilled by free choice: but through the law comes realization of sin; through faith grace is obtained to fight against sin; through grace comes the healing of the soul from the disorder of sin; through the health of the soul comes freedom of choice; through free choice comes delight in righteousness; through delight in righteousness comes the fulfilment of the law. . . . Grace makes the will healthy, so that by that will righteousness may be freely loved. . . . How is it that wretched men have the effrontery to boast of free will before they have been set free? Or to boast of their own strength, if they have by now been set free? . . . It is 'where the Spirit of the Lord is' that 'there is liberty'.[3]

de spir. et lit. 52

The objection may be raised that we must be aware of anyone's supposing that sin which is committed through the use of free choice is to be attributed to God, on the ground that the saying, 'What have you which you have not received?'[4] implies that the will to believe is to be ascribed to the gift of God, since it arises from the power of free choice which we received at our creation. It must be carefully observed that this will is to be ascribed to the gift of God not only because it arises from the power of free choice which was naturally given us at our creation; but also because God acts through the influence of the world of experience to make us will, and make us believe. He acts externally, through the exhortations of the gospel; and here the commandments of the Law have their effect, when they warn a man of his own weakness so as to bring him to take refuge, by believing, in justifying grace. He acts internally; for here it is in no man's power to determine what should come into his mind; but to assent or dissent lies within his own

[1] Rom. 6. 20, 22.   [2] Cf. Luke 2. 14, 'men of (God's) good pleasure'. The AV 'goodwill towards men', translates an inferior reading in the Greek.   [3] 2 Cor. 3. 17.   [4] 1 Cor. 4. 7.

will. These are the ways in which God deals with the rational soul, so that it may believe in him; since it cannot believe anything merely of its free choice, without anything to influence or provoke it to believe. Thus it follows that God produces in man the will to believe, and in everything 'his mercy goes before us':¹ but to consent to the call of God, or to dissent from it, as I have said, lies with man's own will. This fact does not weaken the force of 'What have you which you did not receive?' Indeed it strengthens it. The soul certainly cannot receive and possess the gifts referred to in the text without consenting. Thus it belongs to God to determine what the soul should possess and what it should accept; but the acceptance and possession certainly depends on a man's accepting and possessing. If anyone at this point constrains us to examine the profound question why one man is so influenced as to be persuaded, while another is not, there are at the moment only two things I should be prepared to say in reply: 'Oh, the depth of the riches', and 'Can there be any injustice in God?'² Anyone who finds these answers unsatisfactory may try to find more learned instructors; but let him take care that he does not find glib charlatans.   *de spir. et lit.* 60

(l) Free Choice and Perfect Freedom

'I do not do what I wish to do: I do what I hate': 'The will to do good is present in me: but I do not find the power to achieve it'.³ Did the speaker find that his liberty had been so restored to its original condition (as not to need grace)? 'The desires of the flesh oppose the spirit: the spirit fights against the flesh, so that you cannot do what you will to do.'⁴ I do not suppose you so foolish as to allege that the liberty of man's original condition exists in those to whom this is said. And yet, if they had no liberty at all, they would not be able to will what is 'holy and just and good'.⁵ For there are people who so delight in sin that they refuse and detest righteousness; and no one can wish for righteousness, unless the Lord furnishes him with the will, so that the longing for righteousness precedes the achievement; and this is gradually followed by effectual power, for some more quickly than for others, as God grants to each person; for he alone is able to restore man's health and increase it, in spite of his desperate condition, and even to bestow on him the inability to die. . . . Thus all who are redeemed are redeemed by him who 'came to seek what had perished':⁶ and, before he came in

¹ Ps. 59. 10.   ² Rom. 11. 33; 9. 14.   ³ Rom. 7. 15, 18.   ⁴ Gal. 5. 17.   ⁵ Rom. 7. 12.
⁶ Matt. 18. 11.

the flesh, he redeemed men just through that faith by which they
believed that he would come. Such men are redeemed for the everlasting freedom of happiness, a condition in which it is impossible for
them to be the 'slaves of sin'.[1] If, as you say, 'The only freedom is the
possibility of choosing good or evil', then God is not free, since in him
there is no possibility of sin. If we try to find the free choice of man
which is inherent and inalienable, we shall find it in the will of all men
for happiness, even in those who refuse the paths that lead to happiness.

op. imperf. c. Jul. 6. 11

(m) Calling and Choosing

If this calling is so sure of producing a good will that everyone follows
when called, how can it be true that 'many are called; few are chosen'?[2]
If this is true, and he who is called does not obey the call inevitably, and
it rests with his own will whether he should obey or no, then it could
also be said that 'it does not depend on God's mercy, but on man's will
and man's activity':[3] since the mercy of the caller is insufficient unless
followed by the obedience of the person called. It may be that those
who did not consent when called in this way might be able to adjust
their will to faithful obedience, if called after another fashion; and then
it would be true that 'many are called; few are chosen'; in that, although
many are called in the same way, still, because all are not affected in the
same way, only those follow the call who prove to be capable of receiving it. And so it would remain true that 'it does not depend on man's
will and man's activity, but on God's mercy'; since God called them in
a manner suitable for those who in fact followed the call. Certainly the
call came also to others; but since it was of such a nature as could not
move them, and since they were not fitted to receive it, they could be
said to have been called but not chosen. This being so, it is not true that
'it does not depend on God's mercy, but on man's will and activity';
seeing that the effect of God's mercy cannot be in man's power, so that
his mercy is fruitless, if a man refuses it. For if it were his will to have
mercy on those very men who refuse, he could call them in such a way
as should suit them, so that they would be moved, and understand, and
follow. Thus it is true that 'many are called: few are chosen'; for those
are chosen who have been suitably called; while those who were not
attuned to the calling were not chosen because, though called, they did
not follow. *ad Simplic.* 1, 2, 13

[1] Rom. 6. 17. [2] Matt. 22. 14. [3] Cf. Rom. 9. 16.

(n) Predestination

Those who have not heard the Gospel; those who after hearing have been converted to a better life but have not received the gift of perseverance; those who after hearing the Gospel have refused to come to Christ. . .; those who were unable to believe because they were mere infants and who perished, dying without receiving the washing of regeneration by which alone they could be set free from original guilt; all these are not separated from that mass which, as all agree, is condemned, since all men are bound for damnation because of one man's fault. Men are set apart from this condemnation, not by their own merits, but through the grace of the Mediator; that is, they are justified freely by the blood of the second Adam. . . . We must understand that no one is set apart from that mass of perdition, which results from the first Adam, unless he has the gift which he can only receive by the grace of the Saviour.

The chosen are chosen by grace, not because of their own existing merits; for every merit of theirs is the result of grace.

The chosen are those who are 'called according to God's purpose', who have also been predestined and foreknown. If any of them perishes, God is deceived: but none of them does perish, for God is not deceived. If any of them perishes, God is overcome by man's perversity: but none does perish, since nothing can overcome God. And they have been chosen to share the reign of Christ: not as Judas was chosen, for the task which suited him. Judas was chosen by him who knew how to make good use of evil, so that by an act which brought him damnation an act might be fulfilled which commands our worship, that act for which Christ came.   de corr. et grat. 12–14

The Scripture says, 'God wills that all men should be saved';[1] and yet in fact men do not all attain salvation. This text may be interpreted in a number of ways, some of which I have spoken of in other treatises.[2] Here I will mention only one. 'God wills that all men should be saved' is to be taken as meaning 'all those predestined': for every race of mankind is found among them. The Pharisees were said to 'tithe every vegetable',[3] which is to be understood to mean every vegetable they had: for they did not tithe every vegetable in the world. The same manner of speaking is used in 'I try to please all men in all my actions'.[4] Surely the speaker did not please all his many persecutors? But he

[1] 1 Tim. 2. 4.   [2] e.g. in Enchiridion, 103.   [3] Luke 11. 42.   [4] 1 Cor. 10. 33.

pleased men of every race which was gathered in the church of Christ, whether those who were already within the fellowship, or those who were to be brought into it. *de corr. et grat.* 44

(o) The Number of the Elect

From the children of men who have been deservedly and justly condemned, God by his grace collects a people large enough to make up the loss of the fallen angels, so that the beloved heavenly city shall not be deprived of its number of citizens; in fact it may be that it will rejoice in a more abundant supply. *de civ. Dei* 22. 1

Will anyone dare to say that God did not foreknow to whom he was going to grant that they should believe, or whom he was going to give to his Son, so that he should not lose any of them?[1] If he really foreknew this, then certainly he foreknew his acts of kindness, by which he deigns to set us free. This, and nothing else, is the predestination of saints; God's foreknowledge and preparation of his acts of goodness, by which those who are set free are most surely freed. Where are the rest left, by the just sentence of God, unless in the mass of perdition? Where were the men of Tyre and Sodom left?[2] They could have believed, if they had seen Christ's signs. But since it was not granted them to believe, they were denied the source of belief. It is clear from this that some have naturally a divine gift of understanding, by which they may be moved to faith, if they hear words, or see signs, appropriate to their intelligence. And yet, if they have not been separated from the mass of perdition by the predestination of grace, through a deeper judgement of God, these divine words or acts, which would make faith possible for them, do not reach them. . . . Yet this predestination, which is explicitly asserted in the words of the Gospel, does not prevent the Lord from saying of the beginning of faith, 'Believe in God, also believe in me';[3] and, of perseverance in faith, 'Men ought to pray always, and not give up'.[4] For those hear and act to whom it is granted: those to whom it is not granted do not act, whether they hear or no. *de don. pers.* 35

(p) Inscrutable Justice

That there is no 'injustice in God'[5] must be an unshakable conviction in a mind of rational piety and steadfast faith; likewise it must be believed, with the utmost firmness and tenacity, that the fact that 'God

[1] John 18 .9. [2] Cf. Matt. 11. 22, 24. [3] John 14. 1. [4] Luke 18.1. [5] Rom. 9. 14.

shows mercy as he wills, and as he wills he hardens man's heart'[1] (that is, he shows mercy as he wills, and does not show mercy where he does not so will), depends upon some secret justice, inscrutable by human standards. But in fact in worldly business relations between men something of the same sort is to be observed; for if we did not have in them some sort of vestiges of the heavenly justice, our feebler gaze could never peer up in wonder at the sacred and holy inner chamber of spiritual precepts. 'Blessed are those who hunger and thirst for justice, for they shall be satisfied.'[2] In this state of drought which is the condition of our mortal life we should rather be dried up than feel thirst if there were not wafted upon us from above as it were the faintest kind of breeze of justice. Now men are bound together in society by mutual giving and receiving, and gifts and receipts may or may not be matters of debt. It is obvious that a man cannot be charged with injustice if he demands the payment of a debt. Nor can he be so charged who decides to forgo a debt. And it is clear that it depends on the decision of the creditor, not of the debtors. This is an analogy, or, as I said, a trace of the supreme justice. For since, as the Apostle says, 'In Adam all men die',[3] for from Adam derives the alienation from God which affects the whole human race, all men are, as it were, one lump of sin, incurring the punishment of the supreme justice of God; and whether this is demanded or foregone, there is no injustice. It is arrogance in the debtors to judge in what case the debt should be claimed and in what foregone; as the labourers hired for the vineyard had no right to grumble when others were given the same wages that were paid to them.[4]

Hence comes the Apostle's retort to the impertinent question: 'My good man, who are you, to answer back to God?'[5] A man 'answers God back' when he disapproves of God's finding fault with sinners, as if God compelled any man to sin by bestowing only on certain sinners the mercy of his justification, and by 'hardening' certain sinners; which means that he does not have mercy on them, not that he forces them to sin. He withholds this mercy from those to whom he decides (by a secret justice, far remote from human powers of apprehension) that mercy should not be accorded. 'His decisions are inscrutable, his ways cannot be traced.'[6] He has the right to find fault with sinners, since he does not compel them to sin. At the same time his purpose is that those

---

[1] Rom. 9. 18.   [2] Matt. 5. 6.   [3] 1 Cor. 15. 22.   [4] Cf. Matt. 20. 10–15.   [5] Rom. 9. 20.
[6] Rom. 11. 33.

to whom he shows mercy may also be called to be conscience-stricken, when God finds fault with sinners, and may be turned to his grace. Hence God, in finding fault, acts both with justice and with mercy.

ad Simplic. 1. 16

When two infants are alike bound by original sin, why should 'one be taken, the other left'?[1] When there are two adults, both irreligious, why should one be so called as to follow him who calls; while the other is not called, or is not so called that he follows? 'The decisions of God are inscrutable.'[2] Of two religious persons, why is one granted perserverance to the end, and not the other? The decisions of God are yet more inscrutable. But what must be resolutely held by the faithful is that one belongs to the number of the predestined, the other does not. For 'if they had been of our number', says one of the predestined, who had imbibed that secret from the breath of the Lord, 'they would certainly have remained with us'.[3] What does that mean? Were not both created by God, both born from Adam, both made from the earth, and had received souls of one and the same nature from him who said, 'I have made every breath'?[4] Finally, had not both been called, and followed the caller, both been justified from their irreligion, both renewed by the 'washing of rebirth'?[5]

If such questions as these were to be heard by a man who knew beyond doubt what he was talking about, he would reply: 'True, in regard to all this they were of our number; but they were not of our number in respect of another distinction: if they had been, they would have remained with us'. What distinction? The books of God lie open: let us not avert our eyes. Divine Scripture speaks clearly: let us pay attention. They were not in their number, because they were not called according to God's purpose: they were not 'chosen in Christ before the foundation of the world';[6] they had not obtained a 'share in the inheritance'; they had not been 'predestined according to the purpose of him, whose design is in operation in the whole scheme of things'.[7] If they had been in this condition, they would have been in that company, and they would undoubtedly have remained with them. *de don. persev.* 21

---

[1] Cf. Matt. 24. 40.   [2] Rom. 11. 33.   [3] 1 John 2. 19.   [4] Cf. Isa. 57. 16.   [5] Tit. 3. 5.
[6] Eph. 1. 4.   [7] Cf. Eph. 1. 11.

III. The Status of Christ

(a) *The Equality and Subordination of the Son*

Many statements in the Scriptures imply, or even openly assert, that the Father is greater than the Son; and men have erred because they have not been careful enough to examine the whole tenor of the Scriptures and thus have sought to transfer what is said of Christ Jesus as man to his mode of being[1] before his incarnation, which was and is eternal. And they allege that the Son is inferior to the Father because the Lord himself is quoted as saying, 'The Father is greater than I'.[2] But it is demonstrable that in this respect the Son is also inferior to himself. For if 'he emptied himself, receiving the form of a servant'[3] he must surely have become inferior to himself. For this taking of the form of a servant did not entail his losing the form of God. . . . In both forms he was the same Only-begotten Son of God the Father, in the form of God equal to the Father, in the form of a servant 'the mediator between God and man, the man Christ Jesus'.[4] Then obviously in the form of a servant he is inferior to himself in the form of God. . . . He is equal to the Father in nature, inferior to him in condition.[5] . . . In the form of God he made man: in the form of a servant he was made man. . . . Therefore, since the form of God received the form of a servant, he is both God and man; but God, because God took humanity, man, because of the taking of humanity. And by that taking neither is turned or changed into the other; godhead is not changed into a creature, so as to cease to be godhead; nor creature into godhead, so as to cease to be creature.

de trin. 1. 14

(b) *The Son in Judgement*

[*In capp*. 22–30 *of de trin. A. argues that the presence of two natures in Christ explains the apparent inconsistencies in the Gospels, e.g. John 10. 30 ctr. John 6. 38; John 5. 26 ctr. Matt 26. 39; John 17. 10 ctr. 17 and Mark 13. 32; and, in respect of judgement John 12. 47, 'I will not judge' ctr. John 5. 22 'The Father has given judgement to the Son'.*] Since the Son of God is equal to the Father he does not receive this power of executing judgement, but he has it with the Father, in secret; but he receives it, as Son of Man, that the good and the evil may see him passing judgement; for the vision of the form of God is only shown to the pure in heart: the vision of the Son of Man will be displayed to the evil also. *de trin*. 1, 30

---

[1] *substantia*.   [2] John 14. 28.   [3] Phil. 2. 7.   [4] 1 Tim. 2. 5.   [5] *habitus*.

(c) The Son Derivative

There are, however, some statements in Scripture so put that it is uncertain to what principle they should be referred, whether to that by which we understand the Son to be subordinate in his assumption of creaturehood, or to that by which we understand the Son to be, not indeed less than the Father but equal to him, and yet to be *of* the Father, God *of* God, Light *of* Light; while the Father is simply God, not *of* God. Hence it is clear that the Son has another from whom he has his being, *of* whom he is Son: while the Father has the Son, not having his being from him, but being father in relation to him.

[*e.g. John 5. 26 and* 19.] The meaning of these sayings is that the life of the Son, like the life of the Father, is unchangeable, and yet derived *from* the Father; and the activity of Father and Son is inseparable, and yet this activity is derived by the Son from the Father, from whom he has his being.   *de trin.* 2. 2, 3

(d) Inseparable Operation of Father and Son
The Sending of the Son

There is one will of Father and Son, and one inseparable activity. Thus therefore one may understand that the incarnation and the birth from a virgin, by which the Son is understood to have been 'sent',[1] was effected by one and the same activity of Father and Son, working inseparably, and, of course, with the Holy Spirit not separated from the work, as is plainly said: 'She was found pregnant by the Holy Spirit'[2] ... The sending was done by a word, and he is himself the Word of God and the Son of God. Thus, when the Father sent him with a word, his sending was done by the Father and his Word. Therefore the Son was sent by the Father and the Son. ... The form of the humanity assumed is the person of the Son, not of the Father also. Hence the invisible Father, together with the Son who with him is invisible, is said to have sent the same Son in making him visible.   *de trin.* 2. 9

Now if the Son is said to be sent by the Father in respect that the one is Father, the other Son, this in no way hinders our belief that the Son is equal to the Father, consubstantial and co-eternal; and yet that the Son is sent by the Father. Not because one is greater than the other; but because one is Father, the other, Son: one, begetter, the other, begotten. ... The Son is from the Father, not the Father from the Son.

[1] Cf. John 10. 36.   [2] Matt. 1. 18.

... The Son is 'a kind of clear effluence of the splendour of Almighty God'.¹ And the effluence and its source are of one and the same substance. For it does not flow as water from a hole in the ground or in the rock, but as light from light. 'The brightness of the eternal light'² means the light of eternal light. For the brightness of light *is* light, and is co-eternal with the light from which it springs. . . . If the brightness is less than the light, it is its obscurity, not its brightness.

The Son is said to be sent not just because he is begotten by the Father. But either in that he has been manifested to this world as the Word made flesh [*John* 16. 28]; or in that he is perceived in time by a mind. . . . In this second sense he is said to be 'sent', but not 'sent into this world', for he does not appear to the physical senses; for when we have a mental conception, as far as we can, of something eternal, we are not in this world. . . . But when the *Father* is mentally apprehended he is not said to be 'sent', for he does not derive or proceed from any source. Wisdom proceeds 'from the mouth of the Highest',³ and the Holy Spirit 'from the Father';⁴ but the Father proceeds from none.

de trin. 4. 27, 28

IV. The Person of Christ

(a) Two Natures—One Person

[*In contrast with the temporary manifestations of the Spirit in form of a dove or flame.*] Christ did not take human form for a time, to show himself to man in this guise, an outward appearance which should thereafter be discarded: he took the visible form of man into the unity of his person, the form of God remaining invisible. Not only was he born in that form of a human mother; he also grew up in it, he ate and drank and slept and was put to death in it; and in that human form he rose again, and ascended into heaven; and now he sits at the right hand of the Father in that same human form, in which he is to come to judge the living and the dead, in which he will, in his kingdom, 'be made subordinate to God who made all things subordinate to him'.⁵

c. Maxim. 1. 19

There is no need to fear that God should seem to suffer constraint in the tiny body of a child: for God's greatness is not in size, but in moral

¹ Wisd. 7. 25.   ² Wisd. 7. 26.   ³ Ecclus. 24. 3.   ⁴ John 15. 26.   ⁵ 1 Cor. 15. 28.

power. . . . That moral power, without changing for the worse, took to itself the rational soul, and through that the human body, and the whole man, to change it for the better; in condescension taking from it the name of humanity, in generosity bestowing on it the name of divinity..

ep. 137. 8

As in the unity of a person a soul is united to a body to constitute a man: so God is united to man, in unity of person, to constitute Christ. In the former case there is a mixture of soul and body: in the latter a mixture of God and man. But this should not be interpreted on the analogy of the mixture of two liquids, where neither preserves its identity. . . . When the Word of God was mixed with a soul possessing a body, he assumed soul and body together.

ep. 137. 11

We are changeable, and we are changed for the better by becoming partakers of the Word: the Word is changeless, and suffered no change for the worse when he became partaker of flesh, by means of a rational soul. The Apollinarian heretics[1] wrongly suppose that the man Christ either had not a soul, or had not a rational soul. The Scripture (in saying 'The Word became flesh'[2]) employs its customary idiom of using 'flesh' for 'man', in order to show the humility of Christ more emphatically, to avoid seeming to shun the title 'flesh' as if it were something unworthy. 'All flesh shall see the salvation of God'[3] is not to be taken as excluding 'souls'. 'The Word became flesh' simply means 'The Son of God became a son of man'. . . . As the accession of flesh to soul to constitute one man does not create a plurality of persons, so no plurality is effected by the accession of man to Word, to constitute one Christ. And the statement, 'The Word became flesh', is intended to make us understand the singularity of this person, not to lead us to imagine the conversion of the divinity into flesh.

ep. 140. 12

(b) Christ's Knowledge

In respect of 'the form of God',[4] 'all things belonging to the Father were his';[5] 'All that is mine is thine, and thine is mine'.[6] In respect of 'the form of a slave',[7] the 'teaching was not his own, but that of him who sent him'.[8] 'About the day and the hour no one knows; not the angels in heaven; not the Son: only the Father knows.'[9] His 'ignorance' meant

---

[1] See p. 11 f. [2] John 1. 14. [3] Isa. 52. 10. [4] Phil. 2. 6. [5] John 16. 15. [6] John 17. 10.
[7] Phil. 2. 7. [8] Cf. John 7. 16. [9] Matt. 24. 36.

that he was keeping the disciples in ignorance: he had not the knowledge to reveal to them at that moment. ... Similarly, the Apostle says, 'I decided to know nothing, while I was with you, except Jesus Christ— and a Christ who was crucified'.[1] For he was speaking to people who could not take in the deeper truths about the divinity of Christ. ... He was 'ignorant', while among them, of knowledge which they could not receive from him. His only knowledge, he said, was the knowledge which it was proper for them to receive from him. In fact, he knew among 'the mature', what he 'did not know' among 'the infants'.[2] ... 'Ignorance' is used for 'concealment' by the same idiom which calls a hidden ditch a 'blind' ditch.   *de trin.* I. 23

(c) *The Reality of Christ's Manhood*

Let us not listen to those who say that it was not a real manhood which the Son of God assumed, that he was not born of a woman, but that he displayed to the beholders a false flesh and a feigned appearance of a human body. Those people do not know that the substance of God, which directs the whole creation, is utterly incapable of being con- taminated: and yet they acknowledge that the visible sun diffuses his rays through all manner of physical dirt and corruption, but preserves their spotless purity. If, then, visible purity can be in contact with visible impurity and escape contamination, how much easier was it for the invisible and unchangeable Truth to avoid pollution when it freed man from all his infirmities by assuming the whole man, man's spirit, and, in consequence, man's soul, and, in consequence, man's body.

de agon. Chr. 20

The Son of God assumed human nature, and in it he endured all that belongs to the human condition. This is a remedy for mankind of a power beyond our imagining. Could any pride be cured, if the humility of God's Son does not cure it? Could any greed be cured, if the poverty of God's Son does not cure it? Or any anger, if the patience of God's Son does not cure it? Or any coldness, if the love of God's Son does not cure it? Lastly, what fearfulness can be cured, if it is not cured by the resurrection of the body of Christ the Lord? Let mankind raise its hopes, and recognize its own nature: let it observe how high a place it has in the works of God. Do not despise yourselves, you men: the Son of God assumed manhood. Do not despise yourselves, you women:

[1] I Cor. 2. 2.   [2] I Cor. 2. 6; 3. 2.

God's Son was born of a woman. But do not set your hearts on the satisfactions of the body, for in the Son of God we are 'neither male or female'.[1] Do not set your heart on temporal rewards: if it were good to do so, that human nature which God's son assumed would have thus set its heart. Do not fear insults, crosses and death: for if they did man harm, the humanity which God's son assumed would not have endured them.   *de agon. Chr.* 12

V. The Work of Christ

(a) Reconciliation

Some people ask: 'Had God no other method by which to set men free from their state of mortality? Was it necessary that he should wish his Only-begotten Son, God co-eternal with himself, to become man, by putting on human soul and flesh, and, thus made mortal, to suffer death?' Is it not enough to answer this by asserting that the method by which God deigned to set us free through the 'mediator between God and men, the man Christ Jesus'[2] was good, and congruous with God's dignity? We should show not that God had no other method possible, since all things are equally subject to his power, but that no other more fitting method existed, or could have existed, for curing our unhappy state. For in order to raise our hopes, to free mortal minds, cast down by that very condition of mortality, from despair of attaining immortality, what was needed above all was that we should have proof of how highly God valued us, how much he loved us. And could there be a proof of this more clear and cogent than that God's own Son, the unalterably good, while remaining in himself what he was, should receive from us and for us that which he was not, and without derogation from his own nature should deign to share our nature and should bear our ills, with no previous ill-desert on his part? So that when we came to believe in God's great love for us, and to hope for what we had despaired to attain, he should bestow on us, with undeserved generosity, his gifts of good, without, on our part, any good, but rather ill-desert.

But what is the meaning of 'made righteous in his blood'?[3] What power is there in this blood, I demand, that believers are made righteous in it? And what of 'reconciled through the death of his Son'?[4] Is it

[1] Gal. 3. 28.   [2] 1 Tim. 2. 5.   [3] Rom. 5. 9.   [4] Rom. 5. 10.

really the case that, when God the Father was angry with us, he saw the death of his Son for us, and was appeased? Are we to suppose that his Son was appeased, so much that he deigned even to die for us; while the Father remained so angry that he would not be appeased unless his Son died for us? What of that other passage, by the same 'Teacher of the nations';[1] 'What are we to say, in the face of this? If God is on our side, who is against us? God did not grudge his own Son, but gave him up for us all: with this gift, can he fail to bestow all his gifts on us?'[2] Can we suppose that the Father would have given his own Son for us, ungrudgingly, had he not already been appeased? Is there not a contradiction here? The one passage says that the Son died for us and the Father was reconciled to us by his death: the other speaks as if the Father loved us before, and himself gave his Son. . . . Nor was the Son given up as if against his will, since it has been said of him, 'He loved me, and gave himself up for me'.[3] Everything is the combined work of the Father, the Son, and the Spirit of both, in equal and harmonious activity: yet 'we have been made righteous in Christ's blood', and 'reconciled to God through the death of his Son'. How this can be I will do my best to explain, sufficiently for our present purpose.

de trin. 13. 13, 15

(b) Victory over the Devil

By a kind of divine justice the human race was handed over to the devil's power, since the sin of the first man passed at birth to all who were born by the intercourse of the two sexes, and the debt of the first parents bound all their posterity. . . . The method by which man was surrendered to the devil's power ought not to be understood in the sense that it was God's act, or the result of God's command: rather he merely permitted it, but he did so with justice. When God deserted the sinner, the instigator of the sin rushed in. Yet God did not so desert his creature as not to show himself to him as God the Creator and Life-giver, and the provider, even amid the ills of punishment, of many good things for evil mankind. In his wrath he did not withhold his mercies.[4] Nor did he let man go from the reach of his power, when he allowed him to pass into the power of the devil; not even the devil himself is removed from the power of the Omnipotent, nor from his goodness. Whence could even the malignant angels derive existence,

[1] 1 Tim. 2. 7. [2] Rom. 8. 31, 32. [3] Gal. 2. 20. [4] Cf. Hab. 3. 2.

except through him who is the source of all life? Thus the commission of sins subjected man to the devil through the just anger of God; while the remission of sin, through the generous reconciliation of God, rescued man from the Devil.

However, the devil had to be overcome not by God's power, but by his justice. What is more powerful than the Omnipotent? What creature's power can be compared with the Creator's? But the devil, warped by his own perversity, fell in love with power, and abandoned justice and attacked it; for men also imitate the devil in this way, in so far as they neglect, and even hate, justice and aim at power, gloating in its acquisition or inflamed with lust for it. Therefore God decided that, to rescue man from the devil's power, the devil should be overcome by justice, not by power: not because power is to be eschewed as something evil; but the right order must be kept, and justice has precedence.

And what is the justice by which the devil has been conquered? Surely it is the justice of Christ. And how has he been conquered? Because the devil put Christ to death, although he found in him nothing that deserved death. And it is surely just that the debtors he held should be set free when they believe in him whom he put to death when no debt was owing. . . . 'The Prince of this world is coming, and he finds nothing (that is, no sin) in me. But, so that all may know that I am doing my Father's will, arise, let us go from here.'[1] And he went on from there to his passion, so that he might pay for us debtors what he himself did not owe. Would it be true that the conquest of the devil might have been achieved with perfect equity, had Christ decided to deal with him by power, rather than by justice? But in fact Christ postponed the use of power so that he might first act as was fitting. And for this reason it was necessary that he should be both man and God. For had he not been man, he could not have been put to death; had he not been God, man would have believed not that he did not will to exercise his power but that he had not power to achieve his will; we should suppose him not to have preferred justice, but to have lacked power. As it is, he endured human suffering for us, because he was man. Had he so willed, he could have avoided this suffering, since he was also God. Therefore justice was made more attractive in humility, because the mighty power in his divinity could have avoided humiliation, had he so willed. Thus by the death of one so powerful justice is demonstrated,

[1] John 14. 31.

and power promised, to us mortals in our impotence. He demonstrated justice by his death, he promised power by his resurrection. What could be more just than to go as far as the death of the cross, for the sake of justice? What greater act of power than to rise from the dead, and to ascend to heaven with the very flesh in which he was slain? First justice conquered the devil, then power: justice, because he had no sin and was most unjustly put to death by the devil; power, because he lived again after death, never to die thereafter. Power would have overcome the devil, even if Christ could not have been put to death by him; and yet it showed greater power to conquer death itself by resurrection, than to avoid it by continuing to live.

de trin. 13. 16–18

If Christ had not been put to death, death would not have died. The devil was conquered by his own trophy of victory. The devil jumped for joy, when he seduced the first man and cast him down to death. By seducing the first man, he slew him: by slaying the last man, he lost the first from his snare. The victory of our Lord Jesus Christ came when he rose, and ascended into heaven; then was fulfilled what you have heard when the Apocalypse was being read, 'The Lion of the tribe of Judah has won the day'.[1] He who was slain as a lamb is called a lion: a lion on account of his courage, a lamb on account of his innocence; a lion, because unconquered: a lamb, because of his gentleness. The slain lamb by his death conquered the lion who 'goes round seeking someone to devour'.[2] (The devil is called a lion for his savagery, not for his bravery) . . . The devil jumped for joy when Christ died; and by the very death of Christ the devil was overcome: he took, as it were, the bait in the mousetrap. He rejoiced at the death, thinking himself death's commander. But that which caused his joy dangled the bait before him. The Lord's cross was the devil's mousetrap: the bait which caught him was the death of the Lord.[3]

serm. 261. 1

It is not difficult to see the devil overcome, when he who was slain by him rose again. It is more important, it requires a more profound insight, to see the devil conquered at the time when he supposed he had won, that is, when Christ was put to death. For then that blood, being the blood of one who was entirely without sin, was poured out for the remission of our sins, so that whereas the devil rightly has in his power

[1] Rev. 5. 5. [2] 1 Pet. 5. 8. [3] Cf. p. 142.

those whom he had bound under sentence of death, as guilty of sin,
he should rightly lose control over them because of him on whom he
had wrongly inflicted the death penalty, when he was completely
guiltless. . . . In this redemption the blood of Christ was given for us as
the price: but by accepting it the devil was not enriched, but enchained;
so that we might free ourselves from his toils, and that not one of those
whom Christ had redeemed from every debt by the shedding of his
blood freely (since he had incurred no debt), not one of those should
be dragged by the devil, ensnared in the toils of sin, to the doom of the
second and everlasting death. So that those who attain to the grace of
Christ, who are foreknown and fore-ordained[1] and chosen before the
foundation of the world, should die only so far as Christ died for them
—the death of the body only, not the death of the spirit.   *de trin.* 13. 19

(c) *The Example*

Our reconciliation to God by the death of his Son is not to be understood as meaning that its effect is that God now began to love those
whom he had hated; like the reconciliation of enemies, where mutual
hate turns to mutual affection. We have been reconciled to one who
loves us, with whom we were at enmity because of sin. The Apostle
supports the truth of my statement: 'God gives his own proof of his
love towards us in Christ's death for us while we were still sinners'.[2]

in ev. Jo. tract. 110. 6

The chief cause of the coming of the Lord was that God should give
proof of his love towards us. And it is a cogent proof; for 'Christ died
for us while we were still sinners'.[2] He gave this proof because love is
the purpose and the fulfilment of the law.[3] He gave it so that we should
love him in return, and also that we should lay down our lives for our
brothers, as he laid down his life for us.[4] God's love for us came first; he
did not spare his only Son, but gave him up for us all.[5] If once we
shrank from loving God, can we now shrink from responding to his
love? One can offer no greater inducement to love than to take the
initiative in loving; and it is a hard heart indeed which refuses not only
to give love but even to repay it. . . . Now if an inferior has lost hope
that he could be loved by his superior, he will be wonderfully stirred to

[1] Cf. Rom. 8. 30; 1 Pet. 1. 20.   [2] Rom. 5. 8.   [3] Rom. 13. 10.   [4] 1 John 3. 16.   [5] 1 John
4. 10; Rom. 8. 32.

love if that superior condescends, of his own accord, to show affection; how great then would be his love towards one who should go so far as to offer him such a boon with no thought of his own advantage. Could there be a greater superiority than that of God as judge, a state more hopeless than that of man as sinner? For man had subjected himself to the domination of the powers of pride, and was therefore all the more devoid of the hope that he could be the object of concern to that power which does not aim at exaltation through wickedness, but is exalted by goodness. Thus the principal reason for Christ's coming was that man should recognize the greatness of God's love; and should so recognize it that man should be kindled to love for him whose love came first, and that he should love his neighbours, at the command and after the example of him who, by loving one who was not his neighbour but had wandered far away, became his neighbour.

All Scripture serves to give notice of the coming of the Lord. ... The New Testament is hidden in the Old: the Old Testament is brought to light in the New. The unspiritual fail to see this hidden meaning and now, as of old, they are held in subjection to the fear of punishment. While through this revelation those spiritual men who of old knocked with faith found hidden things opened to them, and now those who seek without pride (lest pride should shut from them even what has been made open) by their spiritual understanding are set free through the gift of love. Nothing is more opposed to love than envy; and the mother of envy is pride. The Lord Jesus Christ, the God-man, is at once the proof of God's love towards us and an example of the humility which men should show to one another, so that the great swelling of our pride should be cured by a medicine of greater power. The pride of man is a great misery: the humility of God is a greater mercy. This love is as it were the purpose set before you, to which you should refer all that you say; and let every communication of yours be such that he to whom you speak may believe through hearing, hope through believing, love through hoping.   *de cat. rud.* 7. 8

In our faith in the Lord Jesus Christ, it is not the mental picture we have of him that effects our salvation; for that picture may be far from the reality. It is rather the kind of notion we have of a human being, in respect of outward appearance. We have, I mean, a notion of human nature fixed in our minds as a norm, which enables us to recognize a man, or the representation of a man, when we see anything answering to this notion. It is this notion which governs our thinking when we believe that God for our sake became man, as an example of humility and as a demonstration of God's love towards us. For it is to our profit to believe, and to hold firmly and unshakably in our hearts, that the humility of God in being born of a woman and being led to death, with all those ignominies, by mortal men is the sovereign remedy to heal the swelling of our pride, the deep mystery to undo the bonds of sin. *de trin.* 8. 7

Man was created righteous in such a way that he could, with divine help, remain in that condition, while he could, by the exercise of his own choice, become perverted. Whatever course he adopted, God's purpose would be fulfilled, either by him or else concerning him. Hence, because he preferred his own will to that of God, God's purpose was done concerning him, in that God made from that 'lump of perdition', which issued from his stock, 'one vessel for honour, another for contempt; so that no one should boast in man;'[1] and, consequently, should not boast in himself. For we would not be liberated even by means of 'the one mediator between God and man, the man Jesus Christ',[2] were he not also God. When Adam was created, he was certainly righteous, and there was no need of a mediator. However, when sins had made a wide rift between mankind and God, it was necessary that we should be reconciled to God, and even brought to the resurrection to eternal life by means of a mediator who alone was without sin in his birth, life, and execution: so that man's pride should be shown up and cured by the humility of God, and man should be shown how far he had departed from God, since it was through the incarnation of God that he was recalled, and through the God-man that an example of obedience was offered to the insolence of man. And so a fountain of grace was opened, not for any antecedent merit, by the taking of 'the form of a servant'[3] by the Only-begotten; and a proof of the bodily resurrection promised to the redeemed was given by anticipation in the person of the Redeemer himself. The devil was overcome by means of that very nature which, he rejoiced to think, he had entrapped. Yet man should not boast, lest pride should arise again. And there are other consequences of this mighty and mysterious work of the mediator which can be seen and described by those who benefit from it; or can be seen, though they cannot be described. *enchir.* 108

[1] Rom. 9. 21.   [2] 1 Tim. 2. 5.   [3] Phil. 2. 7.

'The Word was made flesh, and dwelt among us.'[1] The Wisdom, which came into being from God, deigned to be created also among men. This is the reference of 'The Lord created me in the beginning of his ways'.[2] The beginning of his ways is the head of the Church, that is, Christ endued with human nature, so that we might receive through him an example of humility, which is the sure way by which we may come to God. It was through pride that we fell ('Taste, and you will be as gods'[3] was said to the first created man); we can return only through humility. So our Redeemer himself has deigned to show, in his own person, an example of humility, of the way by which we must return.

de fid. et symb. 6

(d) More than an example

The unspiritual man . . . does not understand the things which belong to the Spirit of God, that is, the grace conferred on believers by the cross of Christ. He supposes that the only effect of the cross is to offer us an example as we contend on behalf of the truth even to death. If men of this stamp, who refuse to rise above merely human standards, knew that Christ in his crucifixion has been 'made by God our wisdom, righteousness, consecration, and liberation; so that, as Scripture says, "if anyone rejoices in his situation, let it be in the Lord"';[4] if they knew this then without doubt they would not find their grounds of rejoicing in men.

in ev. Joh. tract. 98. 3

(e) Christ's death a sacrifice

We came to death through sin, he through righteousness; therefore, since death is our punishment for sin, his death has become a sacrifice for sin.

de trin. 4. 15

By his death, the one most real sacrifice offered for us, he purged, abolished, and extinguished whatever guilt there was which gave just ground for the principalities and powers to hold us in custody for our punishment.

de trin. 4. 17

What priest could be so righteous and holy as the only Son of God, who had no need to purge his own sins by sacrifice, neither original sins nor additional sins committed during a man's life? And what more suitable

[1] John 1. 14.   [2] Prov. 8. 22.   [3] Gen. 3. 5.   [4] 1 Cor. 1. 30, 31 [Jer. 9. 23, 24].

offering for men could be taken from men[1] than human flesh? What more fitting for this immolation than mortal flesh? And to cleanse the faults of mortals what offering so clean as flesh that came to life in a virgin womb, and from a virgin womb, without any pollution of lust? And what could be offered as acceptably, and received as readily, as the flesh of our sacrifice, the flesh that made up the body of our priest? In every sacrifice there are four considerations: to whom it is offered, by whom it is offered, what is offered, for whom it is offered. And so the one true Mediator[2] himself reconciled us to God, and in this he remained one with him to whom he made the offering, and made one in himself those for whom he offered, and was himself one as the offerer and the offering.

de trin. 4. 19

VI. The Holy Spirit

(a) *The Sending of the Spirit*

The Holy Spirit is a unity with the Father and the Son, for those three are 'one thing'.[3] As the Son's 'begetting' is his derivation from the Father, so his 'sending' is the recognition of him as thus derived; and as the Holy Spirit's character as the 'gift of God' means his proceeding from the Father, so his 'sending' is the recognition of him as thus proceeding. Nor can we say that the Holy Spirit does not also proceed from the Son, for then the statement that he is the Spirit of the Father and of the Son is meaningless. Nor can I see what else the Son meant when he breathed on the face of his disciples and said, 'Receive the Holy Spirit'.[4] . . . This was a demonstration, by a fitting symbol, that the Holy Spirit proceeds not only from the Father but from the Son. . . . The Lord says, [The Spirit] 'whom I will send you from the Father'[5] . . . and not, 'Whom the Father will send from me'. That is, he shows that the Father is fountain-head of the whole divinity, or, better, deity. Therefore he who proceeds from the Father and the Son is referred to him from whom the Son has his generation. The statement of the Evangelist, 'The Spirit had not yet been given . . .',[6] can only be taken as meaning that a special giving or sending of the Spirit, such as had never been before, was to take place after the glorification of Christ. Not that there had been no sending before, but there had been none like that.

de trin. 4. 29

[1] Cf. Heb. 5. 1.   [2] Cf. 1. Tim. 2. 5.   [3] Cf. John 10. 30.   [4] John 20. 22.   [5] John 15. 26.
[6] John 7. 39.

(b) 'Procession'

You ask me: 'Since the Son is derived from the Father's substance, and the Holy Spirit also is derived, how is it that the one is Son, and not the other?' I reply ,'The Son is from the Father, the Holy Spirit is from the Father: but the former is begotten, the latter proceeds. So the former is the Son of the Father, of whom he is begotten; the latter is the Spirit of both, since he proceeds from both. But the Son speaks of the Spirit as "proceeding from the Father",[1] because the Father is the source of his procession in that he begot such a Son, and in begetting him granted him also to be the source from which the Holy Spirit should proceed.'

c. Maxim. 2. 14, 1

Anyone who understands the timeless generation of the Son from the Father may understand the timeless procession of the Holy Spirit from both. When the Son says, 'As the Father has life in himself, so has he granted to the Son to have life in himself',[2] it is not meant that the Father has given life to a Son who hitherto was lifeless, but that he has begotten him timelessly, in such a way that the life which the Father has given to the Son in begetting him is co-eternal with the life of the Father who has given it. And anyone who can understand this may understand that, as the Father has in himself the possibility of the Holy Spirit's procession, so he has granted to the Son that the same Holy Spirit should proceed from him, and in both cases timelessly. . . . Whatever the Son has, he has from the Father. . . . Though we do not describe the Holy Spirit as 'begotten', we do not dare to call him 'unbegotten', lest such a term should lead anyone to suppose two Fathers in the Trinity or two underivative beings. For only the Father is underived therefore he alone is called 'unbegotten'; though this term is not scriptural, but of general use in theological debate when men have to use the most adequate language at their command in teaching so difficult a matter. The Son is begotten from the Father; the Spirit proceeds from the Father as the ultimate source, and, by the Father's gift and without interval of time, he proceeds in common from both.

de trin. 15. 47

The Holy Spirit does not proceed from the Father into the Son, and proceed from the Son to sanctify created beings; he proceeds simultaneously from both; although it is by the Father's gift that he proceeds from the Son also, as from the Father himself.

de trin. 15. 48

[1] John 15. 26.   [2] John 5. 26.

(c) The Bond of Love

The Holy Spirit has his existence in the same unity of substance and equality of Father and Son. Whether he is the unity of the two, or the holiness, or the unity because he is the love, and the love because he is the holiness, it is plain that the two Persons are joined together by a bond other than themselves. . . . Therefore the Holy Spirit is something which is common to Father and Son, whatever it is. But their communion is itself consubstantial and co-eternal; if it can fittingly be called 'friendship', that name will serve; but a more appropriate term is 'love'. And this is a 'substance' because God is a 'substance', and 'God is love'. Thus there are three persons, and not more than three. One who loves him who is derived from himself, one who loves him from whom he himself is derived, and their mutual love.   *de trin.* 6. 7

If then one of the three should be called Love, as his proper name, what more fitting than that this should be the Holy Spirit? I mean, that in that simple, supreme nature, 'substance' should not be one thing, love another; but love itself should be 'substance', and love substantial, whether in Father, Son or Spirit, and yet, as a proper name, Love should be the title of the Holy Spirit.   *de trin.* 15. 29

The Spirit is then the gift of God only so far as he is given to those to whom he is given. In himself he is God, existing even if he is given to no one, for he was God, co-eternal with Father and Son, before he was given to anyone. Nor is he inferior to them in that they give and he is given. For as the gift of God he is given, but at the same time he, as God, gives himself. For it cannot be said that he is not free, for it is said of him. 'The Spirit blows where he wills'.[1] And (in the Apostle's writings) 'all these things are due to the activity of one and the same Spirit, dividing to each their own gifts as he wills'.[2] Here there is no constraint on what is given, no control by the givers, but a concord of given and givers.   *de trin.* 15. 36

If the 'Will of God' is to be assigned as a proper name to one of the Trinity, it suits best the Spirit, as does Love. For what else is will but love?   *de trin.* 15. 38

In this analogy [*of the Trinity and human mind*] I have shown nothing which may be compared to the Holy Spirit except our will, or our love, which is a stronger kind of will.[3]   *de trin.* 15. 41

[1] John 3. 8.   [2] 1 Cor. 12. 11.   [3] Cf. p. 234.

A further question has been raised; whether, just as the Son derives from his begetting not merely his Sonship but his actual existence, so also the Holy Spirit derives from his being given, not only his character as a gift, but his actual existence; whether therefore he existed before he was given, but was not yet a gift, or whether he was a gift even before he was given, in that God was to give him. But if he does not proceed except when he is given, he clearly could not proceed until there was someone to whom he might be given. . . . Does the Holy Spirit always proceed, not in time only, but from eternity? But because he proceeded in order to be potentially a gift, he was already a gift before there was any recipient. . . . For a gift can exist before it is given. . . . The Spirit is eternally a gift, but the gift is bestowed in time.   *de trin.* 5. 16

VII. The Trinity

(a) Three and One

[*The Spirit manifested by visible signs, as the dove and the fiery tongues.*] The Father the Son and the Holy Spirit, of one and the same substance, are inseparable in activity as God the Creator, the almighty Trinity. But this activity cannot be displayed as indivisible when operating through such quite different and very physical created things. Just as by means of our voices, which produce a physical sound, the names, 'Father', 'Son', and 'Holy Spirit' can only be uttered in separation, divided by the intervals of time occupied by each name. As they exist in their own 'substance', the three are a unity . . . without any intervals of time, an unchanging unity from eternity to eternity. . . . But they cannot be named simultaneously, and when written down they occupy separate places in space. Again, just as, when I name my memory, intellect, and will, the different names each refer to single entities, yet the three entities all unite in producing the individual names (for each of these names is the result of the activity of memory, intellect, and will); so the voice of the Father, the flesh of the Son, the love of the Holy Spirit—each of those is due to the combined activity of the Trinity, although those manifestations are referred to the respective persons.   *de trin.* 4. 30

The predicates proper to the respective persons in the same Trinity refer to their mutual relations, or to their relations to created beings . . .

but since 'God is spirit',[1] 'Holy Spirit' can be predicated of the whole Trinity; the Father and Son both being 'spirit', and both 'holy'. . . . But the Holy Spirit, as a proper name in the Trinity, is relative to the Father and the Son, since the Holy Spirit is the Spirit of the Father and the Son. . . . The Holy Spirit is the inexpressible communion, as it were, of Father and Son; and that is perhaps the reason for his appellation which fits the Father and the Son as well. . . . The name which fits them both signifying their communion with each other; and thus the Holy Spirit is called the gift of both. And this Trinity is one God, only good, great, eternal, almighty; his own unity, deity, greatness, goodness, eternity, omnipotence. *de trin.* 5. 12

(b) One Source

In the mutual relations of the Trinity . . . the Father is the source of the Son, as begetting him. It is no easy question whether the Father is the source of the Holy Spirit, since 'He proceeds from the Father'.[2] Because, if so, he is not only the source in respect of that which he begets or makes, but also in respect of what he gives. This also throws light on the question, which disturbs many people, why the Spirit is not also a Son, and he 'came from the Father'. For he comes not as begotten, but as given; therefore he is not called Son, since his relation is not that of the Only-begotten; nor is he created, as we are, so as to obtain the adoption to sonship. . . . If a gift has the giver as its source . . . it must be admitted that the Father and the Son are the source of the Spirit; not two sources, but one source in relation to the Holy Spirit, as the Father and the Son are one God, and, in relation to the creation, one Creator and one Lord; while in relation to the Creation Father, Son, and Holy Spirit are one source, as they are one Creator and one Lord. *de trin.* 5. 15

(c) Ousia and Hypostasis

Nothing is predicated of God *per accidens* because nothing in him is subject to change; but that does not mean that everything is predicated of him in respect of 'substance'. There are relative predicates, as Father, in relation to Son: Son, in relation to Father; but those are not 'accidental', for the Father is always Father, the Son always Son . . . since the Son has always been begotten, and never begins to be Son. . . .

[1] John 4. 24. [2] John 15. 26.

Therefore, although being Son is different from being Father, there is
no difference of 'substance'; for those predicates are relative . . . yet not
accidental, because not susceptible of change.   *de trin.* 5. 6

Above all, we must maintain this position, that terms applied to the
sublime and incomparable divinity in respect of itself are understood
as substantial: terms which have external reference are to be taken as
relative. And that such is the force of the same substance in Father, Son,
and Holy Spirit, that whatever is affirmed of each in respect of themselves is to be taken in the singular, not in the plural, when the three are
considered together. For as the Father is God, so the Son is God, and the
Holy Spirit is God; and no one doubts that this is affirmed in respect of
substance: and yet we do not say that the incomparable Trinity is three
Gods, but one God. The Father is great, the Son is great, the Holy
Spirit is great: yet they are not three in greatness, but one. Whatever
predicates are applied to God in his own being are applied to each person severally . . . and together of the Trinity itself—in the singular, not
the plural. For in God 'to be' is the same as 'to be great'; and therefore
as we do not speak of three 'essences', so we do not speak of three
'greatnesses', but one 'essence' and one 'greatness'. By 'essence' I mean
what in Greek is called *ousia*, which we normally call 'substance'.

They also use the term *hypostasis*, differentiating this from *ousia*; so
that many of our writers who deal with these questions in Greek have
adopted the phrase, 'one *ousia*, three *hypostases*'. The Latin for this
would be, 'one essence, three substances'. But in our language 'essence'
has come to mean the same as 'substance', and so we shrink from using
this formula; we prefer to say 'one Essence or Substance, three Persons',
which is the phraseology of many Latin writers of authority. They use
this language for want of a more fitting way of expressing in words
what they understand without words. For indeed, since the Father is
not the Son, and the Son is not the Father, and the Holy Spirit, who is
called the gift of God, is neither the Father nor the Son, they are certainly three. And so the plural is used in, 'I and the Father are one thing'[1]
not 'is one', as the Sabellians[2] say, but 'are one'. Yet when it is asked
what the three are, human speech is embarrassed by the great poverty
of language. However, we say 'three *Persons*', not because that expresses
just what we want to say, but because we must say something.

                                                        de trin. 5. 9, 10

[1] John 10. 30.   [2] See p. 38.

The Father, the Son, and the Holy Spirit compose a unity of one and the same substance in inseparable equality. Thus there are not three Gods, but one God; although the Father has begotten the Son, and therefore the Son is not identical with the Father; the Son is begotten by the Father, and therefore the Father is not identical with the Son; the Holy Spirit is not the Father, nor the Son, but only the Spirit of the Father and the Son, yet he is co-equal with Father and Son, and belongs to the unity of the Trinity. It was not the Trinity that was born of the Virgin Mary, crucified under Pontius Pilate . . .; nor did the Trinity descend as a dove . . .; nor did the Trinity say 'Thou art my son . . .'[1] And yet the Father, Son, and Holy Spirit are inseparable and operate inseparably. *de trin.* 1. 7

The Spirit is certainly not a creature, for worship is offered to him by all the saints, as the Apostle says 'We are the circumcision, serving the Spirit of God',[2] where the Greek word λατρεύοντες means 'worshipping'. This is the reading of most of the Latin codices and all, or almost all, the Greek. But some Latin versions have 'serving by God by the Spirit'[3] . . . [1 Cor. 6. 15, 19, 20.] If then the 'members of Christ' are the 'temple of the Holy Spirit',[4] the Holy Spirit is not a creature . . . we must owe him the service which is due to God alone, which in Greek is called λατρεία. *de trin.* 1. 13

Because God is a Trinity he is not therefore to be thought of as three-fold; for then the Father by himself or the Son by himself would be less than Father and Son together. However, this is an impossible sup-position; for the Father and the Son are always inseparably together. This does not mean that both are Father, or both Son; they exist always in reciprocity; neither exists by himself. . . . Since the Father by him-self, or the Son, or the Holy Spirit, is no less than Father, Son, and Holy Spirit together, God cannot be spoken of as threefold. *de trin.* 6. 9

There are terms applied within the Trinity which refer to the single Person in distinction from the other, in respect of their mutual relation-ship: Father and Son and their Gift, the Holy Spirit. The Father is not the Trinity, nor is the Son, nor is the Gift. But terms used of the several persons in respect of their own being are used of the one Trinity, not of

---

[1] Matt. 3. 16, 17.   [2] Phil. 3. 3.   [3] The principal Greek MSS. have πνεύματι Θεοῦ. But the Greek dative is ambiguous, either 'serving the Spirit' or 'serving by the Spirit'; and the context compels the latter.   [4] 1 Cor. 6. 15, 19.

three persons in the plural: I mean that divinity, goodness, omnipotence are ascribed to Father, and to Son, and to Holy Spirit; but there are not three divinities, three goodnesses, three omnipotences; there is one God, the Trinity of goodness and omnipotence; and this applies to all terms which refer to the person in their own being, not in their mutual relation. . . . Thus we speak of three Persons, or three Substances, not to imply any difference of essence, but in such a sense that one word would suffice to answer the question 'What are the three Persons?' And such is the equality in the Trinity, that not only is the Father not greater than the Son, in respect of divinity, but Father and Son together are not greater than the Holy Spirit, nor is any one Person of the Three in any respect less than the Trinity itself.   *de trin.* 8. 1

(d) Vestiges of the Trinity in Man[1]

What is this charity, which the divine Scriptures so praise and preach, but the love of good? Now love is felt by a lover, and by love an object is loved. So here we have three things, a lover, a beloved, and love. And what is love, then, but a kind of life which links, or seeks to link some two things, the lover and the loved? This is true of physical love. . . . Let us rise higher and consider the mind. What does the mind love in a friend, but the mind? Here then are the three things. . . . It remains to rise even higher and seek those things, as far as man may, on a loftier plane. . . . We have not yet found what we are seeking, but we have found where to look for it.   *de trin.* 8. 14

We are not now speaking of heavenly things, of Father, Son, and Holy Spirit; but about man, the image of God; an image on a different plane, but still God's image. . . . When I love anything there are three things, myself, the object I love, and the love. But . . . when a man loves himself there are two, the love and the loved. . . . Thus it does not follow that where there is love there are three things.

The mind cannot love itself unless it knows itself. . . . When the mind loves itself there are, as it were, two things, mind and love; when it knows itself there are, as it were, three things, and those three are a unity; and when perfect, they are equal.

[*They exist substantially, are predicated relatively, are inseparable, of the same 'essence'.*] There abides the Trinity, mind, love, knowledge; they are not confused, but several in themselves, mutually all in all.

[1] Cf. p. 229.

Thus there is a kind of image of the Trinity in the mind, and its knowledge which is mind's offspring, and its word concerning itself; and love makes a third, and these three are a unity and one substance. The offspring is not less than the parent, seeing that the mind's knowledge is in proportion to its own being; nor is the love less, seeing that the mind's love is in proportion to its knowledge and its being.

de trin. 9. 2, 3, 4, 8, 18

There are those three: memory, understanding, will; not three lives, but one; not three minds, but one; therefore clearly not three 'substances', but one. . . . I remember that I have memory and understanding and will; I understand that I understand, will, remember; I will to will, remember, understand; and at the same time I remember my memory, understanding, and will. . .   *de trin.* 10. 18

[In Books 11 and 12 various analogies in the 'outer man' are considered; e.g. in sight, the object, the act of vision, the act of attention. But these are not equal nor consubstantial—the 'outer man' is not in God's image. None of these human relations provide a satisfactory analogy.]

The mind when it observes itself in thought understands itself and recognizes itself; thus it generates this understanding and cognition of itself. . . . And it does not generate this knowledge . . . as of something unknown before; it was known to it before in the same way that things retained in memory are known, even when they are not being thought of. . . . Those two things, the begetter and the begotten, are united by love as the third, and this love is none other than the will, desiring or retaining something to enjoy. Thus under those three names we have thought that a trinity may be inferred, of memory, understanding, and will.   *de trin.* 14. 8

Thus, you see, the mind remembers itself, understands itself, loves itself. If we observe this, we observe a trinity; not indeed God, as yet, but already the image of God.   *de trin.* 14. 11

This trinity of the mind is not the image of God just because mind remembers, understands, loves, itself; but because it is able to remember, understand, love him by whom it was created. When it does this, it attains wisdom. If it does not it is foolish, for all its memory, understanding, love of itself.   *de trin.* 14. 15

Each individual man, who is called the image of God in respect of his mind alone and not of all that belongs to his nature, is one person, and the image of the Trinity is in his mind. Whereas that whole Trinity, of which this is the image, is none other than God, and the whole Godhead is the Trinity and nothing else. Nothing belongs to God's nature which does not belong to that Trinity; and there are three Persons of one 'essence'; while each individual man is one person.

We remember only through memory, understand only through the understanding, love only through the will . . . [*In the divine Trinity*] you see, there are those three things, memory, understanding, love (or will), in that supreme, immutable 'essence' which is God; they are not Father, Son, Holy Spirit, but the Father alone. And because the Son is also wisdom begotten of wisdom, therefore neither the Father nor the Spirit understands for him, but he for himself; so neither does the Father remember for him, nor the Spirit love for him, but he for himself; for he is his own memory, understanding, love. But his being such is derived from the Father, who begets him. Also the Spirit, as wisdom proceeding from wisdom, does not have the Father as his memory, the Son as his understanding, himself as his love . . ., but he has these three, and in such a way that he *is* them. But his being thus is derived from him from whom he proceeds.   *de trin.* 15. 11, 12

In that supreme Trinity, which incomparably excels all other things, the persons are so inseparable that, while a trinity of men could not be called one man, in the case of that Trinity it is called one God, and is one God; it is not that the Trinity is *in* one God, it *is* one God. Nor again is the Trinity a trinity in the way in which man, that image of God, has three elements but is one person. In the Trinity there are three Persons, the Father of the Son, the Son of the Father, the Spirit of the Father and the Son . . . In that image of the Trinity the three elements are *of* the man, they *are* not the man: whereas in the supreme Trinity itself, of which this is the image, the three are not *of* one God, but there is one God, and they are three Persons, not one. And this is without doubt marvellously ineffable or ineffably marvellous; for although the image of the Trinity is one person while the supreme Trinity itself is three Persons, that divine Trinity of three Persons is more inseparable than this human trinity of one.   *de trin.* 15. 43

VIII. The Church

(a) *The Spirit in the Church*

A man who has the Holy Spirit is in the Church, which speaks with the language of all men. Whoever is outside the Church has not the Holy Spirit. That is why the Holy Spirit deigned to reveal himself in the languages of all nations, so that a man may realize that he has the Holy Spirit when he is contained in the unity of the Church, which speaks with all languages. . . . The body is made up of many parts, and one spirit gives life to all the parts. . . . As our spirit (that is, our soul) is to the parts of our body, so the Holy Spirit is to the parts of Christ's Body, the Church. . . . While we are alive and healthy all parts of our body fulfil their functions. If one part is in pain anywhere, all the other parts suffer with it. But because the part is in the body it can suffer, but it cannot die. To die is to 'expire', which means to 'lose the spirit'. If a part of the body is cut off . . . it retains the form of a finger, hand, arm, ear; but it has no life. Such is the state of a man separated from the Church. You inquire if he has the sacrament? He has. Baptism? He has it. The Creed? He has it. But what he has is merely the form. Unless you have the life of the Spirit, it is in vain to boast of the form.

serm. 268. 2

'In this way we know that we are the sons of God.'[1] What does this mean, my brothers? A little before he was speaking of the Son of God, not the sons, and now Christ is presented for our contemplation, and we are told that 'Everyone who believes that Jesus is the Christ, is born of God; and everyone who believes him who begot him' (that is, the Father) 'loves him who was begotten of him' (that is, the Son, our Lord Jesus Christ). And then: 'By this we know that we love the sons of God'.[2] It seems as if he were going to say, 'by this we know that we love the Son of God', and then, instead of saying the 'Son of God', as he had said just before, he said 'sons of God', because the sons of God are the body of God's only Son: he is the head, we are the members, and thus the Son of God is one. Therefore he who loves the sons of God loves the Son of God; he who loves the Son of God loves the Father. No one can love the Father, unless he loves the Son; and he who loves the Son loves the sons of God also. Who are these sons? The members of God's son. It is by loving that a man becomes a member, welded by

[1] 1 John 5. 2. [2] 1 John 5. 1, 2.

love in the structure of the body of Christ: and there will be one Christ, who loves himself. For when the members love each other, the body loves itself. ... 'In this way we know that we love the sons of God, because we love God.' How is this? Are not God's sons quite different from God? Yes, but a man who loves God loves God's commands. And what are God's commands? 'I am giving you a new commandment: love one another.'[1] Let no one use one love to excuse himself from the other. The nature of this love is such that, as it is itself welded into a unity, so it makes a unity of all those who are dependent upon it: it is, as it were, a fire which fuses them together. Gold is fused with a lamp and becomes a unity: and a multiplicity of men can only be fused into unity when the fire of love is kindled. 'Because we love God, it follows that we know that we love the sons of God.'   *in I ep. Joh. tract.* 10.3

All those [*sacraments, etc.*] the Donatists[2] may have had; but they were of no avail, where charity was lacking. And who can truly say that he has the 'charity of Christ', when he does not embrace his unity? When they come to the Catholic Church they do not receive what they had before: they receive what they lacked, so that what they had may begin to profit them. For here they receive the root of charity 'in the bond of peace',[3] and in the fellowship of unity.   *ep.* 61. 2

(b) Visible and Invisible

In the Song of Songs the Church is described as 'an enclosed garden, my sister and bride, a sealed fountain, a well of living water, an orchard of choice fruit'.[4] I dare not interpret this except as applying only to the holy and righteous, not to the greedy, the fraudulent, the grasping, the usurers, the drunken, the envious. Those share a common baptism with the just: they do not share a common charity. ... How have they penetrated into the 'enclosed garden, the sealed fountain'? As Cyprian says, they have renounced the world only in word, not in deed; and yet he admits that they are within the Church. If they are within, and form 'the Bride of Christ', is this really that bride 'without any blemish or wrinkle'?[5] Is that 'beautiful dove'[6] defiled by such a part of her members? Are those the 'brambles' in the midst of which she is 'like a lily'?[7] As a lily she is the enclosed garden, the sealed fountain: that is, as she exists in the persons of the righteous, who are 'Jews in secret, by the

[1] John 13. 34.   [2] See p. 240.   [3] Eph. 4. 3.   [4] Cant. 4. 12, 13.   [5] Eph. 5. 27; cf. Rev. 21. 2, 9.   [6] Cant. 6. 9.   [7] Cant. 2. 2.

circumcision of the heart'[1] ('All the beauty of the king's daughter is within her'[2]). In them is found the fixed number of the saints, fore-ordained before the creation of the world. That host of brambles sur-rounds her on the outside, above that number, whether openly or secretly separated from her. 'I have proclaimed and spoken: they have been multiplied beyond number.'[3] . . . There are some in that number who live wickedly now; they may even be sunk in heresies or in pagan superstitions: yet even there 'The Lord knows those who belong to him'.[4] For in the ineffable foreknowledge of God many who seem to be outside are within: many who seem to be within are outside.

de bapt. 5. 38

(c) Catholicity
In Teaching and in Extension

[Addressing Vincentius, a bishop who supported the Rogatists, a rigorist party similar to the Donatists (p. 240), and criticized A. for invoking the Imperial power to 'compel them to come in'.]

You suppose yourself to be making a shrewd point when you interpret 'Catholic' with reference not to a world-wide community, but to the observance of all the divine commands and all the sacraments. You imagine that we rely on the testimony of this title of 'Catholic' to distinguish the Church which exists among all the nations: and it may well be that the appellation derives from the fact that this Church retains the whole truth, while some fragments of it are found even in different heresies. But you imagine that we rely on this evidence, and not on the promises of God, and all the many unmistakable oracles of the truth itself. The whole point on which you are trying to persuade us is that only the Rogatists are rightly to be called Catholic, on the basis of their observance of all the divine commands and all the sacra-ments. . . . But how could we be confident that we had received the revelation of Christ in the divine writings if we have not also received from them the revelation of the Church? . . . Just as anyone will be anathema if he proclaims that Christ did not suffer, and did not rise on the third day, since we have learnt in the truth of the gospel that 'Christ had to suffer, and to rise from the dead on the third day':[5] so anyone will be anathema if he proclaims a Church apart from the world-wide community, seeing that we learn, in accordance with the same truth,

[1] Rom 2. 29.   [2] Ps. 45. 13 (44. 14).   [3] Ps. 40. 5 (39. 6).   [4] 2 Tim. 2. 19.   [5] Luke 24. 46.

that 'repentance and forgiveness of sins must be proclaimed in his name
through all nations, beginning from Jerusalem'.[1]   *ep.* 93. 23

[Addressing the Donatist[2] bishop Honoratus.]

Would you please be good enough to reply to this question: Do you
happen to know why it should be that Christ should lose his inheritance, which is spread over the whole world, and should suddenly be
found surviving only in the Africans, and not in all of them? The
Catholic Church exists indeed in Africa, since God willed and ordained
that it should exist throughout the whole world. Whereas your party,
which is called the party of Donatus,[2] does not exist in all those places
in which the writings of the apostles, their discourse, and their actions,
have been current.   *ep.* 49. 3

(*d*) *The Mystical Body*

Sometimes the title Christ appears in Scripture in reference to the Word
equal to the Father. Sometimes in reference to the Mediator. . . . Sometimes in reference to the head and the body, when Paul expounds the
conjugal relationship of 'one flesh' in Genesis . . . as a 'great mystery'
. . . applied to 'Christ and the Church'.[3] The husband–wife relationship
is the same as that between head and body, the husband being 'the head
of the wife'.[4] Whether I say 'husband and wife' or 'head and body', you
must understand me to mean a unity. Thus the same Apostle heard the
voice saying, 'Saul, Saul, why are you persecuting *me*?',[5] since the head
is joined to the body. And when as Christ's preacher he was suffering
from others what as a persecutor he had inflicted on others, he says: 'So
that I may complete, in my flesh, the sufferings of Christ which have still
to be endured',[6] showing that his sufferings were related to the sufferings of Christ. Now this cannot be understood of Christ the head; for
he is in Heaven, and suffers nothing of this sort. It must be understood
of the body, the Church; for the body with its head is one Christ.

serm. 341. 12

---

[1] Luke 24. 48.   [2] The Donatists were a schismatic body in Africa, started by those who
refused to accept Caecilian, bishop of Carthage, because he was consecrated by Felix of
Aptunga, an alleged *traditor* (i.e. one who had surrendered copies of the Scriptures in
Diocletian's persecution). The Catholics contended that the validity of a sacrament did
not depend on the worthiness of the minister. Donatus was the second bishop of the sect.
[3] Eph. 5. 32 f.   [4] 1 Cor. 11. 3.   [5] Acts 9. 4.   [6] Col. 1. 24.

IX. The Sacraments

(a) Baptism

(i) Validity and Efficacy[1]

The reason why the blessed Cyprian and other eminent Christians . . . decided that Christ's baptism could not exist among heretics or schismatics was that they failed to distinguish between the sacrament and the efficacy or working out of a sacrament. Because the efficacy and working out of baptism, in freedom from sins and in integrity of heart, was not found among heretics, it was supposed that the sacrament itself did not exist there. But if we turn our eyes to the multitude within the fold, it is clear that those within the unity of the Church who are perverse and lead wicked lives can neither give nor have the remission of sins. Nevertheless the pastors of the Catholic Church spread through the whole world were quite clear that such men had the sacrament of baptism and could confer it; and through them the original custom was afterwards established by the authority of a plenary council. Even when a wandering sheep has received the Lord's brand-mark at the hands of dishonest robbers, and then comes into the security of Christian unity, it is restored, freed, and healed; but the Lord's brand-mark is recognized, not disallowed . . .

No difference is made to the sanctity of baptism by the demerit of the individual who receives or confers it: a man in schism can confer it, a man in schism can have it; but the possession and the conferment are equally fraught with peril. The recipient of a schismatic's baptism may receive it to his salvation, if he himself is not in schism. . . . But if the recipient is in schism the peril of its reception is measured by the greatness of the good which he has received when in no state of good; its destructive power for a schismatic is measured by its salutary power for one within the unity. For this reason, if the schismatic is corrected from that perversity, if he turns from schism and comes into the peace of the Catholic Church, his sins are forgiven by the power of the same baptism which he has received, by reason of the bond of charity.[2]

de bapt. 6. 1 and 7

(ii) Schismatic Baptism

['*If Donatist baptism is valid, then the Donatists must constitute the true mother church.*'] This assumes that the schism is 'mother' in respect of its

---

[1] On this section and the next, cf. pp. 84-8.   [2] Cf. Eph. 4. 2-4, Col. 3. 14.

separation, not in respect of its conjunction with the Church. It is separated from the bond of love and peace,[1] but joined in the one baptism. And so there is one Church which alone is called Catholic. It is this Church, not those separated bodies, who in fact gives birth to these children; and she does this in virtue of that which she has belonging to her in those communities of separated men which are cut off from her unity. It is not the separation which gives birth, but that derived from her which those separated men have retained: if they let this go, they do not give birth at all. Thus it is she, whose sacraments are kept, who gives birth in every instance; hence some birth of this kind can happen in every place. And yet not all to whom the Church gives birth are attached to that unity which will save those 'who persevere to the end'.[2]

de bapt. 1. 14

(iii) *Minister and Sacrament*

The water over which the name of God is invoked is not profane and polluted, even if that name is invoked by profane and polluted men; for neither God's creation nor God's name can be polluted. The baptism which is consecrated by the words of Christ in the Gospels is holy, even when conferred by the polluted, and on the polluted, however shameless and unclean they may be. This holiness is itself incapable of contamination, and the power of God supports his sacrament, whether for the salvation of those who use it aright, or the doom of those who employ it wrongly. The light of the sun, or of a lamp, is not defiled by contact with the filth on which it shines: so how can Christ's baptism be defiled by the wickedness of any man?   *de bapt.* 3. 15

(iv) *Baptism and Regeneration*

For our reception of eternal life, which will be given to us at the last day, we receive a gift from the bounty of God, the gift of remission of sins, on the basis of faith. . . . That rebirth, when the remission of all past sins comes about, is effected through the Holy Spirit, for the Lord says: 'A man cannot enter into God's Kingdom, unless he has been born anew by means of water and the Spirit'.[3] But it is one thing to be born of the Spirit; to be fed by the Spirit is another. . . . Perfect love is the gift of the Spirit; but this is preceded by the gift which concerns the remission of sins.   *serm.* 71. 19

[1] Cf. Eph. 4. 2, 3.   [2] Matt. 10. 22.   [3] John 3. 5

[*Cornelius received the Spirit before baptism; Abraham was justified by faith before circumcision; Isaac was circumcised before justification.*] So in baptized infants the sacrament of regeneration comes first; and if they hold fast to Christian piety, conversion in the heart will follow, following on the sacramental sign [mystery] of it in the body.

This all shows that the sacrament of baptism is one thing, the conversion of the heart is another; but the salvation of man is effected by these two. If one is missing, we are not bound to suppose that the other is absent: in an infant, baptism can exist without conversion; in the penitent thief, conversion without baptism . . . there can be conversion of the heart when baptism has not been received, but not when baptism has been rejected.   *de bapt.* 4. 31, 32

We all know that if one baptized in infancy does not believe when he comes to years of discretion, and does not keep himself from lawless desires, then he will have no profit from the gift he received as a baby.

de pecc. merit. I. 25

(v) *Unbaptized Infants*

I do not say that those who die without Christ's baptism are to be involved in so heavy a punishment that it would be better for them not to have been born.[1] . . . Who could doubt that unbaptized infants, who have only original sin and are not burdened by sins of their own committing, will suffer the lightest possible condemnation? I cannot define the nature and extent of this, but I cannot bring myself to say that it would be better for them not to exist than to exist in that condition.

c. Jul. 5. 44

[It is to be noted that Augustine generally speaks of the punishment of the unbaptized in controversy with Pelagians, when he is challenging them to explain why they practise and approve infant baptism, seeing that they deny original sin.]

(b) *The Eucharist*
(i) *Sacrifice*

The offering of sacrifices of animal victims by the Fathers in ancient times . . . is to be understood as having just this purpose: to symbolize all our endeavours to be united to God, and our concern to achieve the same end for our neighbour. A sacrifice therefore is the visible sacrament

[1] Cf. Matt. 26. 24.

of an invisible sacrifice; that is, it is a sacred sign. . . . 'A sacrifice to God is a contrite spirit'.[1] . . . What is commonly called a sacrifice is the *sign* of a sacrifice. Mercy, too, is a real sacrifice. 'With such sacrifices God is pleased.'[2] All the divine instructions concerning sacrifice in the service of tabernacle or temple are by their symbolism directed towards love to God and to neighbour. 'On those two commandments depend the whole law and all the prophets.'[3]

A true sacrifice is every act which is performed so that we may be united with God in holy fellowship; directed, that is, towards the achievement of our true good, which alone can bring us true happiness. . . . Although this sacrifice is made or offered by man, still the sacrifice is a divine act. . . . The whole redeemed community, the congregation and fellowship of the saints, is offered as a universal sacrifice to God by the great Priest who offered himself in suffering for us in the form of a servant,[4] that we might be the Body of so great a Head. This form of a servant he offered, in this he was offered; for in this he is mediator, priest, and sacrifice. So the Apostle exhorted us to 'present our bodies as a living sacrifice'[5] . . .; we ourselves are the whole sacrifice. . . . This is the sacrifice of Christians; the 'many who are one body in Christ'.[6] This sacrifice the Church celebrates in the sacrament of the altar, which the faithful know well, where it is shown to her that in this thing which she offers she herself is offered.   *de civ. Dei* 10. 5, 6

(ii) *Corpus Christi and the Body of Christ*

The reason why these [the bread and wine] are called sacraments is that one thing is seen in them, but something else is understood. That which is seen has bodily appearance; that which is understood has spiritual fruit. If you wish to understand the body of Christ, listen to the Apostle's words: 'You are the body and the members of Christ'.[7] If you are the body and members of Christ, it is your mystery[8] which is placed on the Lord's table; it is your mystery you receive. It is to that which you are that you answer 'Amen', and by that response you make your assent. You hear the words 'the body of Christ'; you answer 'Amen'. *Be* a member of Christ, so that the 'Amen' may be true. Why then is he in bread? Let us not put forward any suggestion of our own, but listen to the repeated teaching of the Apostle; for he says, speaking of this sacrament: 'We are many, but we are one loaf, one body'.[9] Understand

[1] Ps. 51. 17.   [2] Heb. 13. 16.   [3] Matt. 22. 40.   [4] Phil. 2. 7.   [5] Rom. 12. 1.   [6] Rom. 12. 5.
[7] 1 Cor. 12. 27.   [8] i.e. the symbol of yourselves.   [9] 1 Cor. 10. 17.

and rejoice. unity, truth, goodness, love. 'One loaf.' What is that one loaf? 'We many are one body.' Remember that the bread is not made from one grain of wheat, but of many. When you were exorcized you were, in a manner, ground; when baptized you were, in a manner, moistened. When you received the fire of the Holy Spirit you were, in a manner, cooked. . . . Many grapes hang in a cluster, but their juice is mixed in unity. So the Lord has set his mark on us, wished us to belong to him, has consecrated on his table the mystery of our peace and unity. If a man receives the sacrament of unity, but does not 'keep the bond of peace',[1] he does not receive a sacrament for his benefit, but evidence for his condemnation. *serm.* 272

(iii) *Symbol and Sacrament*

['*How can baptized infants be said to have faith?*'] We often say 'Easter is coming', or: 'It will be Passiontide in a few days', although it is so long ago that the Lord suffered his passion, and that passion happened once for all. And on the Lord's day we say, 'Today Christ has risen': though so many years have passed since his resurrection. The reason why no one is so stupid as to accuse us of lying when we speak thus is that we give those titles to the various days on account of their likeness to the days on which the events took place, so that a day is called by the name belonging to another day, which resembles it by reason of its position in the year's course. Thus we speak of some sacred event [*sacramentum*] which we celebrate as happening on that day, when in fact it happened long ago. Christ was once sacrificed in his own person; and yet he is mystically [*in sacramento*] sacrificed for the peoples not only throughout the Easter festival, but every day. . . . If the sacraments had not a kind of likeness to those things of which they are sacraments, they would not be sacraments at all. And from this likeness they generally receive the names of the things themselves. As therefore the sacrament of the body of Christ is, in a sense, the body of Christ, and the sacrament of Christ's blood is Christ's blood, so the sacrament of faith is faith. *ep.* 98. 9

The infant eats what the mother eats: but since the infant is incapable of being fed with bread the mother takes bread into her body, which is reduced in the breast to the liquid form of milk by which the infant takes nourishment from that bread. How then does the Wisdom of God

[1] Eph. 4. 3.

feed us on this bread? Because 'the Word was made flesh'[1] ... and thus
man 'ate the food of angels'.[2] ... 'He humbled himself and became
obedient even up to death, and that death was the death of the cross.'[3]
So that now from the cross the flesh and blood of the Lord is entrusted
to us as a new sacrifice.   *enn. in Ps.* 32. 1, 6

(iv) *Figurative Interpretations*

If a command seems to order something immoral or criminal, or to
forbid what is useful or beneficial, then it is figurative. 'Unless', he says,
'you eat the flesh, and drink the blood, of the Son of Man, you will not
have life in yourselves.'[4] This seems to order crime or immorality:
therefore it is figurative, and enjoins that we should participate in the
Passion of the Lord, and store up in our memory, for our joy and our
profit, the fact that his flesh was crucified and wounded for us.

de doct. Christ. 3. 24

(v) *Realist Interpretation*

How was he 'carried in his own hands'?[5] When he gave his own body
and blood, he took in his hands what the faithful recognize; and, in a
manner, he carried himself when he said, 'This is my blood'.

enn. in Ps. 33. 2, 2

Judas, to whom the Lord gave the piece of bread, gave the devil his
chance to enter him,[6] not by receiving something evil, but by receiving
something in an evil way. So when a man receives the sacrament of the
Lord unworthily the result is not that the sacrament is evil because he is
evil, nor that he has received nothing at all because he has not received
it for his salvation. It is just as much the Lord's body and blood when a
man 'eats and drinks judgement to himself'[7] by partaking unworthily.

de bapt. 5. 9

(vi) *Spiritual Food and Drink*

'Adore his footstool for he is holy.'[8] ... Scripture tells me that 'the
earth is the Lord's footstool'[9] ... and 'You shall adore the Lord God'.[10]
... I am in perplexity; and I turn to Christ, for I look for him here. And
I find how 'earth' may be adored without idolatry. ... For he took

---

[1] John 1. 14. [2] Ps. 78. 25. [3] Phil. 2. 8. [4] John 6. 53. [5] 1 Sam. 21. 14 (LXX) '[David]
drummed on the gates of the city, and carried himself in his hands'. [6] John 13. 26.
[7] 1 Cor. 11. 29. [8] Ps. 99 (98). 5. [9] Isa. 66. 1. [10] Deut. 6. 13 (LXX).

earth from the earth; because flesh is from the earth, and he took flesh from the flesh of Mary. And he walked here in the flesh, and he gave this flesh to us to eat for our salvation, flesh which no one eats unless he has first adored. . . . But the Lord himself said, 'It is the spirit that gives life; the flesh is of no use.'[1] . . . 'Interpret what I have said in a spiritual sense. It is not the body which you see which you are going to eat, you will not be drinking the blood which those who crucify me are to shed. I have entrusted you with something sacramental which, when spiritually understood, will give you life. Although it must of necessity be celebrated in visible form, it must still be understood invisibly.'

enn. in Ps. 98. 9

'Work for your food; not the food which perishes, but the lasting food, which gives eternal life. . . .' 'This is God's work, that you should believe in him whom he has sent.'[2] This then is to eat 'the food which does not perish.' . . . There is no need of mastication and digestion. Believe, and you have eaten . . . *in ev. Jo. tract.* 25. 12

When the Lord was going to give the Holy Spirit, he spoke of himself as the bread which comes down from heaven,[3] exhorting us to believe in him. To believe in him is to eat the living bread. He who believes, eats; he is invisibly fed, because he is invisibly reborn. He is inwardly an infant, inwardly new; where a man is renewed, there he is satisfied.

in ev. Jo. tract. 26. 1

'Your fathers ate manna, and they died.'[4] Why? . . . Because they believed only in what they saw: they did not understand what they did not see. They are 'your fathers', because you are like them. As regards the visible death of the body, we shall surely die, although we eat 'the bread which comes down from heaven'. . . . But there is that death with which the Lord threatens them, the death which their fathers died; in respect of that death Moses ate manna, and did not die; and this is true of Aaron, and Phineas, and many others who 'pleased the Lord'. Why? Because they understood the visible food in a spiritual sense; they were spiritually hungry, they tasted spiritually, so that they were spiritually satisfied. We today receive visible food; but the sacrament is one thing, the virtue of the sacrament is another. . . . Take care

[1] Cf. John 6. 63. [2] John 6. 27, 29. [3] John 6. 50. [4] John 6. 49.

then, brothers; eat the heavenly bread spiritually; bring innocence to the altar . . .

'He who eats of this bread will not die.'[1] But that means the man who eats what belongs to the virtue of the sacrament, not to the visible sacrament; who eats inwardly, not outwardly; the man who eats the sacrament in the heart, not the man who crushes it with his teeth . . .

This food and drink the Lord wishes to be understood as the fellowship of his body and his members; which is the holy Church, consisting in his saints and faithful people, who are fore-ordained, called, justified, and glorified.[2] . . . The sacrament of this, of the unity of the body and blood of Christ . . . is made ready on the Lord's table, received from the Lord's table, by some to bring them life, by others to bring them destruction: but the reality itself, of which this is the sacrament, is for every man who partakes of it the means of life, never of destruction.

in ev. Jo. tract. 26. 11, 12, 15

X. The Last Things

(a) Punishment

Those who wish to refer both the fire and the worm to pains of mind, not of body, say that those who repent too late, and to no avail, burn with mental anguish at being cut off from the Kingdom of God. They maintain that the metaphor of fire can be appropriately used for this burning anguish: hence the Apostle says, 'Do I not burn, if any one is made to stumble?'[3] And they suppose that the worm is to be interpreted in the same way. For, they say, what the Bible is saying is: 'As the moth eats into cloth and the worm eats into wood, so sorrow tortures the heart of a man.' But those who are convinced that the punishment will involve pain both of mind and body assert that the body is burnt by fire, while the mind is, as it were, gnawed by the worm of sorrow. Now although this sounds plausible, since it is certainly absurd to suppose that in that state any pain, whether of body or mind, will be lacking; still for myself I find it easier to say that both pains apply to the body rather than to deny that either does. Mental pain is not mentioned in these words of the Bible, because it is understood to follow, without its being expressly stated, that when the body suffers in this way, the mind will be tormented by unavailing repentance.   *de civ. Dei* 21. 9

[1] John 6. 50.   [2] Cf. Rom. 8. 30.   [3] 2 Cor. 11. 29.

He who desires to avoid eternal punishment must be not only baptized but also justified in Christ, and thus really pass from the devil to Christ. Let him be assured that there will be no purgatorial pains except those which precede that last and dreadful Judgement. However, it cannot be denied that even the eternal fire itself will be lighter for some, heavier for others, in proportion to their varying deserts.   *de civ. Dei* 21. 16

How absurd it is to interpret eternal punishment as meaning merely a fire of long duration while believing eternal life to signify life without end. . . . The phrases are parallel: eternal punishment; eternal life. To say, in the same context, 'Eternal life will be without end, eternal punishment will have an end', is utterly ridiculous. Hence, since the eternal life of the saints will be without end, the eternal punishment of those who incur it will without doubt be endless.[1]   *de civ. Dei* 21. 23

(b) The Reward

The reward of virtue will be God himself, who gave the virtue, and promised to give himself; and there could be no better or greater gift. For when he said by the prophet, 'I shall be their God, and they will be my people',[2] he surely meant just this: 'I shall be their satisfaction; I shall be everything that men can honestly desire: life, health, food, abundance, glory, honour, peace, and all good things.' This is the right interpretation of the Apostle's words, 'That God may be all in all'.[3] He will be the end of our desires, and we shall see him without end, love him without revulsion, praise him without weariness. This gift, this emotion, this activity will be shared by all, just as life eternal will be the common condition of all.   *de civ. Dei* 22. 30

(c) The Resurrection Body

The souls of departed saints make light of the death by which they are separated from their bodies. This is because their 'flesh rests in hope',[4] whatever the humiliations it may seem to have suffered, which it is now unable to feel. For they do not (as Plato supposed) long to receive bodies through forgetfulness:[5] but because they remember the promise given them by one who always keeps his word, who gave them assurance of the preservation of the hairs of their head,[6] they look forward with patient yearning to the resurrection of the bodies in which they endured many hardships, but in which they will never feel any further

[1] Lev. 26. 12.   [2] Basil makes the same point; cf. p. 92.   [3] I Cor. 15. 28.   [4] Ps. 16. 9.
[5] Cf. Plato *rep.* 621A.   [6] Matt. 10. 30.

pain. If they did not 'hate their own flesh'[1] when they constrained it by the law of the spirit because through its weakness it opposed their will, how much more do they love it when it is itself destined to be spiritual. The spirit when subservient to the flesh is not inappropriately called carnal: so the flesh in subservience to the spirit is rightly called spiritual, not because it is converted into spirit, as some infer from the scriptural text, 'It is sown as a natural body, it will rise as a spiritual body',[2] but because it will be subdued to the spirit, readily offering complete and wonderful obedience. And this will lead to the fulfilment of their desire, with the secure attainment of secure immortality, with the removal of all feeling of discomfort, all corruptibility and reluctance.

de civ. Dei 13. 20

(d) The Last Judgement

In its confession and profession of faith the whole Church of God asserts that Christ will come from heaven 'to judge the living and the dead': this is what we call the Final Judgement, the Last Day. It is not known for how many days this Judgement may be prolonged: anyone who has read the holy Scriptures, however inattentively, must know that 'day' is habitually used for 'period'. When we talk of the Day of Judgement, we add the epithet 'Final', or 'Last', because God's judgement is happening even now. This judgement began at the start of the human race, when God expelled the first human beings from paradise, and cut them off from the tree of life, because they had committed a great sin. Indeed, it happened when God did not spare the angels who sinned, whose prince first brought about his own ruin, and then through envy brought ruin on mankind: here, beyond doubt, was a judgement. And it is because of God's high and just judgement that the life of men and of demons, on earth and in the sky above us, is most miserable, full of uncertainty and hardship. Even if no one had sinned, it would have been by an act of good and just judgement that God would have kept the whole world of rational creatures attached to himself without faltering. He passes judgement not only generally, on the race of demons and men, so that they are in misery because of the first offences; but also on the particular acts of individuals, the acts of their own free choice. .... What is properly called the Day of Judgement is the day when Christ will come to judge the living and the dead. In that day there will be no place for uninformed discussion of the reason why one

[1] Eph. 5. 29.   [2] 1 Cor. 15. 44.

man is fortunate, another unfortunate. Then the true and full happiness of none but the good will be manifest, and the deserved and complete unhappiness of the wicked. *de civ. Dei* 20. 1

John speaks of the opening of books,[1] and of a book: and he states what kind of a book this is: 'It is the book of life' . . . in which is shown which of God's commandments each man has performed or failed to perform. . . . It is to be understood as a kind of divine power which enables each man to recall to mind all his actions, good or bad, and to observe them with miraculous speed by an act of mental intuition; so that each man's knowledge may accuse or absolve his conscience. Thus each and all may be simultaneously judged. *de civ. Dei* 20. 14

[1] Rev. 20. 12.

Cyril of Alexandria

I. The Person of Christ

(a) The Title 'Mother of God'

[Nestorius, appointed bishop of Constantinople in 428, attacked the use of the title 'Theotokos', 'Mother of God', as suggesting the heresy of Apollinarius (see p. 11 f.).]

I am amazed that there are some who are extremely doubtful whether the holy Virgin should be called Mother of God or no. For if our Lord Jesus Christ is God, then surely the holy Virgin who gave him birth must be God's mother. . . . But you may say; 'Now tell me, was the Virgin the mother of the Godhead?' My reply is that the living and subsistent[1] Word of God is begotten of the substance of God the Father, as all acknowledge, and has his existence without beginning in time, always co-existing with his Father, having his being in and with the Father, and is thus presented to our minds. In the last times of this age, when he became flesh, that is, was united with flesh endowed with a rational soul, he is said to have also been begotten through a woman according to the flesh. This mystery of the incarnate Word has some similarity with human birth. For mothers of ordinary men, in obedience to the natural laws of generation, carry in the womb the flesh which gradually takes shape, and develops through the secret operations of God until it reaches perfection and attains the form of a human being: and God endows this living creature with spirit, in a manner known only to himself: as the prophet says, 'He forms a man's spirit in him'.[2] The condition of flesh is very different from that of spirit. But although those mothers are only the mothers of bodies belonging to this world, still they are said to give birth, not to a part of a man but to the whole man, consisting of soul and body. . . . If anyone maintained that anyone's mother was 'mother of flesh' and not 'mother of soul' he would be talking nonsense. For what she has produced is one living being, a composite of two dissimilar elements, but a single human being, with each element retaining its own nature.

ep. 1, ad monachos Aegypti

---

[1] ἐνυπόστατος.   [2] Zech. 12. 1.

(b) Unity of Person

If his [N.'s] term 'conjunction' [*synapheia*] means the unity [*henôsis*] which we conceive, that is, a unity of person [*hypostasis*], then he would be justified in claiming to teach that 'there is no division in Christ, as Christ; there are not two Christs, two Sons. . .'. But if this is so, how is it that you, Nestorius, allege that the one and indivisible Christ is 'twofold, not in status but in nature?' Because the Word of God the Father took flesh and came forth as man in our condition, he is not therefore to be called 'twofold'; he who in his own proper nature is outside of flesh and blood is one being, in the flesh. If anyone kills an ordinary human being he is not to be accused of two crimes, even if a man is to be considered as composed of soul and body, and the experiences of these two components are by nature different. We should think of Christ in the same manner: he is not twofold; he is one single Lord and Son, the Word of God the Father, in the flesh. I myself acknowledge that there is a very great difference, indeed the greatest disparity, between divinity and humanity: these terms clearly denote things essentially diverse and utterly dissimilar. But when the mystery of Christ is presented to us, then the principle of unity does not ignore the difference, but it excludes division: it does not confuse or mingle the natures: The Word of God partook of flesh and blood, and the Son is conceived of as one, and is so named.   *adv. Nest.* 2. 6

(c) Indivisible Worship of the One Christ

What I would say, my good Nestorius, is that although we speak of Christ as man and at the same time God, we are not making a division in so speaking. Rather we knew this same Son and God and Word of the Father even before his incarnation; and, after that, we knew him as made man, in our condition, and incarnate.[1] Nestorius, in contending that he is not to be thought of as a mere man, but as God and man, attributes the crown of thorns and the rest of his sufferings to the man, separately and exclusively, and acknowledges that he gives to him 'joint-adoration with the divinity': and he goes further in impiety in saying that he worships him not, as is right, as being truly God and Son, but as having become 'the advocate of the authority of the Word'. The division that he makes is clear from his acknowledgement that worship is to be given *with* the divinity: for what is worshipped *with* something else is surely quite distinct from that with which it is said to

[1] σεσαρκωμένος.

be worshipped. But we are accustomed to worship Emmanuel with one single worship, not separating from the Word the body which was personally[1] united to him. *adv. Nest.* 2. 10

(d) Distinction and Unity in the Logos Incarnate

Surely it is beyond dispute that the Only-begotten, being by nature God, became man not by conjunction [*synapheia*], as Nestorius alleges, regarded as a merely external link, or a moral connexion;[2] but by a genuine union [*henôsis*], in a manner beyond explanation or understanding. Thus he is thought of as one single being; all that he says is consistent with himself and will prove to be entirely the utterance of one person [*prosôpon*]. For [3]as soon as this union has taken place there is a single nature presented to our minds, the incarnate nature of the Word himself.[3] Something like this can of course be observed in our experience; for a single man is really a composite being, made up of unlike elements, namely soul and body. Further, it must be observed that we assert that the body which was united to God the Word was animated by a rational soul. It is important to add that there is a great difference between the flesh, considered in its own nature, and the essential nature of the Word: but although the things so named are conceived as different, and separated by their diversity of nature, Christ is still apprehended as one being, made up of the two elements. The divinity and the humanity come together in a real unity of mutual accord ...

Our Lord Jesus Christ compares himself to a pearl, 'The Kingdom of Heaven is like a merchant looking for fine pearls'.[4] ... And I find him using another image to reveal himself to us, when he says, 'I am a flower of the plain, a lily of the glens'.[5] For in his own nature he possesses the divine brightness of God the Father, while at the same time he gives out his own fragrance, a sweet spiritual perfume. In the case of the pearl and the lily the underlying physical body is perceived, while the brightness or fragrance is apprehended after its own manner; and these are apprehended as different from the things in which they subsist: yet they inhere in these inseparably, belonging to them, and not alien from the bodies which possess them. I believe that we should think and judge in the same way about Emmanuel. Divinity and flesh are by nature diverse in kind: yet the Word's body was his own: the Word united

[1] καθ' ὑπόστασιν. [2] συνάφεια σχετική—perhaps 'habitual connexion' (cf. p. 260).
[3-3] μία γὰρ ἤδη νοεῖται φύσις μετὰ τὴν ἕνωσιν, ἡ αὐτοῦ τοῦ λόγου σεσαρκωμένη.
[4] Matt. 13. 45. [5] Cant. 2. 1.

to that body was not separated from it. This is the only way in which we should conceive of Emmanuel, 'God with us'. *adv. Nest. 2. pref.*

(e) 'For our Salvation'

Inspired Scripture says that the Word from God the Father was incarnate, that is, was united to flesh without confusion, hypostatically. The body was united with the Word, the body, born of a woman, was not alien from him; just as the body of each one of us belongs to the individual person, so the body of the Only-begotten belonged to him. . . If the Word had not been begotten, according to the flesh, in the same way as we are, if he had not shared in our condition in this way, he would not have freed human nature from the guilt we inherit from Adam, nor have driven away the corruption from our bodies. . . . But you affect to be afraid that some of us may suspect that the Word, begotten from the Father, had the beginning of his existence from earthly flesh, and you utterly destroy the mystery of the [1]'economy' in the flesh,[1] when you say that we must not give to the holy Virgin the title 'Mother of God'. . . . You would yourself approve the correct and holy faith of those who so believe, if you would bring yourself to consider, and to acknowledge, that Christ is truly God, that he is one, and the only Son of the God and Father, not divided into God and man; that he is one and the same, the Word from the Father, and man from a woman, after our fashion, while remaining God. *adv. Nest. 1. 1*

The Lord of the Universe, the Only-begotten God, submitted himself to deprivation for our sakes, so that he might generously confer on us the privilege of brotherhood with him, and the beauty, all to be desired,[2] of his own inherent nobility. But Nestorius deprives us of all this glory, in saying that it was simply a man who was born to be our brother: and to explain to us what he considers to be a credible argument for this position he adds, 'Observe what immediately follows: "That he might prove to be a merciful and faithful high priest before God; for since he has himself experienced the test of suffering he is able to help those who undergo the test." He who experiences suffering is the merciful high priest: The temple is capable of suffering, not God who gives life to that which suffers.' A man who chooses to hold this opinion, and does not shrink from uttering it, is making a division

---

[1]-[1] τῆς μετὰ σαρκὸς οἰκονομίας—the 'economy' (the fulfilment of God's plan) in the incarnation. [2] Cf. Isa. 53. 2.

again into two hypostases, in fact into two persons, the one being the Word from God the Father, the other being he whom he lately introduced as the 'God-bearing man'. I cannot believe that anyone will doubt this conclusion, assuming the distinction and separation between 'he who experiences suffering' and 'he who gives life'. . .   *adv. Nest.* 3. 2

So you say that it was the flesh alone that was sent by the Father, that the flesh was the visible person? Then that alone is enough for us, to bring to life that which is under the tyranny of death? Why then do the inspired Scriptures vainly rhapsodize about the Word's becoming flesh, insisting on it at all costs? Would the Word be of any use at all, if the human nature were sufficient, considered solely by itself, to be able to abolish death, and to overthrow the power of destruction?
adv. Nest. 4. 4

Nestorius imagines that he gives a notable display of reverence in vigorously maintaining what no one denies: that the Word from God the Father is, as God, far removed, in his own nature, from suffering, and is superior to death; otherwise life itself would, in some manner, have died. But even in this Nestorius flies in the face of the doctrines of the Church, and shows no respect at all for the 'economy' of the Only-begotten in his incarnation, giving no consideration to the depth of the mystery. If we were to inquire into the nature of the Word, or if we had to explain it to others who asked about it and wished to learn, then if we were careful to follow the path of wise and true reasoning, we should be forced to the logical demonstration that death could not approach that nature, and that it is utterly remote from suffering. But since the way in which he became man allows him (as far as concerns the principles of the 'economy') to die in the flesh, should he so wish, without suffering anything in his own divine nature, why do you rob us of our noblest ground of confidence? For you have heard him say, 'The good shepherd lays down his life for the sheep'.[1] Therefore, if he is said to have suffered, we know that he is impassible as God; but we say that he suffered death in the 'economy' in his own flesh, so that he might trample death underfoot, and rise again (being by nature life and giver of life) and refashion for immortality that which had been under death's tyranny, namely the body. Thus the power of his work of restoration reaches to us also; it extends to the whole human race.   *adv. Nest.* 5. 1

[1] John 10. 11.

(f) Incarnation and Eucharist

[Nestorius: 'I will quote the words of his which gave offence. The Lord Christ was talking with them about his flesh. "Unless you eat the flesh of the Son of Man," he said, "and drink his blood, you will not have life in you."[1] His hearers could not take in the sublimity of what he said. They thought, in their folly, that he was suggesting cannibalism.']

Well then, how is it that this is not a matter of cannibalism? In what way is this mystery sublime, unless we say that it was the very Word of the Father who was sent, and acknowledge the fashion of his sending to be his becoming man. Then we shall see that the flesh united with him has life-giving power; it is not alien flesh, but flesh which belonged to him who can give life to all things. Fire, in this world of the senses, can transmit the power of its natural energy to any materials with which it comes in contact; so that it can change even water, which is in its own nature a cold substance, to an unnatural condition of heat. This being so, is it strange or in any way incredible that the very Word from God the Father, who is in his own nature life, should give to the flesh united to himself this life-giving property? For this flesh belongs to the Word; it does not belong to some other being than himself who may be thought of separately as another member of the human race. If you remove the life-giving Word of God from this mystical and real union with the body, if you completely set him apart, how are you to show that body as still life-giving? Who was it who said, 'He who eats my flesh, and drinks my blood, remains in me, and I remain in him'?[2] If it was a man who was born in his own separate nature; if the Word of God did not come to be in our condition; then indeed what is performed is an act of cannibalism, and participation in it is of no value at all. I hear Christ himself saying, 'The flesh is of no value; it is the spirit that gives life'[3] . . .

The rays of light sent from the sun may be said to be radiant on account of their sender or rather on account of their source; but it is not from participation that they have the power to give light. It is by a kind of natural nobility of origin that they convey the excellence of the sender, or rather of the source that flashed them out. In the same way, I suppose, and on the same principle, even if the Son said that he lives 'because of the Father'[4] he would be claiming for himself the nobility which he derives from the Father; he will not be acknowledging that he

[1] John 6. 53.   [2] John 6. 56.   [3] John 6. 63.   [4] John 6. 57.

has life in no distinctive way from that of created things in general, a life conferred from outside. *adv. Nest.* 4. 5

(g) *The Suffering and Glory of the one Christ*

'Until he comes.'[1] Who is it that is coming? 'They will see him whom they pierced.'[2] The one who will come is the one who suffered death in human fashion, but rose again in a divine manner and went up to heaven. He is now glorified on the throne of ineffable Deity, sitting at his Father's side, surrounded by the Seraphim and the Powers on high, who are fully aware of the measure of their subjection: and every Authority and Power and Dominion does reverence to him; for 'every knee shall bend to him, and every tongue shall acknowledge that Jesus is Lord, to the glory of God the Father'.[3] He will come, as I have said, revealed not in human lowliness but in the glory of supreme divinity, with heaven and the celestial spirits escorting him as God and king, attending upon the Lord of the Universe. If he is not the Word of God in flesh (that is, made man) but a 'god-bearing man' with a bodily side, who suffered the piercing of the side, how is it that he is seen on the throne of the supreme Godhead, as if we had a fourth God, recently added to the Holy Trinity? Do you not shrink in horror from conceiving him as an ordinary man, and contemplating the ascription of worship to a creature? *adv. Nest.* 4. 6

(h) *The Dogmatic Letter*

[The 'Second Letter to Nestorius', of February 430, was endorsed at the Councils of Ephesus (431) and Chalcedon (451).]

[*In saying that 'the Word was incarnate, etc.*'] we are not asserting any change in the nature of the Word, or the transformation of the Word into an entire man, composed of soul and body. We are saying that the Word, in a manner indescribable and inconceivable, united personally [*hypostatically*] to himself flesh animated with a reasonable soul, and thus became man, and was called the Son of man. And this was not by a mere act of will or favour, nor by taking to himself a mere personal presentation [*prosôpon*]. The natures which were brought together to form a genuine unity were different; but it was one Christ, and one Son, that was produced out of these two natures. We do not mean that

---

[1] 1 Cor. 11. 26; Rev. 2. 25. [2] Rev. 1. 7; John 19. 37; cited from Zech. 12. 10.
[3] Phil. 2. 10, 11.

the difference of the natures is annihilated because of this union; but rather that the deity and the manhood, by their inexpressible and inexplicable concurrence into unity, have brought about for us the one Lord and Son, Jesus Christ. It is in this sense that he is said to have been born of a woman, in respect of the flesh, though he existed and was begotten from the Father before all ages. . . . It was not that an ordinary man was first born of the holy Virgin, and that afterwards the Word descended on him. The Word was united with the flesh in the womb itself, and thus is said to have undergone a birth in the flesh, inasmuch as he made his own the birth of his own flesh.

In the same way we say that 'he suffered and rose again'. We do not mean that God the Word suffered in his deity . . . for the deity, being incorporeal, is impassible. But the body which was made his own endured these sufferings; and therefore he is said to have endured them for our sake. The impassible was in the body which suffered.

In the same way we speak of his death . . .

Thus it is one Christ and Lord that we acknowledge, and as one and the same we worship him, not as a man associated in our worship with the Word . . .

We must not therefore divide the one Lord Christ into two Sons. Some who do this add an assertion of a 'union of persons' [*prosôpa*]; but this assertion will not serve to restore their doctrine to a sound statement of the faith. Scripture does not say 'the Word united to himself the person [*prosôpon*] of a man', but 'the Word was made flesh'. And that means precisely this, that he became partaker of flesh and blood, just as we do, and made our body his own. He issued as man from a woman: but he did not cast off his being God and his generation from God the Father. He assumed our flesh: but even in doing this he remained what he was.   *ep.* 4 [*ad Nest.* 2]

(i) The Formula of Reunion 433

[At the Council of Ephesus, 431, Cyril obtained the condemnation of Nestorius before the 'Antiochene' bishops assembled: they then held a separate council under John of Antioch and declared Cyril deposed. The Emperor, Theodosius II, confirmed both councils, but C.'s deposition was soon cancelled, and he proceeded to conciliate the moderate Antiochenes.]

Therefore we acknowledge our Lord Jesus Christ, the Only-begotten Son of God, perfect God and perfect man, consisting of rational soul and body: in respect of his divinity, begotten from the Father before the ages; in respect of his humanity, begotten also of the Virgin Mary, for us and for our salvation: he is also of one substance with the Father, in respect of his divinity; and of one substance with us in respect of his humanity. For a unity of two natures[1] has come about: therefore we acknowledge one Christ, one Son, one Lord. In accordance with this principle of the union without confusion, we acknowledge the Holy Virgin as Mother of God, because the Word was incarnate and made man, and from the very conception united to himself the temple taken from her. As for the utterances about the Lord in the Gospels and Apostolic writings, we know that the theologians regard some as common to both natures on the basis of one person;[2] others they distinguish, on the basis of two natures,[3] referring the godlike utterances to the divinity of Christ, and the lowly to his humanity.

ep. 39 [to John bishop of Antioch]

(j) Nestorius distinguished from the Antiochenes

Nestorius pretends to acknowledge that the Word, who was God, was incarnate, and made man: but he does not recognize the meaning of the incarnation, and he uses the term 'two natures' and separates them, dividing off the divinity, and keeping the manhood apart, as being attached to the Godhead by habitual conjunction,[4] merely by equality of honour or authority. What he says is: 'God is indivisible from the visible [i.e. *the manhood*]: therefore I am not separating the honour of that which is not divided; I divide the natures, but unite the worship.' Now the brethren of Antioch[5] have accepted the components in Christ which are presented to our minds, but simply and solely in the sphere of thought: they have spoken of a difference of natures (for, as was said above, Godhead and manhood are not the same in natural quality); but they confess one Son and Christ and Lord, and they say that, since he is really one, there is in him one personality [*prosôpon*]. In no way do they divide the things which have been united. They refuse the notion of a division in nature, a notion which the introducer of these disastrous novelties has decided to entertain.   *ep. 40 [ad Acac. Melit.]*

A number of people find fault with the formula which has been drawn up by the Eastern bishops.[6] They say: 'Why did the bishop of Alexan-

---

[1] δύο φύσεων ἔνωσις.   [2] ὡς ἐφ' ἑνὸς προσώπου.   [3] ὡς ἐπὶ δύο φύσεων.   [4] σχετικῶς— perhaps 'by moral connexion' (cf. p. 254).   [5] i.e. those who accepted the Reunion Formula of 433.   [6] That of 433 (above).

dria tolerate, and even applaud, those who use the term "two natures"? The followers of Nestorius assert that this is his opinion, and they sweep over to their side those who are ignorant of the niceties of interpretation.' The reply to this criticism is that we are not bound to avoid or repudiate all the statements of heretics: much of what they acknowledge coincides with our professions. For example, when the Arians assert that God the Father is God of all things, and Lord, it does not follow that we should reject such statements of belief. Similarly, in the case of Nestorius, when he says that there are two natures, marking the difference between the flesh and God the Word, since the nature of the Word is distinct from that of the flesh. But he does not join us in acknowledging the unity. We unite the two natures, and acknowledge one Christ, one Son, the same being, one Lord, in fact [1]one nature of God incarnate.[1]

ep. 44 [*ad Eulogium*]

(k) Unity of Nature

Now there are some who ascribe to us the opinions of Apollinarius, and say; 'You speak of a Son who is one in virtue of an exact unity of intermixture, the Word of God the Father made man and incarnate: if so, perhaps you have decided to entertain the fancy that what happened was a mixture, a confusion, an amalgam, of the Word with the body, or rather the conversion of the body into the nature of divinity'. For this reason we choose our words with great care, to refute this calumny; and we say that the Word of God the Father, in a way beyond our comprehension and our power of expression, united to himself a body animated by a rational soul; he issued as man from a woman, and entered our condition, not by a conversion of nature but [2]as an act of favour, in pursuance of God's plan for mankind.[2] For he willed to become man, without discarding the godhead which was his by nature. Although he descended to our level, and put on 'the form of a servant',[3] yet even so he continued in the excellences of the godhead, in his natural Lordship . . .

Therefore, in considering the manner of his incarnation, we observe that two natures came together in indissoluble union, without confusion and without change. The flesh is flesh and not divinity, even if it became the flesh of God; and likewise the Word is God, and not flesh, even if he made the flesh his own, for his dealings with man.[4] When we

[1-1] μίαν τὴν τοῦ Θεοῦ φύσιν σεσαρκωμένην.   [2-2] εὐδοκίᾳ οἰκονομικῇ.   [3] Phil. 2. 7.
[4] οἰκονομικῶς.

conceive the matter in this way, we do not misrepresent the coming together into unity, in saying that it was a union of two natures: but we do not divide the natures after the union, nor do we sever the one indivisible Son. We assert the one Son and, as the Fathers have said, [1]one nature of the Word of God, incarnate.[1] The manner of the incarnation of the Only-begotten is visible only to the eyes of the soul.

ep. 46 [ad Succensum 1]

The nature of the Word did not pass over into the nature of flesh, nor that of the flesh into the nature of the Word: Word and body continued alike in their own natural character, and are so apprehended by our minds. . . . He displayed to us a nature of the Son which was one nature, but, as we have said, a nature made incarnate. For unity is truly predicated not only of things which are by nature simple, but also of things united by composition: an example of this is a human being, consisting as he does of soul and body.

The inspired Scriptures speak of his suffering *in the flesh*, and it is better for us to use such language than to say 'in the nature of his humanity': although that form of speech does not misrepresent the principle of the mystery, unless it is maliciously employed. For what is the nature of humanity except flesh animated by reason? And it is in this flesh that we acknowledge that the Lord suffered. And so they show an excessive precision, in saying that he suffered 'in the nature of his humanity': for this suggests a separation of that nature from the Word, isolating it in its own particular character, so that two beings are considered and not one, incarnate and made man, the Word of God the Father.

ep. 46 [ad Succensum 2]

II. The Work of Christ

(a) Restoration

B. [Hermias] I should like to learn what was the purpose of his coming among us; what was the mode of his incarnation, and the reason for it. A. [Cyril] . . . This is what Paul says, in his wisdom; and he had Christ speaking in him: 'The children share the same flesh and blood; and he likewise shared the same, so that he might, through death, stultify him

---

[1]-[1] μίαν φύσιν τοῦ Θεοῦ λόγου σεσαρκωμένην. The phrase was taken from works of Apollinarian origin: but C. thought it derived from Athanasius.

who wielded the power of death, that is, the devil . . .'.[1] And in another passage he explains it in a different way: 'What the law could not do, because the weakness of our flesh made it powerless, God has done by sending his Son in the likeness of sinful flesh, and as an offering for sin: thus he condemned sin in the flesh.'[2] . . . Surely it is quite obvious and unmistakable, that the Only-begotten became like us, became, that is, a complete man, that he might free our earthly body from the alien corruptions which had been brought into it? He descended to become identical with us, in respect of the conditions of life, accommodating himself through the unity[3] of Word and flesh: he made the human soul his own, thus making it victorious over sin, colouring it, as it were, with the dye of the steadfastness and immutability of his own nature. . . . By becoming the flesh of the Word, who gives life to all things, this flesh triumphs over the power of death and destruction: in the same way, no doubt, the soul, since it has become the soul of him who had no experience of doing wrong, has its state secured, immutable in all good, and incomparably stronger than the sin which before exercised domination. For Christ is the first man who 'committed no sin and was convicted of no dishonesty'.[4] He is, so to speak, the root and the first fruits of those who are restored in the Spirit to newness of life, to immortality of the body, to certainty and security of divinity, so that he may transmit this condition to the whole of humanity by participation, and as an act of grace. Paul knew this, and was inspired to write: 'As we have worn the likeness of the man made of earth, so we shall also bear the likeness of the heavenly man.'[5] By 'the likeness of the man of earth' he means the propensity to sin: by 'the likeness of the heavenly man' (that is, of Christ), he means the steady course towards holiness, the rescue from death and destruction, the restoration to immortality and life. So we assert that the Word in his entirety has been united with man in his entirety.   *de incarn. unigen.*

[*The Pharisees said, 'It is not for any good action that we are going to stone you'* (John 10. 33) . . .] But this is how we address him: 'It is for a good action that we regard you with awe and wonderment, because, being God by nature, you became man.' And for what reason? Because the Word of God is, in his own nature, life, and he took as his own a body by nature liable to destruction so that he might abolish the power of

---

[1] Heb. 2. 14 f.   [2] Rom. 8. 3 f.   [3] τῇ καθ' ἕνωσιν οἰκονομίᾳ.   [4] 1 Pet. 2. 22.   [5] 1 Cor. 15. 49.

mortality that was in it, and transform it to incorruption. For just as iron, when brought into contact with extreme heat of fire, has its colour changed straightaway and takes on the appearance of the fire, and is in travail with the power which overcomes it; so the nature of flesh receives the immortal and life-giving Word of God, and the nature remains, but under a changed condition; from now on it is revealed as superior to corruption.   *hom. pasch.* 17 [429]

(b) Sacrifice; Ransom; the Conquest of Death

The true Lamb, portrayed of old in types, the spotless sacrifice for all, is led to the slaughter, to drive away the sin of the world,[1] to overthrow the destroyer of all humanity, to abolish death by dying for all, to do away with the curse laid upon us;[2] that there should henceforth be an end of the condemnation, 'You are earth, and will return to earth';[3] that he should become a second Adam, not from earth, but from Heaven,[4] the source of all good to human nature, freeing us from the corruptibility that had been brought upon us, the mediator to us of eternal life, the cause of our restoration to God, the beginning of true religion and righteousness, the way to the Kingdom of Heaven. For one Lamb died for all, bringing the whole flock on earth back safely to God the Father; one for all, that he might bring all under subjection to God; one for all, that he might gain them all; 'that for the future they might all no longer live for themselves, but for him who died and rose for them.'[5] For when we were guilty of many sins, and for that reason were liable to death and destruction, the Father gave a ransom for us, one for all, since all things are in him, and he is greater than all. One died for all, that we all might live in him: Death devoured the Lamb on behalf of all, and then vomited all in him, and with him. For we were all in Christ, who died and rose again on our account, and on our behalf. And when sin has been annihilated, then death, of which sin is the source and cause, must needs be annihilated too.   *in Jo.* 1. 29 [before 429]

(c) Satisfaction

'Christ has redeemed us from the curse of the Law, by becoming a curse for us. For Scripture says: "Accursed is everyone who is hanged on a tree." '[6] The legal formula pronounces the curse on those who suffer thus for transgression and sin. Christ, who 'had no experience of sinning',[7] submitted to judgement and accepted an unjust sentence, and

[1] Cf. John 1. 29.   [2] Cf. Gal. 3. 10.   [3] Gen. 3. 19.   [4] Cf. 1 Cor. 15. 45, 47.
[5] 2 Cor. 5. 15.   [6] Gal 3. 13 (citing Deut. 21. 23).   [7] 2 Cor. 5. 21.

endured what was justly due to those under the curse: so that by dying on behalf of all men, being himself worth the whole universe, he might free the whole of mankind from the charge of disobedience, and might purchase this terrestrial world by his own blood. One man would not have been a recompense adequate for all mankind, had he been merely a man. But if he is to be conceived of as God incarnate, suffering death in flesh which was his own, then the whole creation would be a small thing in comparison with him, and the death of one flesh an abundant ransom for the flesh of all. For the flesh was the flesh of the Word who was begotten from God the Father.   *de rect. fid.* 2. 7

(d) Vicarious Punishment

The penalty for transgression of God's law and contempt of the Lord's will is death. But the Creator had pity on human nature thus doomed to destruction: and the Only-begotten became man, and wore a body by nature liable to death, and bore the name of flesh, so that, by submitting to the death which hung over us as a result of our sin, he might annihilate sin, and put an end to Satan's accusations: for in the person of Christ himself we paid the penalty of the sins of which we stood accused.   *de ador.* 3

III. The Holy Spirit

'From the Father and the Son'

When he says of the Spirit, 'It is he who will glorify me',[1] we do not assert, if we rightly understand the matter, that the one Christ and Son received the glory that comes from the Holy Spirit, as if he needed glory that comes from another: for his Spirit is not superior to him and above him. But since he used his own Spirit for works of power in order to display his Godhead, he speaks of himself as 'glorified' by the Spirit, just as an ordinary man might say 'they will glorify me', when speaking, for instance, of his strength, or his skill in anything. For though the Spirit exists in his own person [*hypostasis*], and as a separate object of thought, as being Spirit and not Son, yet he is not alien from the Son. He is called the Spirit of Truth, and Christ is the Truth: and he is poured out from the Son, just as, to be sure, he is poured out from God the Father. ... We are not asserting that the Spirit is wise and

[1] John 16. 14.

powerful merely by participation: for he is all-perfect, and not lacking in every perfection. And since he is the Spirit of the Father's Power and Wisdom, that is, of the Son, he is assuredly power and wisdom in himself.   *ep.* 17 [*ad Nest.* 2]

Inasmuch as the Son is God and from God, by nature, since he has been truly generated from God the Father, the Spirit is his own, and is in him and from him.   *com. in XII proph., in Joel* 2. 28

The Spirit exists from him by nature, and being sent from him upon creation, effects the renovation.   *thesaur.*

The Spirit belongs to both the Father and the Son: he is poured forth essentially from both, or from the Father through the Son.   *de ador.* 1

IV. The Church

The Unity of the Body of Christ

'That they may all be one in us, as thou Father in me, and I in thee.'[1] . . . I have already carefully explained that the manner of the divine unity and the identity of substance in the Holy Trinity, and the inter-connexion of the Persons in all respects, ought to be mirrored in the unity of the faithful through their mutual harmony and concord. I am eager to demonstrate in the faithful also a kind of unity of nature, by which we are joined with one another, and we are all joined to God; and this does not, we may say, stop short of a bodily unity with one another, though we are distinguished by our different bodies, and each of us, as a human being, is confined within the limits of his own body, and of his own person . . .

The Mystery of Christ is available for us as a beginning and a way for our participation in the Holy Spirit, and our union with God. For we are all sanctified in him, in the way I have already explained [*viz. He took our humanity so that man might share the divine nature*]. The Only-begotten, through the wisdom that is rightly his, and through the counsel of the Father, devised a means by which we may come into union with God and among ourselves, although we are separated by the distinction which is observable between individuals. By means of

[1] John 17. 21.

one body he blesses those who believe in him and incorporates them in himself and in each other; and that body is his own. And who can divide and remove them from this mutual union of nature, when they have been bound together in unity with Christ by means of that one holy body? We all partake of one loaf, and so we are all made into one body:[1] for Christ cannot be divided. Therefore the Church is called the 'Body of Christ, of which each individual is a member'[2] as Paul understands. For we are all united to the one Christ, by means of his holy body, since we take him, the one and indivisible, in our own bodies: therefore he has a greater claim than we upon our own members. . . . If we are all incorporated with one another in Christ, not only with one another but also with him who comes within us by means of his own flesh—then surely it is clear that we are all of us one, both with one another and in Christ. For Christ is the bond of unity, since he is God and man in one and the same person. In speaking of this unity of the spirit I shall follow the beaten track of the Church's doctrine and repeat that we all receive the one same Spirit, the Holy Spirit, and thus are mingled, as it were, with one another and with God. Although we are many and Christ makes the Spirit of the Father, which is also his own Spirit to dwell in each of us individually, yet the Spirit is one and indivisible. Thus by his own being he joins into unity those spirits which in their own nature as individual persons are sundered from unity with one another, and through his activity they are displayed as a kind of single entity in himself. For just as the power of the holy flesh incorporates with one another those who partake of it; so, in my view, the one indivisible Spirit, dwelling in all of them, brings them all into spiritual unity. *in Jo.* 17. 21

V. The Eucharist

We proclaim the death, in the flesh, of the only-begotten Son of God, Jesus Christ, and acknowledge his return to life from the dead and his ascension into heaven, and as we do this we perform the bloodless sacrifice in the churches: and thus we approach the consecrated gifts of the sacrament, and are sanctified by partaking of the holy flesh and the precious blood of Christ, the Saviour of us all. We do not receive it as common flesh (God forbid), nor as the flesh of a mere man, sanctified

[1] 1 Cor. 10. 17. [2] 1 Cor. 12. 27.

and linked with the Word in unity of standing, or as enjoying a divine indwelling; we receive it as truly life-giving, as the flesh that belongs to the Word himself. For as being God he is in his own nature Life, and when he became one with the flesh which is his own, he rendered it life-giving.   *ep.* 17 [*ad Nest.* 3]

It was necessary for him to be present in us in a divine manner through the Holy Spirit: to be mixed, as it were, with our bodies by means of his holy flesh and precious blood, for us to have him in reality as a sacramental gift which gives life, in the form of bread and wine. And so that we should not be struck down with horror, at seeing flesh and blood displayed on the holy tables of our churches, God adapts himself to our weakness and infuses the power of life into the oblations and changes them into the effective power of his own flesh, so that we may have them for life-giving reception, and that the body of life may prove to be in us a life-giving seed.   *in Luc.* 22. 19

Theodoret of Cyrus

I. The Person of Christ

(a) The Two Natures

[Theodoret's main dogmatic treatise is in the form of a dialogue between Eranistes ('a beggar'), a Monophysite, and Orthodoxus, an orthodox believer.]

Eran: Therefore Jesus Christ is God only.

Orth: You are told that God the Word was made man. Are you going to call him *God only*?

Eran: He was made man, without alteration. He remained what he was; and therefore he is to be called what he was.

Orth: Certainly God the Word was, and is, and will be unchangeable; but he became man by taking human nature. It is right, then, that we should acknowledge both natures, that which assumed, and that which was assumed. *eran.* 2 [*c.* 447]

(b) The One Person

Orth: You said that the divine nature came down from heaven, but that it was called Son of Man because of the union. Thus it is right to say that the flesh was nailed to the tree, but to confess that the divine nature was inseparable from it, on the cross, in the tomb, though that nature did not undergo suffering, being by nature incapable of suffering and death, and having a substance [*ousia*] immortal and impassible. Thus Paul spoke of the 'crucified Lord of glory',[1] applying the epithet of the impassible nature to the passible, since the body ranked as the body of the divinity. . . . I have often said that the one person [*prosôpon*] receives both the divine and the human epithets. That is why the blessed Fathers at Nicaea, after instructing us how we should believe in the Father, when they passed on to the person of the Son, did not immediately say 'and in the Son of God'. . . . They wished to hand on to us a statement both of the divinity and at the same time of the economy,[2] to prevent the notion of two different persons, that of the divinity and that of the humanity.

[1] 1 Cor. 2. 8. [2] The working out of the divine plan in the Incarnation, involving the self-limitation of the Godhead.

Therefore they continued . . . 'and in our Lord Jesus Christ'. Now Christ is the title of God the Word, after his incarnation: so that this title includes all that belongs to his Godhead, and all that belongs to his manhood. . .

[*Isaac and the ram symbolize the two natures of Christ.*] But I have often said that it is impossible for the picture and the original to coincide in all respects: and here is an example to make the point clear. Isaac and the ram correspond to the original [i.e. Christ] in respect of the difference of natures, but not in respect of a division between separate *hypostases*. For we preach such a union of the Godhead and the manhood that we conceive of one indivisible person, and recognize him to be at the same time God and man, visible and invisible, circumscribed and uncircumscribed. And all other qualities which signify divinity and humanity we ascribe to the one person. *eran.* 3

(c) *Unity and Distinction*

[The *reprehensio XII capitum* was written in 431 at the request of John of Antioch, as an answer to Cyril's twelve anathemas against Nestorius: it defends N. and accuses C. of Monophysitism. It was one of the works (the 'Three Chapters') condemned at the Council of Constantinople (Fifth Oecumenical) in 553.]

We acknowledge one Christ, believing in the inspired teaching of the apostles, and we call him God and man because of the union; but we know nothing at all of a 'hypostatic union', since this is a doctrine foreign and alien to the inspired Scriptures and the Fathers who interpreted them. If, however, Cyril, who fathered these notions, means to assert, by the phrase 'hypostatic union', that a mixture of flesh and Godhead took place, then we will vehemently contradict him, and refute his blasphemy. For a necessary consequence of 'mixture' is confusion; and when confusion comes in, it does away with the distinctive character of each nature. For when things are mixed, they do not retain their original character. It would be most absurd to allege this of God the Word and him who was of the race of David. We must believe the Lord, who displayed the two natures, and who said to the Jews, 'Destroy this temple, and I will raise it in three days'.[1] *repr. anath.* 2

[Theodoret takes ὑπόστασις as equivalent to φύσις, 'nature' or 'substance'.]
[1] John 2. 19.

Cyril says that it is not right to conjoin the *hypostases* by connexion,[1] but by a 'coming together', a 'natural coming together'.[2] Either he does not realize what he is saying, or else he knowingly blasphemes. For 'nature' is something compulsive and involuntary. For example, it is 'by nature' that we feel hungry: and we feel this by compulsion, not by our decision. . . . But the saying, 'He reduced himself to nothing, and took the form of a servant'[3] shows that the incarnation was a voluntary act. If then it was by a decision and an act of will that he was united to a nature taken from our human condition, the addition of the phrase, 'natural', is otiose: it is enough to acknowledge the union. Now 'union' is applied to things that are distinct; it cannot be conceived without the existence of division. Therefore, when union is undertaken, division is presupposed. How then can Cyril say that the *hypostases*, or natures, must not be divided? He knows that the complete *hypostasis* of God the Word existed before the ages, and that the complete 'form of a servant' was taken by that *hypostasis*: and therefore he spoke of *hypostases* and not of *hypostasis*. If then each of the natures is complete, and both come together, in the taking of the form of a servant by the form of God, it is true reverence to acknowledge one person and one Son, the Christ. But to speak of two *hypostases*, or natures, is not absurd; it fits the facts. In the case of one man we 'divide the natures', speaking of a mortal body and an immortal soul, but the two, we say, are one man. It is even more reasonable to acknowledge the distinction of the natures of God who assumed, and man who was assumed. *repr. anath.* 3

[*Cyril's 4th anathema condemned those who ascribe certain utterances of Christ, or about Christ, to the human being, others to the Word.*] Let this careful teacher of sacred doctrine tell us how he is to refute the blasphemy of heretics, when he ascribes to God the Word the utterances of humility which are appropriate to 'the form of a servant'.[3] That is what the heretics do, and therefore lay it down that the Son of God is inferior to God, a created being, a servant, coming from non-existence. We hold beliefs diametrically opposed to theirs: we acknowledge the Son as consubstantial and co-eternal with the Father. . . . To whom are we to ascribe, 'My God, my God, why hast thou forsaken me?'[4] . . . and, 'No one, not even the Son, knows the hour'[5] . . . to whom shall we attribute hunger, thirst, weariness, sleep, ignorance, fear? . . . If these

[1] συνάφεια.   [2] συνόδῳ φυσικῇ.   [3] Phil. 2. 7.   [4] Matt. 27. 46 (etc.).   [5] Matt. 24. 36 (etc.).

belong to God the Word, how can Wisdom be ignorant? How can Wisdom deserve that name, if it is liable to the experience of ignorance? ... Surely it is absurd that Abraham should have 'seen his day, and rejoiced';[1] that Isaiah should have foretold his saving passion...;[2] while he himself should be ignorant, should ask to be released from that passion, and to be spared that which was to be for the world's salvation.[3] Those sayings, therefore, were not those of God the Word, but of the 'form of a servant', which feared death, because death had not yet been destroyed. God the Word allowed those sayings, and permitted the fears, so that the nature of him who was born might be apparent; so that we should not suppose that the descendant of Abraham and David was a semblance or a phantom. ... Thus we will ascribe to God the Word the sayings and actions which are appropriate to God; those which show humility we will attribute to the 'form of a servant', so that we may not suffer from the blasphemous disease of Arius and Eunomius.

repr. anath. 4

You can be sure that no one ever heard us proclaiming two Sons: in fact such teaching is, in my view, execrable blasphemy. For Jesus Christ is one Lord, through whom are all things. I acknowledge him as God before the ages, and as man at the end of the days, and I offer one adoration as to the Only-begotten. But I have been taught the distinction between flesh and Godhead; for the union is without confusion. ... The sayings concerning the Lord which show a humility appropriate to the nature assumed we ascribe to him as such: those which befit the Godhead, and are evidence of that nature, we attribute to him as God. However, we make no separation into two persons [*prosôpa*], but we teach that both types of sayings belong to the one Only-begotten: some of them belong to him as God, Maker and Lord of the universe: some to him as made man for us.

ep. 104

This natural union unites things which are equally limited in time, which are created, and equally subject to slavery. But in Christ the Lord everything depends on his good pleasure, his compassion, his grace. Even if there is here a natural union the distinctive properties of the natures have remained intact.

eran. 2

I am not aware that I have ever so far taught a belief in two Sons. For I was instructed to believe in one Only-begotten, Jesus Christ our Lord,

[1] John 8. 56.   [2] Cf. Isa. 53.   [3] Cf. Matt. 26. 39.

God the Word made man. But I understand the difference between flesh and Godhead, and in my opinion it is impiety to divide our one Lord Jesus Christ into two Sons: as also to take the opposite path and to speak of the Godhead of our Master, Christ, and his manhood, as one nature. *ep.* 109

The incarnation of the Only-begotten did not increase the number of the Trinity, so that it became a quaternity. The Trinity remained a Trinity even after the incarnation. When we believe that the Only-begotten Son of God became man, we do not deny the nature he assumed; we acknowledge, as I said, the assuming nature, and the assumed. For the union does not confuse the distinctive properties of the natures. The air, which receives the light throughout its whole extent, does not lose its being as air, nor does it destroy the nature of the light: we see the light with our eyes; we recognize the air by our sense of touch. . . . It would be the extreme of folly to call the union of Godhead and manhood a confusion. . . . When heat is applied to gold, the gold partakes of the colour and energy of the fire: but it does not lose its own nature; it remains gold, while behaving as fire. So our Lord's body is a body, but impassible, incorruptible, immortal; it is the Lord's body, divine, and glorified with divine glory. It is not separated from the Godhead; it does not belong to someone else: it belongs to the only-begotten Son of God. Nor does it display to us another person, but the Only-begotten himself, clothed in our nature. *ep.* 145

II. The Work of Christ

(a) Sacrifice

We incurred the death penalty for our sins, and therefore had received this sentence: but he underwent death for us. We were under the curses, because we had transgressed the law: he became a curse for us.[1] . . . He was free from sin and spotless, and he suffered the punishment on our behalf . . . and granted us peace. *in Isa.* 53

(b) Ransom

When all men had been brought under the dominion of death, although as God he was not subject to death (for he is by nature immortal), nor as man (for he did not commit sin, which is the introducer of death),

[1] Cf. Gal. 3. 13.

he gave himself as a kind of ransom, and freed all mankind from servitude to death.   *interp. in XIV epp. S. Pauli; in Col.* I. 21

(c) A Debt Paid

It was not the law which bestowed this gift (of reconciliation), but the Lord Christ, who paid your debt, and handed over his body to death; so that you who are accounted worthy of the calling[1] are set free from all reproach.   *interp. in XIV epp. S. Pauli; in Col.* I. 21

(d) The Judgement of the Devil

Therefore he takes upon himself the curse that lay on all mankind and removes it by a slaughter that was unjust. He was not under the curse ... but he endured the death of sinners; and he contends in judgement with the vengeful foe of all our human nature, becoming the champion and advocate of our nature. He says, with justice, to our harsh tyrant: 'You are caught, you villain, and snared in your own nets. ... Why have you nailed my body to the cross and handed me over to death? What kind of sin have you observed in me? What breach of the law did you detect? ... If the smallest fault is found in me, you would have every right to hold me; for death is the punishment of sinners. But if you find nothing in me which God's law forbids, but rather everything which it enjoins, I will not allow you to hold me wrongfully. What is more, I will open the prison of death for others also: and I will confine there you alone, for transgressing God's law. ... And since you have taken one prisoner unjustly, you will be deprived of all those justly subject to you. Since you have eaten what was not to be eaten, you will vomit all that you have swallowed. ... I have paid the debt, and it is right that those who were imprisoned for that debt should be set free to enjoy their former liberty and return to their own homeland.' With those words the Lord raised his own body, and sowed in man's nature the hope of resurrection, giving to mankind the resurrection of his own body as a guarantee.

Let no one suppose that this is an idle tale. We have been taught from the holy gospels and the apostolic instructions that this is fact. We have heard the Lord himself say; 'The ruler of this world is coming, and he finds nothing in me'[2] ... and, in another place: 'Now comes the judgement of this world: now the ruler of this world will be cast out.'[3]

de provid. 10

[1] Cf. 2 Thess. I. 11.   [2] John 14. 30.   [3] John 12. 31.

III. The Holy Spirit

Relation to Father and Son

We refuse to admit that God the Word, consubstantial and co-eternal with the Father, was formed in the womb, and anointed at the baptism by the Holy Spirit: we refer these events to the human nature which was assumed in these last days by the Word. The Spirit is the Son's own Spirit, of the same nature with him, and proceeding from the Father: this we accept as a statement of true religion. But if Cyril means that the Holy Spirit has his existence from or through the Son,[1] we repudiate this as irreligious blasphemy. We believe that, in the Lord's words, the Spirit proceeds from the Father. *repr. anath.* 9

We have been taught that the Holy Spirit has his existence from the Father. The mode of his existence is not like that of created beings, for the All-holy Spirit is uncreated. Nor is it like that of the Son; for none of the orthodox has ever spoken of the coming into being of the Spirit as 'generation'. The sacred Scriptures teach that he exists from the Father, and that he is divine. . . . The Father is the source of the Spirit. *haer. fab.* 5. 3

IV. The Eucharist

(a) Symbol and Reality

Orth: If the divine mysteries are symbols of the real body of Christ, then it follows that the body of the Lord is a body, not changed into the nature of godhead, but filled with divine glory.

Eran: You have brought up the subject of the divine mysteries most conveniently for me. For from this I will demonstrate the change of the Lord's body into another nature. . . . What do you call the oblation before the priestly invocation?

Orth: I must not say openly; there may be some of the uninitiated present.

Eran: Answer allusively, then.

Orth: Food of a grain of some kind.

Eran: And what is the name of the other symbol?

Orth: That too is a common name, signifying a kind of drink.

[1] Cf. p. 265 f.

Eran: What do you call them after the consecration?

Orth: The body of Christ, and the blood of Christ.

Eran: And you believe that you partake of Christ's body and blood?

Orth: I do.

Eran: Then the symbols of the Lord's body and blood are one thing before the priestly invocation: after that they are changed into something else. In the same way, the Lord's body was changed into the divine substance, after the Ascension.

Orth: You are caught in the net you have woven! For even after consecration the mystic symbols do not change their nature. They remain in their previous substance, shape and appearance: they are visible and tangible as before. But they are thought of as being what they have become, and they are believed to be so, and are worshipped as being what they are believed to be.

eran. 2

Our Saviour interchanged the names, and gave to the body the name of the symbol, and to the symbol the name of the body. Thus, as he called himself a vine,[1] he spoke of the symbol as his blood. . . . For he wished the partaker of the divine mysteries not to pay attention to the nature of the visible elements, but by means of the interchange of names to believe in the change which has taken place as a result of grace. For he who spoke of his natural body as corn and bread, and again called himself a vine, honoured the visible symbols by calling them his body and blood, not changing their nature, but adding grace to their nature.

eran. 1

(b) The Eucharistic Sacrifice

Christ is a priest . . . who does not himself offer anything, but he acts as the head of those who offer. For he calls the Church his body, and through it he performs the office of priest as man, while as God he receives the offerings. The Church offers the symbols of his body and blood, sanctifying the whole mass through the first-fruits.

in Ps. 109 [110]. 4

If the priesthood established by the law has come to an end, and the priest who is 'in the order of Melchizedek'[2] has offered his sacrifice, and has made all other sacrifices unnecessary, why do the priests of the new

[1] John 15. 1.   [2] Heb. 5. 6. etc. [Ps. 110. 4].

covenant perform the mystical liturgy? Now it is clear to those instructed in divinity that we do not offer another sacrifice, but perform a memorial of that unique and saving offering. For this was the Lord's own command: 'Do this in remembrance of me'.[1] So that by contemplation we may recall what is symbolized, the sufferings endured on our behalf, and may kindle our love towards our benefactor, and look forward to the enjoyment of the blessings to come.

interpr. in XIV epp. S. Pauli; in Heb. 8. 4

[1] I Cor. 11. 24 f.

Leo the Great

The Person of Christ

Eutyches did not realize what he ought to hold concerning the incarnation of the Word of God, and he was not prepared to seek out the light of understanding by diligent study in the wide range of Holy Scripture. But he might at least have received with careful hearing that common and universal confession, in which the whole body of the faithful acknowledge their belief IN GOD THE FATHER ALMIGHTY AND IN JESUS CHRIST HIS ONLY SON OUR LORD WHO WAS BORN OF THE HOLY GHOST AND THE VIRGIN MARY. For by these three statements the devices of almost all heretics are overthrown. God is believed to be both almighty and Father; it follows that the Son is shown to be co-eternal with him, differing in no respect from the Father. For he was born God of God, almighty of almighty, co-eternal of eternal; not later in time, not inferior in power, not dissimilar in glory, not divided in essence. The same Only-begotten, eternal Son of the eternal Father was born of the Holy Ghost and the Virgin Mary. But this birth in time has taken nothing from, and added nothing to, that divine eternal nativity, but has bestowed itself wholly on the restoration of man, who had been deceived; that it might overcome death and by its own virtue overthrow the devil who had the power of death. For we could not overcome the author of sin and death, unless he had taken our nature, and made it his own, whom sin could not defile nor death retain, since he was conceived of the Holy Spirt, in the womb of his Virgin Mother, whose virginity remained entire in his birth as in his conception. . . . That birth, uniquely marvellous and marvellously unique, ought not to be understood in such a way as to preclude the distinctive properties of the kind [i.e. *of humanity*] through the new mode of creation. For it is true that the Holy Spirit gave fruitfulness to the Virgin, but the reality of his body was received from her body. . .

Thus the properties of each nature and substance were preserved entire, and came together to form one person. Humility was assumed by majesty, weakness by strength, mortality by eternity; and to pay the debt that we had incurred, an inviolable nature was united to a nature that can suffer. And so, to fulfil the conditions necessary for our healing, the man Jesus Christ, 'one and the same mediator between God and man,'[1] was able to die in respect of the one, unable to die in respect of the other.

Thus there was born true God in the entire and perfect nature of true man, complete in his own properties, complete in ours.[2] By 'ours' I mean those which the Creator formed in us at the beginning, which he assumed in order to restore; for in the Saviour there was no trace of the properties which the deceiver brought in, and which man, being deceived, allowed to enter. He did not become partaker of our sins because he entered into fellowship with human infirmities. He assumed the form of a servant without the stain of sin, making the human properties greater, but not detracting from the divine. For that 'emptying of himself',[3] whereby the invisible rendered himself visible, and the Creator and Lord of all willed to be a mortal, was a condescension of compassion, not a failure of power. Accordingly, he who made man, while he remained in the form of God, was himself made man in the form of a servant. Each nature preserves its own characteristics without diminution, so that the form of a servant does not detract from the form of God.

The devil boasted that man, deceived by his guile, had been deprived of the divine gifts and, stripped of the dower of immortality, had incurred the stern sentence of death; that he himself had found some consolation in his plight from having a companion in sin. He boasted too that God, because justice required it, had changed his purpose in respect of man whom he had created in such honour: therefore there was need of a dispensation, for God to carry out his hidden plan, that the unchangeable God, whose will cannot be deprived of its own mercy, might accomplish the first design of his affection towards us by a more secret mystery; and that man, driven into sin by the devil's wicked craftiness, should not perish, in defiance of the purpose of God.

The Son of God therefore came down from his throne in heaven without withdrawing from his Father's glory, and entered this lower world, born after a new order, by a new mode of birth. After a new order, inasmuch as he is invisible in his own nature, and he became visible in ours; he is incomprehensible[4] and he willed to be comprehended; continuing to be before time began to exist in time. . . . By a new mode of birth, inasmuch as virginity inviolate which knew not the desire of the flesh supplied the material of flesh. From his mother the Lord took nature, not sin. Jesus Christ was born from a virgin's womb,

---

[1] Tim. 2. 5.   [2] *totus in suis, totus in nostris.*   [3] Cf. Phil. 2. 7.   [4] 'Not spatially circumscribed.'

by a miraculous birth: and yet his nature is not on that account unlike
to ours, for he that is true God is also true man. There is no unreality
in this unity since the humility of the manhood and the majesty of the
deity are alternated.[1] For just as the God is not changed by his compassion, so the man is not swallowed up by the dignity of the Godhead.
Each nature performs its proper functions in communion with the
other; the Word performs what pertains to the Word, the flesh what
pertains to the flesh: the one is resplendent with miracles, the other
submits to insults. The Word withdraws not from his equality with
the Father's glory; the flesh does not desert the nature of our kind. ...
And so it does not belong to the same nature to say 'I and the Father are
one' and 'The Father is greater than I'.[2] For although in the Lord Jesus
Christ there is one person of God and man, yet the basis of the
contumely which both share is distinct from the basis of the glory
which they also share.   *ep.* [28] *dogm. ad Flav.* 2–4

[1] *invicem sunt*, or 'exist in reciprocity'; cf. Augustine *de trin.* 6. 9. p. 233.
[2] John 10. 30; 14. 28.

Appendix

Works cited, with translations of Latin titles

CYRIL OF JERUSALEM d. 386 (see pp. 1–5)

catecheses (348)   Twenty-four 'addresses', delivered mainly in the church of the Holy Sepulchre; the first eighteen to candidates for baptism at Easter, the last five (the *Mystagogic Catecheses*) to the newly baptized during Easter Week.

procatechesis   An introductory address by way of preface to the above.

HILARY OF POITIERS c. 315–67 (see pp. 5–7)

de synodis seu de fide Orientalium (c. 359)   'Concerning the Synods, or Concerning the Faith of the Eastern Church', an historical appendix to his *de trinitate*, explaining the various post-Nicene creeds to Western bishops, and defending the *homoousios* to the homoiousian bishops in the East.

de trinitate   'Concerning the Trinity', a defence of the divinity and consubstantiality of the Son.

tractatus super Psalmos (c. 365)   'Treatises on the Psalms' (not completely preserved).

BASIL OF CAESAREA c. 330–79 (see pp. 7–9)

contra Eunomium (c. 364)   'Against Eunomius', a leader of the extreme Arian party, the Anomoeans.

de spiritu sancto (375)   'On the Holy Spirit'.

epistolae   'Letters', 365 letters are preserved (some of them written to Basil). Not all are authentic.

homiliae variae   'Various Homilies.' Some twenty-three are regarded as genuine.

homiliae in Psalmos   'Homilies on the Psalms.' Eighteen devotional treatises, of which thirteen are probably authentic.

regulae brevius tractatae   'The Rules Treated More Briefly.'

regulae fusius tractatae   'The Rules Treated More Fully.' Two monastic rules, mainly in the form of question and answer on the duties of the religious life.

GREGORY OF NAZIANZUS 329–c. 390 (see pp. 9–13)

epistolae	245 letters were mostly written in Gregory's retirement at Arianzum. Nearly all of them are personal; but *epp.* 101, 102, and 207 are attacks on Apollinarianism.
orationes	Forty-five orations, of which five doctrinal sermons (*or.* 27–31) were distinguished as 'Theological Orations'. They were delivered at Constantinople in 380, in defence of the Catholic doctrine of the Trinity against Eunomians and Macedonians.
poemata	Poems written at the end of his life to rebut the charge that Christians were uncultured. The 'dogmatic' and 'moral' verses here have no literary value; and for this we must go to the autobiographical *de vita sua* and *poemata historica*.

GREGORY OF NYSSA d. 394 (see pp. 13–16)

antirrheticus adversus Apollinarem (c. 386)	'A Refutation of Apollinaris', the most important of surviving anti-Apollinarian documents.
contra Eunomium (380–3)	'Against Eunomius.' A combination of four different treatises: Book 1, a reply to an attack by E. on Basil; Book 12b, 13, a reply to E.'s second book; Book 3–12a, an answer to yet another work by E.; Book 2, a refutation of an *expositio fidei* by E. (Werner Jaeger, *Greg. Nyss. opera*, 1, 2, 1921).
(*de Spiritu sancto*) *contra Macedonianos*	'Against the Macedonians' (who denied the divinity of the Holy Spirit).
(*dialogus*) *de anima et resurrectione qui inscribitur Macrina*	'On the Soul and the Resurrection', a dialogue in imitation of Plato's *Phaedo* in which G.'s sister Macrina is represented as discoursing on her death-bed on the Christian doctrine of death, resurrection, immortality, and the final restoration. (M. died in 379.)
(*adversus Graecos*) *de communibus notionibus*	'On Common Notions; against the Greeks', examines the expressions used in describing the Trinity, and seeks to refute opponents on philosophical principles.

de opificio hominis (c. 379)	'On the Creation of Man', intended to complete Basil's on the Hexaemeron
de oratione dominica	'On the Lord's Prayer', five sermons, mainly ethical in content.
(in diem luminum sive) in baptismum Christi (?383)	'On the baptism of Christ', a sermon for Epiphany ('the Day of Lights').
oratio catechetica (magna) (c. 385)	'The (Great) Catechetical Oration', a compendium of Christian teaching for the benefit of teachers 'who need system in their instruction'. A statement of Catholic dogma, and a defence against pagans, Jews, and heretics, representing the first attempt at systematic theology (on a philosophical basis) since Origen's *de principiis*.
(ad Ablabium) quod non sint tres dii (c. 390)	'That there are not three Gods', a treatise in answer to a query from Ablabius, an ecclesiastic otherwise unknown.

THEODORE OF MOPSUESTIA d. 428 (see pp. 16–18)

epistola ad Domnum	'Letter to Domnus', bishop of Antioch. Only fragments remain.
de incarnatione (before 392)	On the Incarnation', in refutation of Arius, Eunomius, and Apollinaris. Discovered in 1905, the manuscript perished in the first world war, and only fragments in Greek, Latin, and Syriac now remain.
homiliae catecheticae (between 388 and 382)	'Catechetical Sermons.' Sixteen sermons discovered in a Syriac translation and published 1932–3. 1–10 explain the Nicene Creed, 11 expounds the Lord's Prayer, and the rest deal with the baptismal liturgy (12–14) and the Eucharist. They correspond to the work of Cyril of Jerusalem.

JOHN CHRYSOSTOM c. 350–407 (see pp. 18–20)

ad neophytos (c. 388)	'An address to the Newly Baptized', extant in an early Latin translation, and identical with the fourth of the eight baptismal catecheses discovered in 1955.
de coemeterio et cruce (date unknown)	'On the Burial and the Cross', a Good Friday discourse at Antioch.
de proditione Judae (date unknown)	'On the Betrayal of Judas', a Maundy Thursday discourse at Antioch.

de sacerdotio (before 392)   'On the Priesthood', a dialogue between C. and his friend Basil, in which C. attempts to justify his avoidance of episcopal office by flight, while inducing B., by deceit, to accept that dignity.

homiliae in Genesin (308)   'Homilies on Genesis', a complete commentary in sixty-seven sermons delivered at Antioch.

homiliae in Matthaeum (prob. 390)   'Homilies on Matthew', the first complete commentary on the Gospel that has survived; in ninety sermons, delivered at Antioch.

homiliae in Johannem (prob 391)   'Homilies on John', eighty-eight short sermons.

homiliae in epistolam ad Romanos (c. 393)   'Homilies on the Epistle to the Romans'. Thirty-two sermons, given at Antioch. C.'s masterpiece.

homiliae in epistulam primam ad Corinthios (uncertain date)   'Homilies on the First Epistle to the Corinthians.' Forty-four sermons at Antioch.

homiliae in epistolam ad Philippenses (prob. after 396)   'Homilies on the Epistle to the Philippians.' Probably at Constantinople. Fifteen sermons.

in eos qui ad synaxim non occurrerunt (uncertain date)   'An address to those who have not come to the Synaxis [public worship].'

(panegyricus) in quatriduarium Lazarum (date unknown)   'A discourse in Honour of Lazarus, Dead for Four Days.' One of a large number of encomia delivered by C. in honour of saints of the old and New Testaments, and of martyrs of the Church.

AMBROSE 339–97 (see pp. 20–2)

apologia prophetae David (c. 383)   'A Defence of the Prophet David.' Preached at Milan.

(oratio) de excessu fratris Satyri (378)   'An Oration on the Death of his brother Satyrus', the second of his funeral sermons.

de fide ad Gratianum (381)   'On the Faith, addressed to Gratian'. Five books against Arianism, written at the emperor's request.

de incarnationis dominicae sacramento (381–2)   'On the Mystery of the Lord's Incarnation', a refutation of Arianism, arising out of objections raised by two of Gratian's court officials.

de mysteriis (390–1)	'On the Mysteries', addressed to the newly baptised, treating of baptism, confirmation, and the eucharist.
de officiis ministrorum (after 386)	'On the Duties of the Ministers', to the clergy of Milan; the first systematic treatment of Christian ethics.
de sacramentis libri VI (390–1)	'On the sacraments.' The same subject-matter as *de myst.*, together with an exposition of the Lord's Prayer. Its authenticity, formerly questioned, is now generally accepted.
enarrationes in Psalmos XII	'Explanations of Twelve Psalms.' On psalms 1, 35–40, 43, 45, 47, 48, 61.
epistolae	'Letters.' Ninety-one are extant, mostly official and theological.
expositio evangelii secundum Lucam (386-8)	'An Exposition of the Gospel according to Luke.' The longest of all his works and his only commentary on the New Testament. Twenty-five sermons and several treatises, contained in ten books.
expositio in Psalmum CXVIII	'An Exposition of Psalm 118 (119)', in twenty-two sermons, answering to the twenty-two sections of the psalm.

JEROME *c.* 345–420 (see pp. 22–4)

(dialogi) contra Pelaganos (libri III)	'Dialogues against the Pelagians, in Three Books.'
epistolae (408–10)	'Letters.' 150, of which 117 are authentic.
in Isaiam (408–10)	'Commentary on Isaiah.
in Matthaeum (398)	'Commentary on Matthew.'
in epistolam ad Ephesianos (387–9)	'Commentary on the Epistle to the Ephesians.'
in epistolam ad Titum (387–9)	'Commentary on the Epistle to Titus.'
praefatio in librum Salomonis (406)	'Preface to the Book of Solomon (Ecclesiastes)'.
prologus in Samuelem et Malachiam (*c.* 407)	'Prologue to Samuel and Malachi.'

AUGUSTINE OF HIPPO 354–430 (see pp. 24–7)

(de diversis quaestionibus) ad Simplicianum (397)	'To Simplicianus, on Various Questions.' A number of exegetical topics, in Romans and Kings, in reply to queries from the bishop of Milan.
contra duas epistulas Pelagianorum (421)	'Against Two Letters of the Pelagians', in six books.
contra Julianum (422)	'Against Julian' of Eclanum, a leading Pelagian.
contra Maximinum (428)	'A Reply to Maximinus', a Gothic bishop who disputed with A. about Arianism.
de agone christiano (369)	'On the Christian Struggle'—with sin and the devil.
de baptismo contra Donatistas (400–1)	'On Baptism, against the Donatists', in seven books.
de civitate Dei (413–26)	'On the City of God.' Twenty-two books; A.'s apologetic masterpiece.
de catechizandis rudibus (c. 400)	'On the Instruction of the Unlearned', written for a deacon, Deo-gratias.
de correptione et gratia (426–7)	'On condemnation and Grace', a companion work to de gratia et libero arbitrio (see below).
de doctrina Christiana (397–427)	'On Christian Doctrine', mainly exegetical, in four books.
de dono perseverantiae (428–9)	'About the Gift of Perseverance.' To A.'s followers, Prosper and Hilary, in opposition to the monks of S. Gaul.
de fide et symbolo (393)	'On Faith and the Creed', a brief explanation.
de Genesi ad litteram (401–15)	'A Literal Commentary on Genesis.' Twelve books; treats only chapters 1–12.
de gestis Pelagii (417)	'On the Career of Pelagius', a documentary account of the beginnings of the Pelagian controversy.
de gratia Christi (et peccato originali) (418)	'On the Grace of Christ (and Original Sin).' Two books.
de gratia et libero arbitrio (426–7)	'On Grace and Free Will', addressed to the monks of Hadrumetum, to clear away doubts about grace and predestination.
de natura et gratia (413–15)	'On Nature and Grace' against the Pelagians.
de nuptiis et concupiscentia (419–21)	'Marriage and Concupiscence.' Two books, against the Pelagians.

de peccatorum meritis (et remissione, et de baptismo parvulorum) (412)	'On the Due Reward of Sins (and the Forgiveness of Sins; and on the Baptism of Little Children)'.
de spiritu et littera (412)	'On the Spirit and the Letter', against Pelagianism.
de trinitate (399–419)	'On the Trinity.' A.'s principal dogmatic work, in fifteen books.
enchiridion (ad Laurentium, sive de fide, spe, caritate) (421)	'A Manual (for Laurentius, or On Faith, Hope, and Charity).' A summary of A.'s teaching written at the request of a Roman layman.
enarrationes in Psalmos (c. 416)	'Explanations of the Psalms', lengthy homilies, mostly allegorical.
[*epistola ad Demetriadem* (412–13)	'A Letter to Demetrias', written by Pelagius on D.'s decision to become a nun.]
epistolae	'Letters'. 270 items, including forty-seven addressed to A., and six to his friends.
in evangelium Johannis tractatus (414–16)	'Treatises on St. John's Gospel.' 124 sermons.
in primam epistolam Johannis tractatus (c. 413)	'Treatises on the First Epistle of St. John.' ten sermons.
opus imperfectum contra Julianum (contra secundam Juliani responsionem imperfectum opus)	'An unfinished Treatise against Julian' ('An Unfinished Treatise in Answer to Julian's Second Reply').
retractiones (426–8)	'Revisions', two books reviewing A.'s ninety-four works, and adding corrections and clarifications.
sermones	'Sermons'. More than 400 are probably authentic.

CYRIL OF ALEXANDRIA d. 444 (see pp. 27–30)

adversus Nestorii blasphemias (430)	'Against the Blasphemies of Nestorius', a critical examination of a volume of N.'s sermons.
de adoratione in spiritu et veritate (uncertain date)	'On Worship in Spirit and Truth.' Seventeen books in dialogue form on O.T. exegesis.
(*scholia*) *de incarnatione unigeniti* (after 431)	'Comments on the Incarnation of the Only-begotten.' Only fragments are extant in Greek; but the whole survives in Old Latin, Syrian, and Armenian.

de recta fide (c. 430)	'On Right Belief.' Three anti-Nestorian memorials sent to court, one addressed to Theodosius II, the two others 'to the royal ladies', probably one to Th.'s younger sisters, Arcadia and Marina, the other to his older sister Pulcheria, and his wife Eudoxia.
epistolae	'Letters', ninety-three of them, seventeen being addressed to Cyril. Some are probably spurious.
homiliae paschales (414–42)	'Easter Sermons.' Twenty-nine discourses, of moral and practical content.
(*commentarius*) *in XII prophetas* (uncertain date)	'Commentary on the Twelve Prophets.'
(*commentarius*) *in Lucam* (after 430)	'Commentary on St. Luke.' 156 homilies, preserved in Syriac; only fragments extant in Greek. Practical in tone.
(*commentarius*) *in Johannem* (before 429)	'Commentary on St. John.' Dogmatic in tone.
thesaurus (*de sancta et consubstantiali trinitate*) (?423–5)	'A Repository of Discourses concerning the Holy and Consubstantial Trinity.' Thirty-five anti-Arian theses.

THEODORET OF CYRUS d. c. 466 (see pp. 30–1)

de providentia orationes X (c. 458)	'Ten Discourses on Providence.' Sermons to a cultured auditory in Antioch.
epistolae	'Letters.' 232 are extant.
eranistes (*seu polymorphus*) (c. 447)	'The Beggar (or Mr. Multiform).' T.'s chief dogmatic work, in four books. Books 1–3 comprise dialogues between a Monophysite, the Beggar (because his doctrines are filched from earlier heretics, and their heterogeneity suggests the alternative name) and an orthodox respondent: book 4 gives a summary of the argument in forty syllogisms.
haereticarum fabularum compendium (c. 453)	'A Handbook of Heretical Fables', a history of heresy in five books.
(*commentarius*) *in Psalmos* (between 441 and 449)	'A Commentary on the Psalms', a continuous exposition of the whole psalter.
(*commentarius*) *in Isaiam* (date uncertain)	'A Commentary on Isaiah.' Text found in 1899, published 1933.

interpretationes in XIV epistolas sancti Pauli (after 450)	'Detailed Commentaries on the Fourteen Epistles of St. Paul.' T.'s only work on the N.T.
reprehensio (XII capitum seu) anathematismorum Cyrilli (431)	'A Refutation of the Twelve Chapters or Anathemas of Cyril.' A defence of N. written at the request of John of Antioch. Text preserved in Cyril, *ep. ad Euoptium.*

LEO THE GREAT 440–61 (see pp. 31–3)

epistola [28] *dogmatica ad Flavianum* (449)	'A Doctrinal Letter to Flavian.' 'The Tome of Leo'; the classical Christological formulation.

Index